DEAD STRAIGHT GUIDE TO

S K A

MICK O' SHEA

The publisher makes no representation, express or implied, with regard to the accuracy of the information contained in this publication and cannot accept any responsibility in law for any errors or omissions.

The right of Mick O' Shea to be identified as author of this Work has been asserted by him in accordance with sections 77 and 78 of the Copyright, Designs and Patents Act 1988.

A catalogue record for this book is available from the British Library

This edition © Red Planet Books Ltd 2018. Text © Mick O' Shea 2018

ISBN: 978 1 9113 4667 8

Printed in the UK

Page design/layout/cover: Harry Gregory
Publisher: Mark Neeter

Red Planet Publishing Ltd,
Tremough Innovation Centre,
Penryn, Cornwall TR10 9TA

www.redplanetzone.com
Email: info@redplanetzone.com

AUTHOR'S NOTE

B efore we start, I feel I must hold my hand up and confess to having never previously heard of ska until The Specials burst on to the scene with their debut single, 'Gangsters', during the summer of 1979. Things might have been different had I grown up in Brixton, Notting Hill, Hanworth or some other inner-city area with a thriving Caribbean community, but to the best of my knowledge there were no sound systems or shebeens to be found in Accrington or its environs while I was growing up.

Seeing as I'm being truthful, aside from the obligatory Thursday evening ritual of watching *Top of the Pops*, I hadn't shown much interest in any form of music before having my head turned by the Sex Pistols. Indeed, *Never Mind the Bollocks* was the first album I ever bought. I was a punk at the time 'Gangsters' was released, and my overriding thought upon hearing the song for the first time, therefore, was why would a band choose to reference The Clash's recently deposed manager, Bernard Rhodes? (Call him "Bernie" at your peril.) And I don't mind admitting it took a good few listens to the record before I accepted my hearing wasn't fucking with me. Of course, had I known of Rhodes' involvement with The Specials – or The Special AKA as they were calling themselves at the time – and also been familiar with Prince Buster's 'Al Capone', I would have recognised Neville Staple's opening gambit in 'Gangsters' as a playful rewording of "Al Capone's guns don't argue". But in those halcyon, sepia-toned, pre-internet days, when all I had to rely on for my musical education were the *NME*, Sounds and *Record Mirror*, there was much that I remained in ignorance of; for example, that ska had been a forerunner to reggae, much the same as pub rock had proved a precursor to punk.

The connection betwixt the enigmatic Rhodes and The Specials came from their being invited on to the Clash on Parole tour during the summer of 1978 owing to Rhodes' having temporarily taken the Coventry-based six-piece under his wing (Neville Staple wouldn't be promoted from stage toaster to fully fledged Special until after the tour). Having already undergone a couple of name changes – from The Hybrids to The Automatics, to the Coventry Automatics – the band were still undecided as to what they should call themselves, or they surely would have got their name in small print on the poster (spot the *Give 'em Enough Rope* reference, anybody?).

The Specials would crop up occasionally in one or other of the leading music weeklies, and though I was always keen to check out any new band showing promise, my interest in 'Gangsters' or The Specials (either with or without the "AKA" tag) probably lasted until the next Clash, Jam, or Skids single hit the record shops.

My perspective was set to change, however. For just as punk had grabbed centre stage following the Pistols' now-legendary appearance on Today in December 1976, the dawning of the Eighties heralded the 2-Tone explosion.

Whereas punk had seen a myriad of bands forming up and down the country, the 2-Tone acts could be counted on one hand. And who would have foreseen Coventry usurping London to become the country's new youth subculture capital, with every music journalist worth their salt suddenly begging their editor to be sent there.

Though no one amongst my tight-knit circle of friends would have dared to admit it, punk was already on its way to becoming a clichéd caricature of itself by the summer of 1979; its initial vibrancy having long-since dissipated and assimilated into the mainstream. However, with Britain still in the grip of the wintry discontent that had swept Margaret Thatcher into power on the back of a landslide general election victory, another generation of disaffected kids walked out of the school gates and straight into seemingly ever-growing dole queues. Just as punk had done for their elder siblings, 2-Tone provided these kids with an exciting distraction from their otherwise humdrum existence. It became the soundtrack to their lives, giving them an identity and a sense of belonging that I, for one, readily recognised.

Music must evolve in order to continue setting the trends, and the latest changing of the guard saw an army of "Walt Jabscos" emerge seemingly overnight. There was never any chance of my shedding my battered biker jacket and ripped T-shirts and donning a two-tone suit or pork pie hat. Thankfully, with The Clash tipping their hat to ska on *London Calling*, it was cool to like 2-Tone whilst keeping one's punk credibility.

Mick O'Shea

Still Living the Dream

May 2018

PROFESSIONAL THANKS TO

Mark Neeter and everyone at Red Planet Publishing, Ayesha Plunkett, David Fairman, Stephen "Roadent" Connelly Bernard Rhodes, Eliot Moses Cohen and Roddy Byers.

SPECIAL MENTION TO

Tasha "Bush" Cowen, Shannon "Mini B" Stanley, Matt Whapshott, Lisa "T-bag" Bird, Paul Young (not the singer), Tony Makin & Pads, Drezzie & Catherine, Kev Gray, Joel & Aggie at The Old House at Dorking, Ziggy P & Mel King, Michelle West, Luke Dillon, Gemma and Donna (aka "The Girls"), Dan, Jeannie & "Pinks", Fay and Richard at The King's Arms in Winkleigh, Roop & Debs, "Scouse Mark" Rudge, Rob and Debbie, P&D Dan, Tiler Dan and Steph, Chris "Hammy" Hamilton, "Crazy Annie" Chamberlain, Johnny Diamond, Johnny "Doris", Helena CW Hamilton, and Simone Jackson.

SOURCES

Books: Horace Panter: *Ska'd for Life: A Personal Journey with The Specials* (Sedgwick & Jackson, 2007); Pauline Black: *Black by Design: A 2-Tone Memoir* (Serpent's Tail, 2011); Heather Augustyn: *Ska: The Rhythm of Liberation* (Scarecrow Press, 2013); Neville Staple: *Original Rude Boy* (Aurum Press, 2009); John Reed: *House of Fun: The Story of Madness* (Omnibus Press, 2010); Belinda Carlisle: *Lips Unsealed: A Memoir* (Crown Publishing, 2010); Johnny Green: *A Riot of Our Own: Night and day with The Clash* (Orion, 2003).

Magazines: Periodicals and TV Documentaries: *The Daily Gleaner; NME; Sounds; Record Mirror; Melody Maker; The Guardian; Daily Mirror; The Sun; Evening Standard; Caribbean Beat; Chicago Tribune; Rebel Music: The Bob Marley Story; The Express; The Telegraph; Coventry Telegraph; M; Mojo; Rolling Stone; Village Voice; The Scotsman.*

Websites: *www.redbull.com; www.reggaevibes.com; www. interviewmagazine.com; hanspeterkuenzler.com; www.rocksgodiva. tripod.com; marcoonthebass.blogspot.com.*

CHAPTER

ONE

IT'S ALL IN THE RHYTHM

"You comin' from town, your face turn to dis sound, on your way up, or on your way down. I want you to stop at dis station for identification. I'm going to turn you over to your sound dimension, your music producer, everybody on the ball."

COUNT MACHUKI

CHAPTER

There is still much confusion as to the etymology of the term "ska", or indeed its correct original spelling. The Oxford English Dictionary cites *Evening Standard* journalist Maureen Cleave with first coining the term in her "The 'Ska' hits London" article featured in the March 17, 1964 edition of Jamaica's national newspaper, *The Daily Gleaner*. Cleave, in turn, credits a pre-Island Records Chris Blackwell, whom she befriended in London a couple of years after the latter's arrival from Jamaica, as being the source. (Though it should, perhaps, be noted that in the same article Blackwell was keen to stress the genre was known as "blue beat", owing to the majority of ska records being issued via the London-based label.)

The *Gleaner* also takes centre stage regarding the confusion over the correct spelling, as the paper was carrying ads using "sca" some twelve months prior to Cleave's article. It's more likely, however, that – regardless of the spelling – ska was the abbreviated term Jamaican musicians used among themselves to denote the "scat-scat-scat" scratching guitar style that sits behind the beat – a beat with a heritage dating back centuries and intertwined with the rhythms and cultures of Jamaica's indigenous people (primarily the Arawak and Tano), their colonial Spanish and British masters, and the slaves brought over from Africa to work the land. Indeed, calypso, which grew to become the dominant music in the Caribbean, is linked to the gayup – the "call and response" work song sung by the slaves toiling in the fields to help alleviate the mundanity of their back-breaking toil; the lilting, topical and frequently risqué songs initially sung in an African-French patois before subsequently switching to English as calypso began to attract the interest of American record labels such as Decca and Bluebird.

Jamaica had been a British dominion since the mid-seventeenth century, but its proximity to the US meant that by the early twentieth century it had become a cosmopolitan playground for America's idle rich. Tourism was soon vying with mining and sugar as the island's dominant source of income; palatial hotels such as the Myrtle Bank in Kingston, Tower Isle in Ocho Rios, Casablanca Beach in Montego Bay, Oracabessa, Ocho Rios, Negril, and elsewhere along the island's shoreline, began booking their own orchestras to perform big band and jazz standards for the ever-growing influx of wealthy Americans.

Jazz soon swept through Jamaica, as it has the US and elsewhere around the globe. Kingston, being the island's capital, was naturally the main hub for the latest music craze, with dance halls such as the Palace Theatre, the Jubilee Tile Gardens, the Bournemouth Beach Club and the Silver Slipper all staging weekly events featuring bands made up of Jamaican jazz musicians, or bringing over leading American singers of the day.

The US military would also inadvertently play its part in the ska story. In June 1941, in accordance with the 1940 Destroyers for Bases Agreement between Britain and America, the US Air Force opened air bases at Vernam Field, some thirty miles south-west of Kingston in Clarendon Parish, and Portland Bight in southern St. Catherine, situated slightly to the east of Kingston Harbour. The influx of American soldiers stationed at the bases would bring a variety of music with them as a means of off-duty entertainment. And it wouldn't have taken those same airmen long to recognise there was money to be earned in catering to the ever-increasing demand for jazz records.

Only the wealthiest of Jamaicans could afford to gain entry to Kingston's theatres and dance halls, but the jazz blaring out of the USO Club (United Service Organizations) located on Old Hope Road in St. Andrew's Parish most nights was accessible to all. The next step in the musical progression came with the more entrepreneurial locals purchasing jazz records from the soldiers and playing them on gramophones imported from the US, or crude, home-made turntables, and charging a small admission fee.

Another relatively cheap and easy means available to the average Jamaican to hear the latest jazz records came with befriending someone who owned a transistor radio, such as the landlords of their tenement yard. The island's sole radio station, ZQI, didn't broadcast anything other than news, BBC World Service, or classical music during its one-hour-per-week broadcasts, but a carefully tuned transistor radio – weather conditions permitting – could tune into jazz-playing radio stations in Florida, Louisiana, Tennessee and other southern US states. By the early-to-mid-Fifties, however, those same southern US radio stations had moved with the times and were switching from jazz to rhythm and blues, or "R&B" as it was more colloquially known.

R&B soon proved as musically mesmeric to Jamaicans as jazz had done three decades earlier. As a result, more and more of the island's youth began turning away from the bland American folk and country pap foisted on them by Radio Jamaica Rediffusion (formerly ZQI) and the Jamaican Broadcasting Corporation and tuning into the sinewy new music being played on southern stations such as Miami's powerful WINZ. (It's long been mooted that the delay effects integral to the reggae/dub sound may have initially been inspired by the oscillations in the signal from these faraway US radio stations.)

Seizing on R&B's burgeoning popularity, those same palatial hotels that had once brought Sarah Vaughn, Dave Brubeck, Jelly Roll Morton et al over to the island began staging shows by Louis Armstrong, Amos Milburn, Rosco Gordon and Bill Haley and the Comets. But with more and more of America's wealthy choosing to abandon Jamaica in favour of other Caribbean idylls such as Cuba, St. Lucia and Anguilla, the island's economy had seen a steady downturn since the end of the Second World War.

One of the knock-on effects of the downturn in Jamaica's economy was that fewer Kingstonians were going out to a theatre or club to see the latest singers or bands. Indeed, for the average Jamaican, entertainment of any form was now regarded as a frivolous luxury. Yet, everyone still wanted to hear the latest R&B hits coming out of America.

Necessity has long been the mother of invention, of course, and the more enterprising club owners decided that if the people could no longer come into the city, a profit might still be turned by taking the music out into the townships. These mobile discos – or "sound systems" as they became known – quickly became big business. Indeed, it was as though a major Jamaican industry was spawned overnight.

Sound systems were nothing new to Jamaica, of course, as from the 1920s onwards clubs would hire someone to play records during the intervals betwixt live acts. But these pick-up truck behemoths – consisting of a generator, turntable and huge speakers built into wooden cabinets colloquially known as "houses of joy" – were designed to attract attention as well as entertain. The DJ, or "selector", would travel around from township to township hosting what best be described as open-air parties, turning sizeable profits charging attendees a small fee and selling alcohol (predominantly cans of Red Stripe) and a variety of easy-to-cook food. It wasn't unusual for thousands of people to turn up to any one party, and if each reveller spent a pound then huge profits could be made in a single day. Those operators with the rarest records could expect to draw the bigger crowds, and rivalry between operators grew so intense that each would scratch the names of songs and artists from the record labels for fear of other DJs trying to locate them elsewhere.

CHAPTER

Sound systems quickly became more popular than named live acts, and by the start of the 1960s most of the crude, cobbled together systems had been replaced by ones custom-built by audio specialists such as Hedley Jones. Amongst his many notable achievements, Jones designed Jamaica's first traffic light systems, as well as one of the first solid-bodied electric guitars.

One of the first to call upon Jones' audio expertise was Tom Wong, a local Chinese-Jamaican hardware store owner-cum-budding selector who billed himself as Tom "the Great" Sebastian. There were a dozen or so sound system operators of renown with equally outlandish comic book sobriquets, such as Admiral Comic, Lord Koo's the Universe, and Count Smith the Blues Blaster. By far and away the three most popular operators were Vincent "Vin King" Edwards, "Sir Coxsone" Dodd and Arthur "Duke Reid".

When Coxsone died in May 2004 aged 72, *The Guardian* lauded him as being an "integral force in the development of ska". He was also something of a father figure to nearly every reggae artist of international renown, having cut the first recordings by a certain Nesta Robert Marley at his legendary Studio One facility.

Clement Seymour Dodd was born in Kingston, but spent several formative years living in the parish of Saint Thomas, before returning to the Jamaican capital to complete his schooling and train as a mechanic. During this time, he also learned the skill of cabinet making courtesy of his contractor-cum-mason father, who'd helped build the Carib Theatre, one of Kingston's best known landmarks. "I did a course in automobile mechanics, used to train at the Ford Garage on Church Street," Dodd told *Caribbean Beat*'s David Katz during interviews conducted during the autumn of 2003.

Dodd's mother owned Nanny's Corner, the restaurant at the downtown junction of Lawes Street and Ladd Lane, which proved to be a popular meeting place for jazz aficionados. Prior

to this, Ma Dodd ran the family liquor store at Love Lane and Beeston Street, and it was here that the young Dodd would receive his jazz education, as he himself would reveal: "I had a Morphy Richards radio at her establishment. In those days, thirty watts was a whole heap of sound. I would stay in my room and play stuff like Fats Navarro, Dizzy Gillespie, Coleman Hawkins, Illinois Jacquet and Charlie Parker. Guys would hang out in the store and out on the piazza. Maybe have some drinks, but a lot of food was sold too. When I arrived on the scene it was because I played jazz and my followers could execute the dance for the sound I played."

In the same *Caribbean Beat* interview, Dodd said how he'd attended a "lot of orchestra dances" in the early days before getting into rhythm and blues circa 1953.

It was during the early Fifties that Dodd migrated to Florida to work as a sugar cane cutter; saving up money each week to fund regular forays to record stores such as Randy's Records in Gallatin, Tennessee, and Rainbow Records in Harlem, New York. He would then ship the records back to Kingston. Upon his return to Jamaica, he arrived home with a game plan on how to get a foothold in the island's music business.

The leading sound at the time was the Duke Reid, aka "The Trojan", established by Arthur Reid, a former policeman and a friend of Dodd's parents. It was Reid's friendship with Dodd's parents that paved the way for his doing guest spots spinning his records on Reid's set, adopting the name "Sir Coxsone". While at school, Dodd's friends had nicknamed him "Coxsone" owing to his impressive batting skills reminding them of Alec Coxon, a noted Yorkshire CC cricketer during the Forties.

"I used to attend dances when Duke Reid was playing and play some of my sides," Dodd told David Katz. "His (Reid's) fans always look forward to seeing me coming with my little case of records, so I eventually went into the sound thing myself; the highlight of the sound system was after I came into it.

"Duke was a close friend of the family, and [so] the rivalry was clean. I respected Duke because he was my senior by a couple of years, but I was more musically knowledgeable. With importation, I had the stronger set of records, and when we started recording locally, I had the stronger set of records, but Duke was so strong financially that, even if I had a contracted artist, Duke would still insist and use them, and that kept me on the ball, trying to produce better stuff."

Having said how he believed Reid looked at music as a business, whereas music was the "love of my life", Dodd went on to add that Reid didn't have much of an ear for music, relying on others to tell him the merits of a particular tune, whereas he'd only need to hear the opening couple of bars to recognise the tune's potential. "I could identify whether [the song] would be a hit, and I thank God for that. As a matter of fact, I am the person who discovered the musicians, then other producers would use the same musicians that I use."

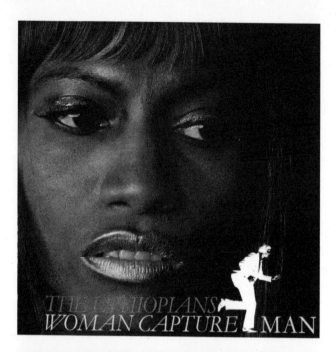

THE ETHIOPIANS
WOMAN CAPTURE MAN

reggae
power

WOMAN CAPTURE MAN

ethiopians

CHAPTER

TWO

KINGSTON AFFAIR

"Ska is not a matter of speed. Ska is a matter of arrangement. I can play you ska and it's slow; you can have slow ska and fast ska, slow rocksteady and fast rocksteady. The snare drum and the bass drum, the way they drop on your riff, that's the main thing. The bass can be any way, the bass can be slow as ever. Rocksteady is the one drop. It's the drum."

LEONARD DILLON

CHAPTER

A rthur "Duke Reid" was quite a bit longer in the tooth than Dodd, having been born in July 1915 in Portland, Jamaica. He'd joined Kingston's constabulary at sixteen and spent the next ten years or so as a police officer before leaving the force to open the Treasure Isle Grocery and Liquor store with his wife. Powerfully built, yet softly spoken, Reid was an imposing figure on the mid-Fifties Jamaica music scene, if only for his never being seen without .45 and .22 pistols tucked into the waistband of his trousers. He was also reputed to juggle a live grenade on occasion. Reid's liquor store, a sprawling property located on Bond Street in western Kingston, soon became the preferred hangout by the criminal elements operating out of the nearby slum, "Back-o-Wall", and Reid himself counted notorious gang leaders such as Woppi King and Dapper Dan amongst his closest associates.

He launched his "Duke Reid, The Trojan" sound system (named after the British-made Trojan vans he used to transport his system) in 1955, always leading with 'My Mother's Eyes' by American jazz saxophonist Tab Smith, which soon came to be regarded as Reid's theme tune. He initially concentrated on mento-styled releases – most notably Lord Power's 'Penny Reel' – on his newly launched Trojan label, before turning his attention to R&B. The following year saw Reid crowned "King of Sounds & Blues" at the Success Club in central Kingston – a title he was to hold for three successive years.

The key to Reid's success was his drive and determination, coupled with an astute business mind and a savvy understanding on the musical demands of his public. Yet his being able to call upon the likes of Woppi King and Dapper Dan to sabotage and intimidate Tom "the Great" Sebastian into submission was undoubtedly a contributory factor in his rise to prominence. By the end of the Fifties, he was sponsoring and hosting *Treasure Isle Time*, a weekly half-hour music show broadcast on RJR, via which he advertised his latest Trojan releases.

With his superior collection of R&B and jazz records, Dodd's Sir Coxsone's Downbeat soon became Reid's main competitor. Dodd was the first to employ a "toaster" in Count Machuki, a wisecracking, machine gun-mouthed DJ. Legendary producer Lee "Scratch" Perry would also start out working for Dodd in varying capacities.

Exclusivity was to prove a key component in Reid and Dodd's ongoing battle for sound system dominance, both men going to any lengths to get the upper hand. There can be little argument that the prolonged rivalry betwixt Reid and Dodd was responsible for instigating seismic shifts in Jamaican music, yet throughout their fight for sound system supremacy the two maintained a close camaraderie. Indeed, their friendship seemed to intensify – this despite Dodd's deliberately aimed barbs casting aspersions on Reid's temporary alliance with Buster in playful releases such as Don Drummond's 'Schooling the Duke' and Lee Perry's 'Prince and Duke' and 'Me Sir'.

In 1956, Dodd began making his own recordings at Federal studio, applying R&B echoes to songs by Bunny and Skully, and Theophilus Beckford's 'Easy Snappin'', which was to top the Jamaican chart following its release in 1959; the single remaining on the chart for a whopping 18 months. The emphasis on the off-beat on 'Easy Snappin'' would be widely imitated and is now viewed as a forerunner to ska. Despite being credited as the writer, Beckford didn't receive any royalties. He recorded several other singles for Dodd, including follow-up hit 'Jack & Jill Shuffle', before leaving to set up his own King Pioneer label.

Speaking with *www.redbull.com*'s Hattie Collins in August 2014, "Vin King" Edwards revealed the origins of the King Edwards sound system which he started up with his brother, George: "I entered the sound system in 1954/55 and the first night was what we call a 'flop'. When my sound came on, it was a little 'fi-fi', no good. So, I had to go and rebuild.

"The popular artists at that time were Fats Domino and these rock 'n' roll artists from America. I'm a patriotic Jamaican, but the reality is that we listened to them the whole time – we emulated them! So, I looked at it like, in those days, the man who has the best tune is the man who commands the crowd."

Identifying Dodd and Reid as his primary competition, Reid realised the only realistic means of becoming the man who could "command the crowd" was to get hold of tunes that neither Dodd nor Reid possessed. Reid had a sister living in Philadelphia at the time, so, leaving brother George to operate their sound system, he headed over to the US. Using his sister's home as a base, he travelled around America – primarily the southern states – by Greyhound bus. "I would go see the musicians and get the records," he explained. "Then I started to have better records than both Duke Reid and Coxsone."

Never being one to shy away from situations that might threaten his livelihood, Reid paid Edwards a visit. "Duke came to me one night and I flopped him," Edwards recounted. "When you flop Duke, really it's trouble. He sent someone to call on me the next morning. So I went down to him and I found him a reasonable fella. He said, 'Where you get these tunes?' So we went to America, me and Duke. We went from Montego Bay to New Orleans, then Houston, San Antonio, Dallas, Los Angeles, and that's where we found the tunes.

"We went to Pico Boulevard and they had all the old records. Duke was bigger than me, so I could jump over the boxes faster and pick up a tune. I found this song, 'Sweepstake', that Coxsone had had for over two years. Now I could come home because I had the tune."

By the mid-Sixties Reid's fortunes were on the decline, his dwindling sales due in part to Dodd's own rise. Yet rather than take delight in kicking Reid while he was down, Dodd readily acquiesced to Reid's request to a production swap, which saw him cutting a version of Drummond's 'Green Island' in return for Dodd cutting 'Eastern Standard Time' (which subsequently appeared on Dodd's *Best of Don Drummond* album. But this wasn't the end of Dodd's largesse as he also allowed Reid the use of several Studio One acts in the hope of reviving the fortunes of his supposed rival. Dodd could afford to be so magnanimous because by this juncture he was pumping out hit after hit with The Maytals, The Gaylads, and his latest recording acquisition, The Skatalites.

The Skatalites were a nine-piece instrumental ensemble made up of Jamaica's most talented session players and lead singer Doreen Schaeffer. Speaking in 1997, alto saxophonist Lester Sterling (the sole surviving founding Skatalite musician at the time of writing) said that while most Jamaican musicians would talk about calypso, he and his fellow Skatalites would only be interested in talking about jazz. In the same interview, double bassist Lloyd Brevett (who died in 2012) explained how each of them had learned their respective chops playing jazz. "When we started, we never started in ska. We started in jazz. We were in separate bands at that point in Jamaica. Big band we started. I was 14 when I started to play in big band. It was jazz and ballads. We started to play rhythm and blues, but jazz was still with it."

The other founding Skatalites were band leader Tommy McCook (tenor saxophone and flute), Roland Alphonso (tenor saxophone), Lloyd Knibb (drums), Don "Cosmic" Drummond (trombone), Jerome "Jah" Jerry Haynes (guitar), Donat Roy "Jackie" Mittoo (piano) and Johnny "Dizzy" Moore (trumpet).

Drummond, Alphonso, Mittoo and Haynes were contracted to Studio One from 1961 onwards according to Dodd, while McCook, Knibb, Brevett and Moore played weekly sessions. "After the ska became dominant and these musicians were the major recording backing band, I decided to form the band The

*Don 'Cosmic' Drummond (centre)
of the Skatelites*

Skatalites," Dodd explained. "I really had the edge, because of all the other sound system men, I was really in the studio more often, and had a lot of releases that hit, so anybody looking for a producer, most would head to me."

The Skatalites recorded their first album for Dodd, *Ska Authentic*, at Studio One in 1964, the same year they made their live debut at the Hi-Hat club, which was operated by Dodd's friend, Orville "Billy" Farnum, in Kingston's Rae Town district, on June 27. "At the formation of the band I supplied the PA system, microphones and whatever it is," Dodd revealed. "Also, the guitar amplifier. I helped with transportation and I supplied storage for equipment and instruments. I was a part of promoting the first gigs to get it off the ground, because I figured more or less, if I am recording The Skatalites, it's good to get them popular out in the streets."

Aside from backing leading artists of the day, including Justin Hinds & The Dominoes, Stranger Cole, Eric "Monty" Morris, and Owen & Leon Silveras, The Skatalites also cut a plethora of quality instrumentals – including their 1965 hit 'Guns of Navarone', the theme tune from the film of the same name which would, of course, be covered by The Specials.

The Skatalites were the toast of Jamaica and would surely have gone on to achieve wider recognition had Drummond, the band's unstable-less-medicated primary composer, not been convicted for the murder of his girlfriend, Marguerita Mahfood, the self-styled "Rhumba Queen of Jamaica", in 1965. Such was the highly erratic trombonist's prowess as a composer (he was already said to have over 200 tunes credited to his name) that the morning after he was hauled away in handcuffs, Knibb snuck inside Mahfood's blood-splattered apartment and grabbed up all the sheet music he could find.

Drummond was subsequently ruled criminally insane and imprisoned at Kingston's Bellevue Asylum, where he died four years later. The official cause of death was listed as "natural causes", but rumours soon abounded that Drummond was either the victim of a government plot against the Kingston music scene or was murdered by local gangsters in revenge for Mahfood's murder.

The Skatalites never recovered from the loss of their primary tunesmith, and within a year of Drummond's internment they had disbanded; the band splintering off to form the nucleus of two other influential instrumental outfits: Roland Alphonso's Soul Brothers and Tommy McCook's Supersonics.

A Skatalites reunion of sorts occurred in 1974 when McCook, Alphonso, Knibb and Mittoo came together to work on Lloyd Brevett's solo album, *African Roots* (since credited to Lloyd Brevett and The Skatalites). 1979 brought another brief reunion, this time to record an album for Chris Blackwell. The album, tentatively entitled *The Big Guns*, was recorded but would end up not being released owing to a dispute between McCook and Blackwell. The album remains unreleased to his day. (*The Return of the Big Guns*, recorded in April 1984, and based around charts originally written by Drummond, was released in the UK via Mango Records.)

June 1983 saw all surviving eight Skatalites came together for the fifth annual Reggae Sunsplash at the behest of the festival's Skatalites-loving director, Ronnie Burke; this despite McCook and Moore not having spoken since the original split some 18 years earlier. The public reaction to the reunion brought about further shows in Jamaica as well as overseas tours; one of the highlights coming at "London Sunsplash" the following July at Selhurst Park (home to Crystal Palace FC in south-east London), where they were joined on stage by Prince Buster.

With Jackie Mittoo at the helm, The Skatalites went into Music Mountain Studio in late 1983 to record a new album, which featured 'Big Trombone', the band's touching tribute to fallen comrade Don Drummond. The album, however, wouldn't be released until 2007 (*Rolling Steady: The 1983 Music Mountain Sessions*).

Having each relocated to the US during the mid-to-late-Eighties, The Skatalites reunited again, and have continued to perform and record – albeit in varying guises owing to deaths and disputes – to the present day; their most recent album being 2016's *Platinum Ska*.

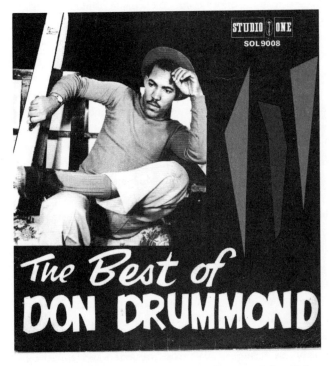

The majority of The Skatalites were graduates of the Alpha Boys School, the vocational residential school in south-central Kingston run by Roman Catholic nuns. Originally established in 1880 as an orphanage, Alpha Boys School would go on to become one of Jamaica's leading schools for training musicians. Many would hone their jazz skills, as well as learn the esoteric rhythms of the Burru and Rasta, in the Wareika Hills (also known as Long Mountain), located to the east of Kingston Harbour. What was known as the "Far East" sound, the sound said to have breathed life into reggae, first came to ska through the Wareika Hills.

Of the handful of innovators and pioneering figures credited with giving reggae its distinctive contours, Oswald Williams, aka "Count Ossie", takes pride of place in the genre's history. Born in 1927 and raised in Bitu, a quarrying village located in the hills of Bull Bay, a few miles east of Kingston, Ossie had played drums in the Boys' Brigade as well as a local marching band. When his family moved on to Slip Dock Road, a then underdeveloped stretch of east Kingston, he'd been drawn to a Rasta camp in Salt Lane, a notorious west Kingston slum, where he soon found himself being spiritually adopted by Brother Job, a Burru man who had himself been taught by Watto King, one of Jamaica's most prominent and respected drum-makers.

The Burru were shunned by Jamaica's Eurocentric society, but found in their fellow outcasts, the Rastafari, so it was only to be expected the two would come to live together in peace. By 1948, Kingston's leading jazz musicians could be found at Salt Lane, playing late into the night with Ossie and other Burru drummers. The Burru and Rasta fraternity would be forced to relocate to Adastra Road in the heart of Rockfort owing to Hurricane Charlie laying waste to the Salt Lane camp when it ripped through the Caribbean in August 1951. The "groundations" (spiritual reasoning, chanting and drumming) Ossie held in the new Wareika Hills encampment during the mid-to-late Fifties would prove crucial to the spread of Rastafari amongst the Jamaican musical fraternity; the end result being a unique form of music intrinsic to Jamaica as the island geared itself for independence from British colonial yoke.

TWO

It cannot be overstated the musical talent coming through to Wareika around this time. Aside from Ossie's close friend, Wilton "Big Bra" Gaynair, a colossally talented tenor saxophonist who would make a name for himself on London's avant-garde jazz scene, trombonist Rico Rodriguez was also a firm fixture; the latter having been mentored by Drummond.

Future "honorary Special" Emmanuel "Rico" Rodriguez was born in the Cuban capital of Havana in October 1937. Owing to his mother being Jamaican, the family relocated to Kingston when Rodriguez was a boy. He was said to be something of an unruly child; so much so, that his despairing mother had sent him to the Alpha Boys School. Though he wasn't above truanting on occasion, Rodriguez would later say that he'd thrived on the school's strict regimen of music and more formal classes: "I always give thanks to Alpha, them give me start musically." Whilst at Alpha, he also learnt bookbinding and printing, but on leaving the school he would spend two years training as a car mechanic while moonlighting with the Eric Deans Orchestra.

Speaking about how he came to learn the trombone at Alpha in March 2010, Rodriguez said he'd started out on percussion, and that it was only one of the older players gifting him his trombone on leaving the school that led to his taking up the instrument he is forever associated with. He also spoke of his learning at the hands of the master. "Don Drummond was my teacher. Me and Don were close because he lived three streets away from me in Allman Road in Kingston. And sometimes when I didn't have a trombone I used to borrow his. Sometimes he didn't want to lend it to me because he thought I wouldn't look after it," he added light-heartedly.

Rodriguez then went into more detail about the school itself: "People in music usually have a lot of trades that they have learned at Alpha. Trades like carpenter, shoemaker, tailor. Some of the boys were very educated and went as far as senior six. When they reached a certain standard in school they sent them to colleges around the island. I spent a long time learning to play the trumpet and the French horn and all those other instruments, so I didn't get to the trombone till a long time after."

Don Drummond's future fellow Skatalites, Alphonso, Knibb, Mittoo and Moore, had also resided at the Wareika encampment; the latter remaining there till his death in 2008. Tommy McCook hadn't long returned from an eight-year stint playing in a jazz ensemble at the Zanzibar Club in Nassau, The Bahamas, when Coxsone Dodd made his approach either in late 1962 or early '63. He'd already "discovered" Alphonso and Drummond while visiting Ossie's Wareika Hills encampment, using the pair on a recording of 'I Cover the Waterfront' (released in 1962). Though aware of ska, McCook initially resisted Dodd's offer as he saw himself as a committed jazz man.

Ossie and his fellow Burru drummers would appear on Prince Buster's production of The Folkes Brothers' 1960 hit 'Oh Carolina', the Jamaican vocal trio having recorded the song (b/w 'I Met a Man') at Kingston's RJR Studios. The elder Folkes Brother, John, had penned the lyric several years earlier about a girlfriend of his whose real name had been "Noelena". Buster heard 'Oh Carolina' for the first time while The Folkes Brothers were auditioning at Duke Reid's liquor store, and having decided he'd like to record the song, offered the trio £60. Buster already knew the sound he was looking for and headed up into the Wareika Hills to speak with Count Ossie.

'Oh Carolina' was licensed to Blue Beat Records for release in the UK in 1961 and is now lauded as being the landmark single in the development of ska, rocksteady and reggae – especially owing to the incorporation of Ossie's African-influenced Niyabinghi-style drumming and chanting.

CHAPTER

THREE

PRINCE FAR OUT

"The fact that he [Prince Buster] came from the streets and he had a terrific sense of humour and energy – it really appealed to us and it had a huge impact on everything we did, really. It's like the Monty Python thing about the Romans: 'What did Prince Buster ever do for us? A great deal indeed."

SUGGS

CHAPTER

P rince Buster, the man who could be said to have single-handedly proved the inspiration behind the late-Seventies 2-Tone explosion, was born Cecil Bustamente Campbell in Orange Street, Kingston, in May 1938; his middle name being in honour of Jamaica's first post-independence prime minister, William Bustamante. After a spell living with his grandmother, "Buster", as he was known to the family, returned to live with his parents in Orange Street. His schooling suffered owing to his performing several evenings a week at the Glass Bucket Club as part of Frankie Lymon's sing and dance troupe.

"I used to have problems going to school because I stayed up so late at night," Buster explained during an interview with Heather Augustyn in August 1997. "I paid less attention to singing and was more into boxing and wanted to be in fights, but really there was no money in boxing. You'd get punched up and then there was no money. So I leave that and go back to singing."

Growing up in Orange Street, one of Kingston's more notorious neighbourhoods, meant the teenage Buster often had to think with his fists. He'd learned how to box at the hands of Jamaican boxing greats Kid Chocolate and Speedy Baker, his prowess at the pugilistic arts earning him the nickname "Prince". By the time of his first foray into the boxing ring at the National Stadium in front of a 15,000-strong crowd in early October 1964, Buster had befriended Muhammad Ali during a trip to London, the latter having recently renounced his "slave name", Cassius Clay, earlier in the year upon his converting to the Islamic faith.

Buster would also convert to Islam and changed his name to Yusef Muhammad Ali; his adopted boxing name, "Prince Mohammed the Great", was emblazoned in black lettering on his glowing scarlet and white robe. Buster's singing renown was already drawing attention, and in the run-up to his fight against Gene Coy, the *Daily Gleaner*'s sports writer, LD Roberts, wrote in anticipation of the fight: "Prince Buster is to make his ring debut in a four-rounder and this in itself should be a treat. But if the Prince forgets he is in the ring and starts to do the ska instead of throwing leather he may get his block knocked off."

Buster, mimicking Ali's fondness for verse, had declared he'd see off Coy in the opening round. However, owing to suspicions that the fight hadn't been fair, the Jamaica Boxing Board of Control had withheld the purses of both boxers pending an investigation. Buster would receive his prize money, yet while continuing to support other boxers by appearing at their bouts, his fight against Coy was his sole professional fight.

As Vin King Edwards says, rock 'n' roll was hugely popular amongst Jamaican teenagers during the mid-to-late-Fifties and early Sixties, and the Glass Bucket Club was the "in place" for rock 'n' roll-themed sock-hops. Once rock 'n' roll started giving way to R&B, however, it was perhaps inevitable that Buster would be drawn to the sound system scene; first with Tom "the Great" Sebastian, then Duke Reid, and then Coxsone Dodd before going it alone.

"Tom had a hardware store and he'd play music there all day long on Fridays and Saturdays," Buster recounted. "They used to play rhythm and blues. I used to play at Tom's and Coxsone came around one day and asked if I would help him, because of my popularity and a lot of people followed me at the time, and I helped Coxsone."

Dodd had initially struggled to draw a crowd to his Downbeat system because people feared falling victim to reprisal attacks by Reid's criminal associates. Having the rough-and-ready and ever-fearless Buster to call upon soon redressed the balance. At a dance staged at Forrester's Hall in late 1957, Buster brazenly broke Reid's stylus to bring the evening to a premature close; brandishing a knife to keep Reid's thugs – until recently his compadres – at arm's length while calmly making his escape.

"Coxsone took off by himself, but I was the one who used to help Coxsone to find who were the artists on the records that Duke Reid played at the dance," Buster continued. "In those days they would scratch the labels off the record, so you could read nothing. But Tom didn't do that, and when I was at Tom's, I read the names on the label and I identified the players who played and told Coxsone the labels they were recording on in the United States and he'd buy these records and bring them back and the agreement was that a certain portion would be for me. But every time he came back he had something to fix or something to do, I didn't get my work."

Whilst with Dodd, Buster fulfilled a variety of roles, from handling ticket receipts, identifying and sourcing music, as well as providing a bit of muscle on occasion. The experience and knowledge he gained under Dodd's tutelage put Buster in good stead for when he started up his own sound system, Voice of the People; the venture being funded in part by his family and a local radio shop owner. "Knowing I was the one keeping up his sound system," he explained, "I went off and did my own system and challenged Coxsone and Duke Reid and dethroned them and became king of sound system."

Following Buster's defection, Dodd brought in Lee "Scratch" Perry to fulfil the general dogsbody role. Perry had initially started out working for Reid, but a dispute over stolen lyrics had resulted in Reid flattening Perry with a single knock-out punch.

Taking another leaf from Dodd's book, Buster applied to America's Farm Work Program as a guest worker so that he too could source the records that might control the crowd. His application was refused, however, but this would prompt him to start recording his own music. His first port of call came with sounding out Arkland "Drumbago" Parks, a professional drummer working out of the Baby Grand Club. Parks agreed to help, and Buster was soon working with Parks and Jah Jerry Haynes. Parks and Haynes would subsequently appear on Buster's debut 1961 single, 'Little Honey' (b/w 'Luke Lane Shuffle'), along with Rico Rodriguez.

Having reflected on the disappointment of having his application on to the US Farm Work Program refused, despite having passed all the requisite tests, during the aforementioned interview with Heather Augustyn, Buster goes on talk about his collaborating with Parks: "I went to Drumbago and asked him to come with me and play a march, similar to a procession. I would wander off in processions to the beat of the drum, and that is what I did. I put the march on the track and I asked him to put the accent on the one and three [beats] and I had Jah Jerry come up with the strum of the guitar and I had Rico Rodriguez do the 'pop-pop-pop' on the tenor sax [sic] and recorded the sound that took over Jamaica. And that was called ska."

Edwards was already familiar with Prince Buster from the days when the latter was still working with Dodd. Upon their return from their record-buying forages in the US, Edwards and Reid staged a dance in Jubilee Hall so as to get the word out about all the new songs they'd amassed. "Buster talked too much," Edwards explained. "He would come to King Edwards and say, 'Country boy, can't find this, can't find that. Coxsone is the greatest!' I'm a politician so I know when to keep things cool. So when we went up to Jubilee the place was blocked! I couldn't believe it; thousands of people.

"Coxsone came to see. I played tune after tune. The place got mad. As big as Duke was, they lifted him up. Coxsone was humiliated because we mashed him up. The sound system was split; there was Coxsone, and there was Duke, and there was Edwards. So me and Duke joined up and that went on until the system became exhausted."

The "mashing up" was to come courtesy of Buster. On discovering Reid was now in possession of a copy of American jazz tenor saxophonist Willis "Gatortail" Jackson's 'Later for Gator' (most likely through his recent visit to the US with Edwards), which Coxsone had adopted as his theme tune and renamed 'Coxsone's Hop', Buster cajoled Coxsone to accompany him to the Jubilee Hall dance. It was on hearing Reid playing 'Later for Gator' that had caused Coxsone's apoplexy.

Another well-publicised "ska spat" was that between Buster and Derrick Morgan, another of the genre's founding fathers, whose 'Tougher than Tough' is also widely credited as being the first rocksteady song.

Morgan, the son of a church deacon, was born in the parish of Clarendon. The family moved to Kingston when Morgan was three years old to seek medical treatment for his night blindness. Retinis pigmentosa was a common eye ailment, but as no one else in the family had ever suffered night blindness, his mother was taking no chances. With both his parents having good singing voices, it was only natural that Morgan started singing at an early age. "My father was a great singer, but he didn't taught [sic] me to sing. My mother had a strong voice and sang in the choir. We used to sing in church a lot."

Morgan would also sing with his grandmother, making up songs about things that sprang to his febrile mind – even the bugs that flitted about the lights in his bedroom. It was only once he got to school that the future "undisputed king of ska" started taking his singing seriously. "I sing about from eleven, they used to have a concert every Friday, and that really taught me to sing proper. After school I could not take the work I liked, I used to like a job they call stenography, which is book-keeping. I couldn't take it, so after that now I decide to try singing. We heard of Vere Johns taking audition [for a] competition called *Opportunity Hour*."

Vere Johns was a one-time newspaper man who now managed a variety of Kingston clubs such as the Palace Theatre, the Ambassador, the Queens and the Gaiety. Vere was always looking at ways to keep his theatres turning a profit and thought a variety show tapping into the local talent might prove another sure-fire winner. *Opportunity Hour* (a forerunner to the execrable 1970s ITV show *Opportunity Knocks* and later *Britain's Got Talent*) would see ten acts battling it out in front of a live audience for a cash prize of £2; the winner being decided solely on audience approval.

Derrick Morgan's rip-roaring impression of Little Richard's 'Long Tall Sally' nigh on raised the Palace Theatre roof. Aside from the £2 prize, and the much-coveted prestige that came with being a "Vere Johns winner", Morgan was invited to accompany popular Jamaican comedy duo Bim and Bam on to the island club circuit. "They (Bim and Bam) had a show which travelled around the island and they took me with them," Morgan told *www.reggaevibes*.com in October 2017. "It really started my singin' officially in the public at the age of 17. Somebody told me after the tour about Duke Reid the Trojan; he had audition for the recording. Duke was a nice man… he was jus' a stern man, him nice. Him say, 'Oh, can you sing?' An' me say, 'Yeah', so him say, 'Well, sing.' He was a liquor store man, and while he's selling he was listening to me too. So he say, 'Okay, do another one, and do another one,' and he say, 'Yes, you can come to the radio station for rehearsal. He was just an outstanding [and] outspoken man; nice man to deal with. Straightforward and demanding.

"When he's in the studio and the musicians are not playing what they do, like the drummer not sounding good, he take away the sticks in the middle of the session and start clapping the sticks his way, so he'd sound good. He was a very good producer, because he tell the musician what he wanted. He didn't allow the musician to just want to play music as they'd like; they have to play what he want. That was very good."

In 1959, Morgan was invited by Duke Reid to record for his Treasure Isle label. The tracks cut that day were popular shuffle-boogie boppers 'Lover Boy' (aka 'S-Corner Rock') and 'Oh My'. A second hit came soon thereafter with 'Fat Man'. The following year saw Morgan claim the top seven placings on the Jamaican chart – the only artist ever to do so. Amongst these were 'Don't Call Me Daddy', 'In My Heat', 'Be Still', 'Meekly Wait' and 'Murmur Not'. But it was the ska-tinged 'Don't You Know' (subsequently retitled 'Housewife's Choice' by a local DJ) that would provide Morgan with the biggest and best-known hit of his career following its release via Treasure Isle in 1962.

"In those days when we work, we worked for… it is just a ten pound," Morgan recounted. "We make them [producers] pounds for each song we recorded. So I make a lot of hits. I go around, I sing for any producer. So everybody was releasing them songs, making hit songs out of everyone. So with everyone releasing it's in the chart.

"It's two radio stations, so you know, I dominated the stations with the songs that sell, on both stations. From one to seven, all hit songs. I would have songs coming in at 14, 15, 16, an' so on – they had a label, the other ones they come into the top ten. I was dominating those days, because the songs I used to sing, you see, the people really loved them. They used to call me 'the hit-maker'. I used to steal the chart away from everyone."

Morgan was hogging the limelight, but he wasn't above offering sanguine advice to those singers nibbling at his heels. Speaking with the *Chicago Tribune* in May 2013, Morgan revealed how Bob Marley tended to wear himself out on stage. "He was always dancing while he was singing, and he would get very tired. So, I told him, 'If you dance straight on with the song, you're going to be overtired. Just sing, then dance during the instrumental solo.'"

Morgan readily acknowledges Duke Reid, Coxsone Dodd and King Edwards as being the three biggest operators, but he aligned himself to another operator. "Duke, Coxsone and Edwards was the big sound. Big sounds, what you call bid sound, it would tremble the whole worl' when they were playing. But the sound that I follow, V Rocket, was a hi-fi sound. They used to play at parties, when they played they play for, y'know, selected parties. I used to follow those sound. They played different from Coxsone, Duke and Edwards and Count Bells the President, those people play different. Heavy duty.

"T'ings like these it look like when you stan' up sometime an' Duke is playing an' dropping all to Derrick Morgan, you really heard about it. Or Coxsone, I used to do a recording with Coxsone called 'Leave Earth', an' he would draw that an' put them amongst Hi-Lite an' Derrick Morgan, an' play other songs. It's nice listening then beca' you have crowd a people following those sets. I like to go to them places where you can hold on to a girl an' dance, but with Duke and Coxsone you jus' stand up outside an' listen the deep bass and drum."

The spat between Morgan and Buster supposedly started when Morgan opted for another singer than Buster to record his song 'Forward March', a song celebrating Jamaica's independence from Great Britain on August 6, 1962 (though it has been written elsewhere that 'Don't You Know' was the cause of their fallout). To compound the situation, Buster got it in his head that Morgan had poached one of his studio instrumentalists, "Deadly Headley" Bennett, to perform a solo on the recording. Buster retaliated not with violence, but rather in song – even if the subject matter of the song, 'Blackhead Chiney Man', was blatantly directed at Morgan's Chinese-American studio producer, Leslie Kong, with its derisive putdown, "I didn't know your parents were from Hong Kong." (The song would subsequently be banned by Radio Jamaica for its overtly racist lyric.)

As many of Morgan's songs were centred around rude boy culture, Buster began penning Judge Dread songs, Dread being the apocryphal judge that sentenced the rude boys to "400 years behind bars", regardless of their crimes or pleas for mercy.

Buster has since played down the rift by saying he and Morgan remained friends throughout their musical stick fight, call-and-response capers. "Derrick came down to [my] shop [studio] because we had a lot of young singers we were bringing along," he explained. "And he sang 'Hey Fat Man' and all that but we said we could do better with him, so he joined the group with us and we took him to the studio and we made records."

Buster says that he actually referred to Morgan as a "Black Head Chinaman", which makes no sense given Morgan's Jamaican ethnicity. Morgan had retorted with 'Blazing

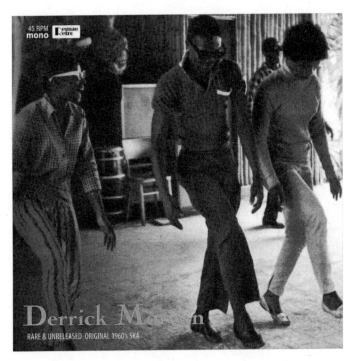

45 RPM mono

Derrick Morgan

RARE & UNRELEASED ORIGINAL 1960's SKA

Fire', which in turn begat Buster's own 'Praise and No Raise', but Buster insisted that it was purely in the spirit of competitiveness in support of making better music. "I counted him [Morgan] close to me. We had a war, but we don't have a physical war. I don't remember ever talk to Derrick that hard for a war, you know, more than for the music, to get things done. It was always a friendship because with me, he's got a voice to speak and it's a democratic kind of thing."

When giving his own version of events about the feud, Morgan said he was already singing with Buster when Jimmy Cliff came to see him to tell him that Leslie Kong was interested in him singing a song called 'Dearest Beverley'.

Cliff hadn't yet started singing, according to Morgan. "Jimmy say [Kong] wanted me to take care of it, take it back to Leslie and say,

'This song sound good', an' so on. So, I listened to Jimmy and his song and it sound alright to me, but I didn't like the slow song, ca' he had another song called 'Hurricane Hattie'.

"After he [Cliff] sang it I say OK, yes it sounds good, and from that we tek it to Leslie Kong. Leslie wanted to go into business also, and he asked me what he should do. I told him about Drumbago an' the All Stars band and about Jimmy Cliff, that Jimmy was soundin' good. Jimmy was at that time called Jimmy Chambers, it was Leslie who named him 'Jimmy Cliff', yunno? So, after bringin' Drumbago to Leslie we start to record then, and Prince Buster didn't like it when he hear about that.

According to apocryphal folklore, Kong first encountered the young Cliff when the latter arrived at his restaurant/ice-cream parlour-cum-record store and started singing 'Dearest Beverley' in the hope that hearing mention of Kong's family-run emporium would convince Kong to sign him up, and this was how Kong decided upon "Beverley's" as the name for his record label.

"In 1962, I made 'Forward March', the Jamaican independence song," Morgan continued. "Buster heard that song and he said the solo in that song was his, he claimed it was part of one of his songs, the melody where it come from, that he do [referring to Headley Bennett]. So, he wrote a song called 'Black Head Chinaman', because Leslie Kong was the Chinaman. And that's where he an' I start the musical war. It was just a musical war."

The musical feud betwixt Morgan and Buster was producing some very fine music, but Morgan says there was never any ulterior motive behind it – in other words, "Let's keep doing this as long as the records keep selling." "No, we never really sit an' talk about it," says Morgan. He [Buster] was a producer and Leslie was a producer, so might be the two of them jus' talk, they never reach out to me, you understan'? When I was with him, Prince Buster was a producer also, an' he go ahead and do his thing, so that's how get to beat me out because I was only singin' and collecting a little pay every now and then."

The musical dispute rivalry was amicable enough between the two, but many of their followers were in rival street gangs that were happy for any excuse to attack each other. The violence on Kingston's streets got so bad that the Jamaican prime minister, Hugh Lawson Shearer, was forced to step in by approaching the *Daily Gleaner* for help by having the paper (the largest in Jamaica at the time) publish a staged photo of Morgan and Buster shaking hands.

"Some gangs defended Buster, and some defended me," says Morgan. "It would get bad, in bars man would cut up one another, and the government would have a problem. Now, it was Buster's plan or Mr Seaga [Edward Seaga, Jamaica's minister of culture and future prime minister], he was also a producer an' doing recording for him before him become a politician. Well, he tell us to go to the *Gleaner*, and they took picture we hugged, and it said on the headline that we are the best of friends."

Dodd would subsequently lay claim to his being the first producer to record what he termed "Rastafari music". "I was the first person ever to use Count Ossie on a recording session with 'Rockaman Soul' and 'Another Moses'. At that time Prince Buster was working for me, then Buster came long after and used them for 'Oh Carolina'. I also used to invite them [Ossie and his drummers] to dances that we had, away from the sound system. We would have them coming on and chanting, so we knew the Rasta thing was popular and would make sense to invest into."

Buster would subsequently reissue 'Oh Carolina' on his own Prince Buster label, while Ossie himself would record the song for inclusion on his 1973 album *Groundation*. Though his own recording output had slowed down considerably by this juncture, he continued to produce excellent results with Dennis Brown, Gregory Isaacs and Big Youth. When he became embroiled in legal wrangling with the Jamaican government over the mosque he'd established in downtown Kingston, however, he turned his back on both his recording career and his homeland by moving to Miami to pursue business interests.

In 1993, Buster would become embroiled in yet another feud following Shaggy's UK chart-topping success with his version of 'Oh Carolina'. As was common with all Jamaican releases at the time of the original recording, the song was credited on the label to the producer rather than the songwriter or artist – in this instance "C. Campbell", which was, of course, Prince Buster's real name. Sensing a larger share of the spoils from Shaggy's hit, Buster claimed he had written the song about one of his ex-girlfriends. When the case went before the high court in 1994, the judge ruled in favour of the original writers, the Folkes' brothers.

The 2-Tone revival brought Buster's talents back to the fore, but he continued to maintain a low profile and wouldn't resume his career until the late Eighties, performing with The Skatalites as his backing band. He started recording again in 1992, subsequently guesting on The Skatalites' 1994 album *Hi Bop Ska*. His own future recordings were primarily in collaboration with Gaz Mayall, lead singer with UK ska act The Trojans.

1997 saw Buster reunited with The Skatalites for his contribution to Island Records' fortieth anniversary album, *Ska Island*, while the following year brought about a return to the UK chart after 30 years owing to Levi Strauss' using his 1967 hit, 'Whine and Grine', as part of their long-running TV campaign. The single gave Buster a Top 30 hit, and a belated debut on *Top of the Pops*. He was awarded the Order of Distinction in 2001.

Paying tribute to Buster following his death in September 2016, Jerry Dammers spoke of the "enormous debt of gratitude" The Specials and the other 2-Tone bands owed to Buster, while hailing him as being "among the most influential figures in late 20th century music".

Count Ossie's drummers would subsequently feature on a number of recordings for Dodd, as well as other producers. Their performances at Jamaica's annual Festival of Arts yielded the gold medal in 1965, and again the following year. They would also perform before Haile Selassie at King's House, during the Ethiopian Emperor's state visit to the island, the clearest indication of Ossie's Wareika Hills project being more than musical get-togethers. Another significant collaboration Ossie undertook came with The Mystic Revelation of Rastafari, which saw Ossie's drummers merge with The Mystics, a group led by saxophonist and spiritual seeker Cedric Brooks.

Ossie's drummers were set to appear alongside The Mystic Revelation of Rastafari at Kingston's National Stadium on October 18, 1976, the public holiday to honour Jamaica's national heroes. Tragedy struck when a torrential downpour caused stampeding amongst the crowd, resulting in two children being trampled to death. Worse was to follow, however.

With the festival's running order now delayed, the man deemed responsible more than any other for bringing unity in a musical genre that has come to be defined by backbiting rivalries was heading back to St. Thomas when he was run off the road by a drunk bus driver, the impact killing him instantly. He was 50 years old. Later that same day, Ossie's eight-month-old son died as a result of a freak accident at the family home.

Rico Rodriguez would pay tribute to the man he regarded as his "bosom brother", saying that Ossie was "the only person in this society that I really talked to, the only person that really loved me".

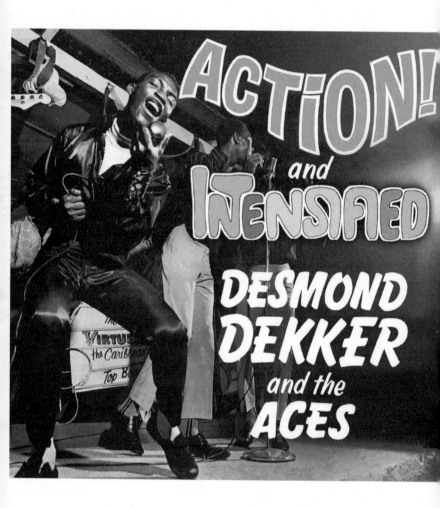

CHAPTER

FOUR

ROCKIN' STEADY

"One day, I went to buy something for my dad at the shops, and I heard a song by Nat 'King' Cole called 'Stardust Melody'. It was like I went into a trance or something. I forgot all about my dad sending me to the shop. When I got home, I explained to him what happened. I thought I was going to get a whipping but he understood."

DESMOND DEKKER

CHAPTER

In October 1963, Coxsone Dodd opened the Jamaica Recording and Publishing Studio (forever known thereafter as "Studio One") on the site of a former nightclub on Brentford Road, a short walk from the Carib Theatre his father had helped build. It was undoubtedly Dodd's opening Studio One that cranked up the rivalry between himself and Reid. The ex-Skatalites would also inadvertently play a part in the unfolding drama as Roland Alphonso's Soul Brothers would serve as the mainstay of Dodd's Studio One output, while Reid snapped up Tommy McCook's Supersonics and installed them as his in-house studio band at Treasure Isle studio.

Ska had reigned supreme, but its style – coupled with Jamaica's torrid climate – was to bring about its downfall; musicians struggling to maintain the tempo and dancing to it carried the risk of heat exhaustion or worse. By the close of 1966, ska had been supplanted by the slower style of rocksteady; its demise coinciding with the opening of Duke Reid's Treasure Isle studio. With Tommy McCook installed as the studio's musical arranger, Treasure Isle would dominate the Jamaican chart for the next couple of years.

Rocksteady's rise would be mirrored by its equally fast demise, but those two years would see Reid come into his own as a producer, releasing a number of superbly crafted songs by some of Jamaica's finest musical talents, including The Melodians, Phyllis Dillon, The Techniques, The Paragons, and Ken Parker and The Three Tops. He also enjoyed sizeable hits with Justin Hinds and Alton Ellis, the "Godfather of Rocksteady". (One of the songs Reid recorded with The Paragons was the 1966 single 'The Tide is High', which was to give Blondie a transatlantic smash 14 years later.)

Ellis had started his career working for Dodd as part of singing duo Alton & Eddy with Eddy Parkins, their first Studio One recording being 'Muriel', a slow R&B-style

ballad that Ellis had written while working as a building site labourer. This was soon followed up with a second ballad, 'My Heaven'. Further syrupy success followed with 'Lullabye Angel', 'I Know It All', 'I'm Never Gonna Cry' and 'Yours'. Alton & Eddy were also recording with Vincent Chin's Randy's label around this time, but Parkins' winning a prestigious talent contest brought a parting of the ways, with the latter relocating to the US.

Ellis remained in Kingston and took up work as a printer, and it was only due to his losing his job that he decided to have another crack at a singing career. He initially formed another duo with John Holt, but when Holt went off to replace Leroy Stamp in The Paragons, Ellis formed the short-lived Anton Ellis and The Flames with his brother, Leslie. The Flames scored hits with 'Girl I've Got a Date' and 'Cry Tough', but it was Ellis' solo release 'Rock Steady' (backed by Tommy McCook and The Supersonics) that heralded the latest direction in Jamaican music, ultimately serving as the genre's new name.

Dodd briefly found himself in Duke Reid's shadow, but he bided his time and when the opportunity presented itself, he lured Ellis back to Studio One and had him re-record many of the songs he'd cut with Reid. With rocksteady having begun its metamorphism into reggae, Dodd, having already signed Bob Marley and The Wailers, meant he was the one reaping the lion's share of the rewards. Further reggae signings came with The Heptones, The Abyssinians, Bob Andy and Marcia Griffiths.

It was The Wailers' percussionist, "Seeco" Patterson, who first brought the band to Dodd's attention. "I was amazed," Dodd reflected. "It knocked me out because I admired the harmony that they had. They came as 'The Juveniles', and two girls was in the group; they had that team sound, so I was crazy about them, because we had nothing like that before in Jamaica – that was coming from a Frankie Lymon kind of thing."

At the time of Patterson's approach, The Juveniles were fronted by "Junior" Braithwaite, and it was only due to his quitting the band and relocating to the US in the hope of pursuing a career in medicine that Marley assumed the role – something that Dodd readily takes credit for. "I selected Bob as the singer," he explained. "Looking back, and seeing that he's such a big star, I feel good to know that I'd seen that in him at a very early stage."

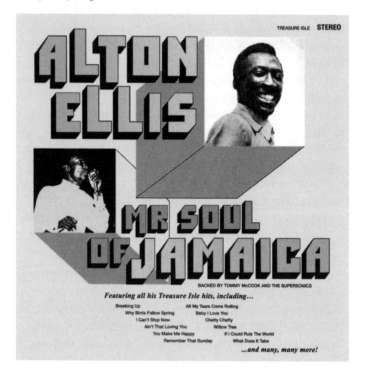

Marley was born in February 1945 on the farm of his maternal grandfather in Nine Mile, Saint Ann Parish. He was primarily raised by his mother, Cedella, as his father – who was employed as a plantation overseer – was rarely at home. To all intents and purposes, Cedella was a single mother, and in order to support herself and young Nesta (as Marley was known for much of his early life) she departed for Kingston to find domestic work, leaving young Nesta in the care of relatives in Nine Mile. Marley subsequently joined Cedella in Trenchtown, one of Kingston's most impoverished ghettos. By this juncture, though she was still married, Cedella had taken up with a man called Toddy Livingston, who ran a local bar.

Marley soon befriended Livingston's son, Neville, who was some two years younger than Marley and known to all as "Bunny". As with most Jamaican teenagers, Marley and Bunny Livingston shared a passion for the R&B that was becoming the island's musical heartbeat. When Cedella fell pregnant to Toddy Livingston, resulting in a half-sister, Claudette Pearl, Marley and Bunny were now family.

Though brighter than most of his peers, Marley left school in 1960 with no qualifications and little hope of ever amounting to anything owing to the colour of his skin. Independence was still some two years hence, and as such Jamaica's economic and political power almost exclusively resided with the small white minority, and the gap betwixt the ruling elite and the island's indigenous black underclass was just as wide as it was while slavery was still in operation. Educational opportunities were virtually non-existent in Trenchtown, and with jobs hard to come by, Marley avoided what would otherwise have proved a restless existence by teaching himself rudimentary guitar-playing along to the songs emanating from every window.

Bunny Livingston had also taken up the guitar, and he Marley would sit

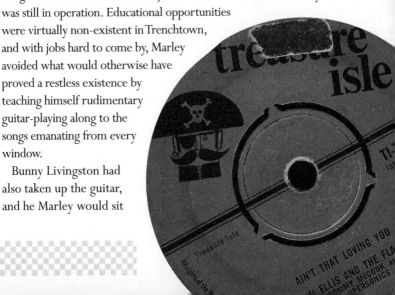

on the porch listening to the radio, keeping their ears tuned for doo-wop bands such as The Ink Spots, The Platters and The Drifters that were merging pop and R&B into a style that would lay the foundation for Sixties soul music. Frankie Lymon and The Teenagers had been the first doo-wop act to come to the fore over in America with their mid-Fifties hit 'Why Do Fools Fall in Love'. Speaking about this time on *Rebel Music: The Bob Marley Story* many years later, Bunny Livingston cited doo-wop as being a key influence on the early Wailers' sound.

Marley and Livingston, along with their more musically gifted friend, Peter Tosh (born Winston Hubert McIntosh), formed a trio, naming themselves "The Teenagers" in homage to Frankie Lymon. Through Tosh, who was a year older than himself, Marley had found work as a trainee welder, but gave the job up to concentrate on making music as slowly but surely – thanks to the likes of Duke Reid and Coxsone Dodd opening recording studios – opportunities were now opening up for young Jamaican artists.

By the time they came to Coxsone Dodd's attention, The Teenagers had expanded to a five-piece and were writing their own material. They were now rehearsing under the watchful eye of Joe Higgs, who was already well known on the Jamaican music scene as part of the successful vocal duo Higgs and Wilson. Given their age, the music they were making was lacking in both experience and refinement, but Higgs saw something worth tutoring and was happy to help the five develop their vocal harmonies. He also reportedly taught Marley how to play the guitar. They'd undergone several name changes, first to the Wailing Rudeboys, then the Wailing Wailers, before finally settling on The Wailers. Had they been aware of a Tacoma, Washington-based rock band of the same name having scored an instrumental hit in 1959 with 'Tall Cool One', they would surely have continued in their search.

Speaking with Stephen Davis for the latter's book, *Bob*

Marley, Higgs noted that while Junior Braithwaite was the singer, Marley was a leader in waiting. "Person to person, they were each capable of leading at any given time because I wanted each person to be a leader in his own right, able to lead anyone, or to be able to wail."

And while The Wailers had a cache of singing talent, with Braithwaite, Tosh and Livingston each having their own distinctive style and range, it was as a solo artist that Marley was to make his recording debut following his being introduced to Leslie Kong in early 1962. Kong at the time had only recently started his Beverley's label as an extension to the restaurant-cum-ice-cream parlour he ran with his brothers. Of the three songs Marley recorded with Kong – 'Terror', 'One Cup of Coffee' and 'Judge Not' – it was the latter that was released as a single. 'Judge Not' (with Marley credited as "Robert Marley") might not have sold well, but aside from showcasing Marley's poetic lyrical style, the tune was undeniably a highly infectious slice of early Sixties ska. Kong released 'Once Cup of Coffee' (with Marley this time credited as "Bobby Martell") as a follow-up. Again, while the record didn't cause much of a stir, it set Marley on his way.

When Kong and Marley's paths next crossed in 1971, Kong was the most successful record producer in Jamaica, while Marley and The Wailers were still searching for that elusive mainstream hit that would "break" the band either in the US or Europe. The sessions were somewhat tumultuous, and within a few months of the recording Kong suffered a fatal heart attack aged just 37.

Legend has it that Bunny Livingston (aka Bunny Wailer) was so angry at what he considered a sub-standard recording on *The Best of The Wailers* (which despite its title isn't a compilation album) that he placed a curse on Kong.

Another tale has Kong meeting with his accountant, and that upon being informed how much money he could expect to make from The Wailers' album, he'd gone home and suffered the fatal heart attack soon thereafter.

Desmond Dekker, who would also come to be regarded as a reggae great, was hanging about Kong's studio at the time Marley made his first forays into recording, yet it would be another two years before he got his chance. "Desmond used to be my back-up singer," Derrick Morgan explained. "He was with Beverley's for two years before he sang a song called 'Honour Your Mother and Father', so while he was there, he was doing back-up with me.

Dekker's actual name was Desmond Dacres. His singing talent was noted from an early age, happily singing along to the likes of Little Richard, Nat 'King' Cole and Sam Cooke for anyone willing to listen. His mother died when he was still quite young, and owing to his father being unable to support him, Dekker was taken in at Alpha Boys School. On leaving Alpha he began working as an apprentice welder, alongside Bob Marley, and only tried his luck as a singer after being encouraged to do so by his fellow workers. Imbued with renewed confidence, Dekker had approached Leslie Kong, and on returning to his place of work, he'd apparently encouraged Marley to do the same.

Dekker performed on Vere Johns' *Opportunity Hour*, and as with many of his contemporaries, took time off work to audition for Duke Reid, Coxsone Dodd and other leading studios. Reid and Coxsone both passed on Dekker, but Leslie Kong recognised his potential and (having suggested a change in surname) duly signed him to the Beverley's label in 1961 – even if two years were to pass before Kong put Dekker in a recording booth.

'Honour Your Mother and Father' (released as Desmond Dekker & The Beverley's Allstars) was to prove an immediate hit in Jamaica. Following a second hit in 1964 with 'King of Ska' (backed by The Cherrypies, who would subsequently undergo a name change of their own to The Maytals), Dekker assembled his own backing band, The Aces, consisting of four brothers – Carl, Patrick, Clive and Barry Howard.

Dekker continued to score hits in Jamaica, but it was his 1967 offering '007 (Shanty Town)' that propelled him to mainstream attention, the single reaching Number 15 on the UK singles chart, and it was also a hit in the US owing to its inclusion in the film *The Harder They Come*.

The following year, Dekker won the 1968 Jamaica Festival song contest with 'Intensified'. That same year he recorded 'The Israelites', the song that was to cement his position as one of Jamaica's all-time greats.

'007 (Shanty Town)' would become a favourite dance track in clubs up and down Britain, proving so popular in fact that a budding music entrepreneur financed Dekker's first visit. "Desmond was signed to Starlight Artists and we paid to bring him over with The Aces to play some shows," says Eliot Moses Cohen, co-founder of Red Bus Recording Studios in Marylebone. "I was studying for a degree at the London School of Economics at the time. I was managing a couple of bands that played on the uni scene, but I'd never put a tour together. It was to prove a real learning curve because I didn't know anything about overheads. Desmond came out ahead though, which is the main thing. Desmond was a great guy, a true gentlemen, and we remained good friends. There was something like 15 or 16 dates across the country and those shows were complete sell-outs because of Desmond's popularity with the mods. They followed him wherever we went.

"Desmond loved London and explored the city every chance he got. He'd just get on a bus and away he'd go. One day he ended up getting lost. There were no mobile phones back then, of course, and Desmond was going off without bothering to take anyone's telephone numbers with him. It was hours before he returned. The tour was early in the year if I remember rightly, because Desmond came down with a cold. He'd never had a cold before and he was quite ill. He was so ill that it looked like we'd have to cancel a couple of shows, but the venue owners weren't having any of that. Desmond said he was okay to sing but wasn't sure he'd be able to remain standing through a whole show. So someone suggested putting a piece of wood down the back of his trousers and under his shirt so that he would stand bolt upright. No one in the crowd noticed thankfully, and he got through the show."

Cohen's naivety would almost prove his undoing. "It was after the show in Birmingham. The owner paid me in silver coins. He did it on purpose, of course. There I was in a strange city late at night carrying a heavy bag filled with crowns and half crowns – that's how long ago it was. The idea, I know, was to have a couple of his people rob me, but thankfully a friend of mine that had driven up to see the show spotted me and picked me up and drove me back to London."

Cohen also took Dekker to Count Suckle's Cue Club on Praed Street. Suckle (born Wilbert Augustus Campbell) was a known face on the London club scene. Prior to leaving Kingston for London with his friend Vincent "Duke Vin" Forbes in 1952, he'd supplied records for Tom "the Great" Sebastian. By 1956 he was running the Count Suckle Sound System – in direct competition with Duke Vin's own sound system – from his Ladbrook Grove base. Suckle quickly built up a large following within west London's African-Caribbean community, and in 1961 he was installed as the resident DJ at the Roaring Twenties club on Carnaby Street, where he thrilled revellers with a blend of obscure rhythm and blues and previously unheard ska; the latter in the form of exclusive records obtained from Prince Buster, Duke Reid and other close associates back in Kingston. It is said that it was owing to the popularity of Suckle's all-night sets that the club's owners agreed to open its doors to black patrons.

Georgie Fame was a regular member of the club's house band. Future Led Zeppelin bassist John Paul Jones was often in attendance, as were members of The Who, The Animals and The Rolling Stones – with Mick Jagger reportedly borrowing Suckle's records on occasion. Suckle also played host to visiting Jamaican performers at the club, including Prince Buster and Owen Gray.

However, with the club being regularly targeted by the police, Suckle took over a run-down billiard hall to open the Cue Club (later Q Club) at 5a Praed Street, playing a variety of ska, reggae, soul and funk music, as well as featuring live performances by Prince Buster and Edwin Starr, amongst others. In 1970 he set up Q Records, a short-lived subsidiary of the Trojan record label. Speaking about the Cue Club's success in 1974, Suckle said: "We lead the field because we've always moved with the times at the Q Club. When we opened ska music was the thing, Prince Buster, Don Drummond, Reco, Tommy McCook, Roland Alphonso, Baba Brooks, y'know. They all played here when they toured London. We played all the latest things and the new dances caught on quick."

"The Cue Club really was the hottest ticket in town," says Cohen, "the Tramps of the late Sixties and early Seventies. Count Suckle was always immaculately dressed and would walk around with at least £200 in five pound notes in his hand. That was his thing. He really had everything going for him. I truly believe if he'd have put a bit more effort into his record label he would have been as big as Branson and Virgin."

Cohen was still studying for his degree at the LSE when Chris Blackwell called out of the blue enquiring about one of the bands he was managing. "'Eliot, I hear you've got a great black band,'" he said. "'I'd like to come and see them rehearse, and so long as they have a great brass section we'll be able to do business.' Chris picked me up in a beautiful black Ford Mustang. I remember there was something like 20 parking tickets stuck to the dashboard, but because the car had an

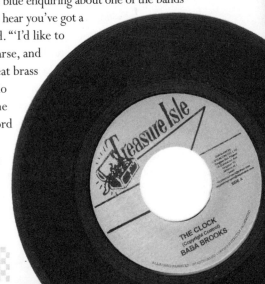

American or Jamaican licence plate I don't think they could ever enforce the tickets. Chris didn't seem to care one way or the other.

"On the way to see my band rehearse, Chris explained about The Skatalites and how they'd scored a big hit over in Jamaica with 'Guns of Navarone'. He was looking to promote the record over here in the UK and wanted to use my band. I don't want to risk being sued by Chris, but that's what happened – my band recorded and toured as The Skatalites. Very few people in England would have recognised anyone from the band so what was the harm? And it was because of Chris approaching me that I was able to start the Red Bus booking agency at 33-37 Wardour Street, the former Whisky a Go Go. So thank you, Chris."

The power pendulum might have swung back Dodd's way, but Reid was far from idle during this frenetic period. As the Sixties ended he was the leading light in what would become the next significant development of Jamaican music: DJ recordings. In placing the then relatively unknown U-Roy's fluid toasts over his old rocksteady rhythms, Reid scored three number ones on the Jamaican chart, while U-Roy's ground-breaking 1970 album, *Version Galore*, would spark a DJ explosion; the tremors of which are still evident in world music today.

Treasure Isle would secure further hits by U-Roy's fellow DJ, Dennis Alcapone. But as the decade unfolded, Reid became disaffected with how Jamaican music was developing along dub and roots reggae lines. His health was also in decline, and acting on his protégé Justin Hinds' advice, sought medical opinion. The doctors confirmed Reid's worst fears: it was cancer. He returned to Kingston, where he sadly passed away at St. Joseph's Hospital in September 1976, his body subsequently laid to rest at Black Rock in Portland.

In October 2007, Reid's sizeable contribution to Jamaican music was finally recognised when he was posthumously awarded the prestigious Order of Distinction (in the rank of Commander), for outstanding and important services to Jamaica.

In a fitting postscript to the Reid/Dodd saga, Reid is believed to have summoned Dodd to his bedside at St. Joseph's to say a final farewell and to discuss certain issues that have understandably remained private.

Unlike Reid, Dodd had readily embraced dub reggae, advancing the career of Dennis Brown along the way. Bob Marley would cite Brown as being his favourite singer, dubbing him the "Crown Prince of Reggae". Brown's first session with Dodd resulted in 'No Man is an Island', which became a huge hit throughout Jamaica.

Recuts of Dodd's rhythms recorded at another of his rivals, Channel One, were to find greater favour, but Dodd would have the last laugh with a Studio One renaissance, which coincided with the emergence of 2-Tone over in England during the summer of 1979.

When armed bandits attacked Studio One that same year (most likely in search of prized vinyls rather than the studio equipment), Dodd transferred the studio to Brooklyn, New York, where he continued recording through to the early 1990s, working with the likes of Frankie Paul and JD Smoothe, occasionally voicing on new mixes of old rhythms. Regular reissues of his best-known work helped keep Dodd in vogue. He would be awarded the Order of Distinction in 1991.

Dodd returned to Kingston in 1998 and reopened Brentford Road, working with veteran musicians as well as up-and-coming talents; the crippling arthritis that had plagued his later years failing to diminish his unswerving passion for making music. A few days before his passing, the Jamaican government paid Dodd another great honour in renaming Brentford Road "Studio One Boulevard", while the island's newspapers wished him "maximum respect".

CHAPTER
FIVE

BLUE BEAT BOP

*"Everybody was learning on the chop;
everybody was learning, a new business was
being created as we went along. With everybody,
not just with the musicians, with the managers,
it was an incredibly exciting time, because you
were breaking new ground. It had never
existed anything like this before."*

CHRIS BLACKWELL

' O h Carolina' is recognised as being the first ska record released in the UK, but ska itself was already being played in basement shebeens in Brixton, Birmingham, Bristol and Coventry by Jamaican musicians who had migrated to Britain in the wake of the SS Empire Windrush in June 1948. At the time of writing, the British government had come under fire for wrongly targeting the so-called "Windrush Generation" as illegal immigrants, according to the guidelines set out in the Home Office's "hostile environment policy". What tends to get overlooked is that those Jamaicans that took up the then British government's offer to resettle here and help with the rebuilding of the country's infrastructure were migrants rather than immigrants and could enter and stay in the UK free from restriction until the implementation of the Commonwealth Immigrants Act in 1962. While many Jamaicans did indeed settle in Britain permanently, others would stay for six months or so then return home for a similar period before repeating the process; the result being a steady transmutation of cultures.

The musicians who came over from Jamaica in the initial late 1940s wave to resettle in Britain in the hope of carving out a career in the clubs of Soho and elsewhere would have all been schooled in jazz. But by the mid-to-late-Fifties, those musicians coming over would have been schooled in jazz, R&B and their hybrid offspring, ska.

From 1960 onwards, the more discerning jazz and R&B enthusiasts in Britain were already attuned to the ska-tinged records being issued by Blue Beat Records, the newly founded London-based subsidiary of Emil Shallit's Melodisc, which had been specialising in calypso and mento for the past 13 years.

Many legends surround the enigmatic Shallit (who died in 1983 aged 71); the one talked about most is of his penchant for walking around Kingston with a red suitcase stuffed with wads of cash and records, with "Danger: High Explosives" written on the outside in large letters to deter would-be thieves.

Shallit had started Melodisc with the proceeds of a reportedly sizeable war pension he received for spying for the Allies behind enemy lines in Nazi-occupied France during World War II. Having encountered Sigmund "Siggy" Jackson on London's famous musical thoroughfare Tin Pan Alley in 1953, Shallit invited the then-aspiring music publisher to join him at Melodisc. When subsequently asked where he'd thought up the name for the label that would come to define a genre, Jackson said the idea came to him whilst listening to some demos of Jamaican music an American acquaintance of his had sent over. Because it had a good beat and was bluesy, I decided to call it 'Blue Beat'.

It was to prove something of an uneasy alliance betwixt the two. Jackson would often bemoan Shallit's spending his days either at his home in France or schmoozing in New York and Kingston, only showing up at their London offices to raid the till, while Shallit often accused Jackson of emptying the till in advance of his arrival.

Prior to Prince Buster's 'Oh Carolina', Blue Beat's catalogue was entirely made up of Duke Reid productions, but from then on Buster would be the label's most prolific artist, spending the next few years hopping between London and Kingston for live shows, TV appearances such as on ITV's newly launched *Ready Steady Go!*, as well as working at Blue Beat's London studios. "The studio would be like a dancehall," Jackson told *The Guardian* in December 2018. "There would always be a bottle of whisky on the table and everyone would be dancing – having a good time was a big part of making music."

Record Mirror was probably the first British music weekly to focus on the new, exciting music flooding in from Jamaica. An article titled "It's the Blue-beat craze" (that appeared in the paper's February 15, 1964 issue) defined Blue Beat as a "strictly Jamaican sound with a pulsating on-beat played on non-stop chords throbbing mercilessly through the disc". Having cited the tunes being secondary to the beat, the article went on to explain how the Blue Beat craze had been "in" with Britain's growing army of mods since the previous summer "because of the marvellous dance beat and of course has been bought by the West Indians in Britain for many years now".

The good times at Blue Beat weren't set to last, however, as Shallit and Jackson's shaky alliance finally broke down in 1967. Buster would side with Shallit and oversee Blue Beat's Melodisc successors, including rocksteady-heavy fab, releasing some of the first DJ and dub cuts. Jackson went off and formed Columbia Big Beat, releasing a string of skinhead-reggae classics such as The Bees' 'Jesse James Rides Again'. Jackson is also still in possession of many of Blue Beat's own classics (allegedly holed away in a bedroom safe), but apparently has no desire to release them any time soon. "I decided a while ago to get out of London and the whole music business," he said in the same interview, "because it's full of liars and cheats. I haven't got time for it anymore."

By 1963, Blue Beat was taking London by storm; it's infectious rhythms also serving as a backdrop while mods clashed with rockers on the beach at Brighton, Margate and elsewhere. The racial integration Jerry Dammers would strive towards with 2-Tone 15 years later was already in evidence on London's early Sixties Soho scene, most notably at the gay club Le Duce, where sharp-dressed Jamaicans performed their "arms-outstretched ska dance and shared spliffs with mods and it-girls".

One of the songs that was certain to have filled the dancefloor at Le Duce (on D'Arblay Street) was Millie Small's 'My Boy Lollipop', a reworking of The Cadillacs' 1956 song produced by Chris Blackwell and issued through Fontana Records, a subsidiary of Philips Records (not Island Records, as is generally assumed).

Speaking with his one-time Island collaborator, Hooman Majd, in March 2009 for *www.interviewmagazine.com*, Blackwell revealed his reasoning behind licensing 'My Pop Lollipop' elsewhere. "I licensed it to Philips because of something I'd learned from understanding the American independent record business, which was that if an independent label had a hit, then it was pretty much guaranteed that they'd be out of business, because most of the time these small labels couldn't collect the money from the stores fast enough to pay for the pressing plant to make more records in order to meet the demand. When I heard 'My Boy Lollipop', I knew it was a hit."

Blackwell was already aware of Millie Small from her recording of 'We'll Meet' as part of singing duo Roy & Millie (with Roy Panton). "This little girl came on in the second verse of the song," he explained in a May 2009 interview with journalist Hans Peter Kuenzler. "She had this very high-pitched and funny voice, and everyone said, 'I've got to have that record.' That encouraged me to bring her over to England to see if I could make a record with her here because her voice was so distinctive. And it was very successful."

Millie Small had started singing at an early age. When she was 12 she entered the Vere Johns *Opportunity Hour* staged at the Palladium in Montego Bay, performing in front of an estimated 2,000 people. "I don't remember what I sang, but most of it was with my eyes shut because I was so shy," Small recalled for the *Express* in August 2016. "I won the second prize of thirty shillings and it was the beginning of my new life as a singer. I never had any singing lessons, my voice was just something I was born with."

It was hearing 'We'll Meet' that led to Blackwell stepping in and inviting her over to London. "I arrived in London in 1963," Small continued. "It felt like I was coming home; that this was where I was meant to be. I made a few songs ['Don't You Know', b/w 'Until You're Mine'] which didn't go anywhere, and then recorded 'My Boy Lollipop' [b/w 'Something's Gotta Be Done'] in 1964, which got to number two over here [UK] and number one in many parts of the world."

In the same interview, Small echoes the urban legend of it being a then relatively unknown Rod Stewart playing the song's tell-tale harmonica solo, something Stewart has always denied.

The original version of 'My Boy Lollypop' was one of the records Blackwell had snapped up on one of his New York shopping trips to sell on to one of the sound system operators. Before selling the records on, however, he would first copy each song on to a reel-to-reel tape. "When I brought Millie over to England I sat down trying to work out if we could find a song for her, and I found this tape which had the original version of 'My Boy Lollipop' [sic] on it," he told Kuenzler. "And I said, that's the song we should do. It was really lucky that I found the tape."

Blackwell rightly cites 'My Boy Lollipop' as being the hit that changed his life; getting him that all-important foot in the door in the music business. There was, however, a cloud accompanying the silver lining, for while he was now on his way, he wasn't able to sustain Small's career. "I felt very bad to open up somebody like what happened with her," he continued. "She had such a big hit and became a star, and then not to be able to sustain it. And I didn't like that.

"I don't know if she took it badly, but there was clearly a disappointment of being on the front of every newspaper, as she was, with The Beatles. At the time it was The Beatles and after that it was her, to sort of being disregarded, and I felt very bad about that. I felt in a sense almost – guilty, really. Thereafter I was always interested in people I felt could have a long-term career."

WELCOME BACK MILLIE TO "SWINGING U.K."

WELCOME BACK millie

SWINGING U.K.

The "Blue Beat Girl", as Small was billed, would continue touring and performing through to the early Seventies. Though she never came close to emulating her breakthrough success, in August 2011 she was awarded the Order of Distinction (rank of Commander) by Jamaica's Governor-General for her contribution to the Jamaican music industry.

Blackwell had founded Island Records in Jamaica in July 1959 with Graeme Goodall and Leslie Kong, reportedly lifting the label's name from Harry Belafonte's 1957 hit, 'Island in the Sun'. He was born in London in June 1937 but had spent much of his childhood in Jamaica, where his father, Joseph, served as a major in the Jamaica Regiment (a non-mechanised infantry regiment that assists the island's constabulary with local law enforcement).

Through his father, Blackwell was related to the founder of Crosse & Blackwell, the long-established purveyors of jarred foods and relishes, while his mother, the colourful and quixotic Costa Rica-born Blanche, came from the powerful Lindo family, said to be one of the 21 families that had controlled Jamaica in the twentieth century, having made its vast fortune in sugar and Appleton rum. Blanche, who died at the grand old age of 104 in August 2017, owned several thousand acres of land near Oracabessa. She was said to have been romantically linked to Ian Fleming in the James Bond author's later life, becoming his muse and the inspiration for one of the best-known Bond girls, Pussy Galore.

Blackwell's parents divorced in 1949 when he was 12, and while he still considered Jamaica his home, he abided by his father's wishes and went to England to continue his education at Harrow. Reflecting on his childhood in Jamaica in a May 2009 interview with *The Daily Telegraph* to commemorate Island's fiftieth anniversary, Blackwell said how he'd returned to Jamaica aged 17 and tried his hand at several businesses, including serving as an aide to Jamaica's then Governor, Sir Hugh Foot, running a small jazz club, renting motor scooters, real estate, teaching water-skiing, and managing jukeboxes to supplement the £2,000 annual allowance he received from his mother. "I managed 63 jukeboxes," he explained, "which meant I had to go all around the country and change the records and argue about the provision of threepenny pieces with the owner of a bar in a little fishing village or up in the hills. It was great stuff to absorb – real life."

Given the opportunities his belonging to one of Jamaica's most prominent families afforded him, setting up his own record label raised one or two eyebrows amongst the island's genteel elite. "It wasn't considered a serious business," he revealed, "more a quasi-outlawish business, sort of like the gambling business might be seen today, or a bookmakers. It was a similar world, full of characters and semi-misfits, of which I was definitely one. It certainly wasn't a thing people had serious careers with. It was right at the start of something, which is always exciting because you're feeling your way."

To Blackwell's mind, it was the Jamaican musicians' feeling their way that had inadvertently given rise to what was to become known as ska. "The early music you heard in Jamaica was kinda soppy. The only thing you'd hear approaching jazz was what Jamaicans called blues music. Now, their blues music wasn't what the English called blues music. It was more like 'Saturday Night Fish Fry' by Louis Jordan – it had this really pumping rhythm to it. So that rhythm was something that people in Jamaica tried to emulate, but they got the accent of it wrong, and that's how ska started – because the rhythm was on the off-beat instead of the on-beat."

Blackwell's idea behind Island Records was to cater for London's burgeoning West Indian communities by pressing up old ska hits. While Jamaica was gearing up for the impending handover from British rule, Blackwell went around striking up deals with Duke Reid, Coxsone Dodd and other producers before returning to London. He'd then return to the island every three months or so, listen through the latest records, and pick the ones he felt the most marketable. He did have competition from a rival London-based label, of course: "I was up against Blue Beat, and the music became known as 'bluebeat', so it was a bit like trying to sell vacuum cleaners against Hoover."

Blackwell revealed how he'd travelled to New York to purchase records which he then shipped back to Jamaica to sell to Duke Reid, Coxsone Dodd, King Edwards et al. "Today, it's impossible to think that you wouldn't know what a record was because everything is so readily available," he told Hooman Majd for the March 2009 interview. "But in those days, that was not the case. So, I would buy these records, scrape off the labels, and sell them to these sound system guys.

"Now, the sound system guys were in the business of selling liquor, and what would happen was that people would have dances on their 'lawns', as they were called, which were far from lawns – they were sort of dirt patches."

The Blackwell name was obviously already well known in Jamaica, so he had an advantage of sorts when he approached Reid, Coxsone and the other leading operators. He was also familiar with all the recording artists, of course: "I knew all these guys when I started. And I eventually started recording with people in Jamaica. Laurel Aitken, Owen Gray, Wilfred Edwards – the first three records that I put out were by those guys, and each of them went to Number 1 [in Jamaica]. The reason they went to Number 1 is because Jamaicans were thrilled to hear Jamaicans singing."

Blackwell's struggle with Blue Beat didn't just extend to procure the latest acetates. When he invited Owen Gray over to London to play some live shows, the latter had no sooner arrived from Kingston when he was spirited away by Jackson and signed to Blue Beat.

Undeterred, Blackwell set about building up his Island empire, travelling about the country in his Mini Cooper. "Boy, that thing could move fast," he enthused. "It was tiny, and I could whisk around the periphery of central London, where all the Jamaicans lived. It was great fun."

Blackwell wasn't above pulling one or two stunts of his own, as he revealed: "There was a guy, Nat Fox, who had a stall in Dalston market – he was a rough character. I remember inviting him in to play some new music in my office. I had two hi-fi systems, one for buying, one for selling. My buying system never sounded so great, but the selling system sounded fantastic. I played him these records on my selling system and he bought the lot, then when he got them back to his stall, he didn't seem to sell them quite as quick as he thought."

As Chris Blackwell would come to appreciate in the 50 years Island Records has been in existence, music must be allowed to evolve in order to survive, with rock and pop proving the two mainstays from which all subgenres emerge. Viewed in that context, ska wasn't intended as a means to a particular end, and in hindsight can be seen as a link – albeit a vital one – in the chain betwixt Jamaican jazz and mainstream reggae.

Ska's original progenitors didn't set out with any game plan other than to emulate the early Sixties R&B emanating from America. Indeed, it could be argued that had it not been for Bob Marley's subsequent global success, ska might well have slipped into obscurity, forever destined to remain a quaint Caribbean curiosity for occasional scholastic debates.

Ska's heyday is generally accepted as spanning 1959 to 1966, plenty enough time to leave an indelible mark before succumbing to the fabled "seven-year itch". And just as psychedelic Sixties garage-rock is now credited with giving rise to the mid-Seventies CBGBs punk scene, ska would in turn engender an equally exciting subculture of its own.

CHAPTER

SIX

A NEW ERA DAWNING

"I got into reggae from when I first heard it around 1969, Desmond Dekker and all that. I was trying to get my school rock band to play it as early as 1971, but no one took reggae seriously in rock circles in those days. Yes, it was a conscious effort to combine ska with punk, but it still seemed natural to me. We injected a bit of that funky African offbeat energy, which most rock could do with, I reckon."

JERRY DAMMERS

By its very definition, a youth culture (or subculture) differs from the cultures of older generations, regardless of whether said previous generations had a youth culture of their own – particularly if said generations had a youth culture of their own! Music, of course, is one of the fundamental core elements of any youth culture: Teddy boys had rock 'n' roll, mods had R&B, soul and ska, while the punks had… punk. Merseybeat was evidence enough that a commercial music scene could thrive outside of London, but who could have foreseen Coventry becoming the epicentre of a seminal youth culture movement?

While it could be argued that all youth cultures are politicised rebellion of one guise or another, be it against parents, the establishment, or, to paraphrase Marlon Brando's immortal line from *The Wild One*, rebelling against "whatever you got", 2-Tone stands out from all others – at least in Britain – for bringing black and white youths together under one banner. Of course, that isn't to say black kids were discouraged from embracing mod or punk for example, but 2-Tone emerged at a time when race relations in Britain were in something of a crisis.

The National Front was on the rise and staging intimidatory marches in areas with large immigrant communities seemingly at will. The spring 1977 elections had seen the NF push the Liberal Party into fourth place in nearly a quarter of the constituencies, and an electoral breakthrough appeared increasingly likely. Somewhat ironically, the Front's membership had been in decline by the mid-Seventies, only for its ranks to swell again following the Labour government's agreeing to allow an influx of Malawian Asian refugees into the country in 1976. With the government seemingly turning a blind eye to the Front's steady rise, Red Saunders, a professional photographer and political activist, got together with some like-minded friends to set up Rock Against Racism (RAR).

Folk music has long been a medium for channelling protest. Journalist Colin Irwin cites the Campaign for Nuclear Disarmament's inaugural "Aldermaston March" over the Easter weekend of 1958 as being the catalyst for the modern-day British protest movement. The 53-mile march, from Trafalgar Square to Britain's Atomic Weapons Establishment situated outside of Aldermaston in Berkshire, staged in protest of Britain's recent testing of the H-bomb, served to fire up angry young singer-songwriters such as Ewan MacColl, Peggy Seeger, John Hasted and Eric Winter to pen songs arguing the case against nuclear weapons.

John Lennon's 1972 album, *Some Time in New York City*, brims with protest songs such as 'Woman is the Nigger of the World' (sexism), 'Luck of the Irish' (British colonialism) and 'Attica State' (the poor living conditions in US penitentiaries), while the ex-Beatle's anti-war rant, 'Give Peace a Chance', was adopted as its anthem by the American anti-war movement. Brummie rockers Black Sabbath got in on the anti-war movement with 'War Pigs', but no British musicians appeared willing to rail against racism in song.

Punk had yet to burst into the public consciousness when the first Malawian refugees began arriving in Britain during the autumn of 1976, but it was coming in for criticism in certain quarters for the overt use of Nazi ephemera, most notably by Sex Pistols bassist-in-waiting Sid Vicious and "Siouxsie Sioux" Ballion. That same summer David Bowie was snapped giving a Nazi salute outside Victoria Station, while in an interview that appeared in the September '76 issue of *Playboy*, he brazenly proclaimed Adolf Hitler to be "one of the first rock stars".

Bowie's antics paled into insignificance compared with Eric Clapton's recent outbursts during a show at the Birmingham Odeon, however. Having drunkenly declared Britain was "in danger of becoming a black colony", he went on to proclaim the controversial Conservative politician Enoch Powell a "prophet" before telling the bemused audience that voting Tory at the next general election was needed to "keep Britain white".

It was Clapton's buffoonery that had galvanised Red Saunders and his friends into action. His protest letter, which was duly published in all three leading UK music weeklies, *NME*, *Sounds* and *Melody Maker*, asking how someone that had built his career on appropriating black music, and had scored a transatlantic hit with a cover of Bob Marley's 'I Shot the Sheriff', could espouse such racist claptrap. Saunders used the letter to announce his intention to "organise a rank and file movement against the racist poison music", while urging those readers wanting to join Rock Against Racism to write back to them. Six-hundred people responded within two weeks, and three months later, in November 1976, Rock Against Racism staged its first-ever gig, featuring singer-songwriter Carol Grimes, at the Princess Alice pub in London's east end. Eighteen months on, some 80,000 people attended the RAR Victoria Park carnival with a line-up boasting Steel Pulse, X-Ray Spex, the Tom Robinson Band and The Clash.

Speaking with *The Guardian* in April 2008 on the eve of a festival to commemorate the thirtieth anniversary of the Victoria Park carnival, Dammers (who was set to play a DJ set at the commemorative festival) explained how RAR was beginning to take off around the same time The Specials had started out (albeit as The Automatics). "It was all part of the same thing. For me, it was no good being anti-racist if you didn't involve black people, so what The Specials tried to do was create something that was more integrated. Music gets political when there are new ideas. Punk was innovative, so was ska, and that was why bands such as The Specials and The Clash could be political."

Bob Marley's 'I Shot the Sheriff' was set to play a prominent role in the 2-Tone story, as Horace Panter (born Stephen Graham Panter) remembers Jerry Dammers bawling out the song's chorus at the top of his voice as he came sauntering into the Art Faculty at Lanchester Polytechnic (now Coventry University), where the two were enrolled. Dammers' flared tartan trousers also made a lasting impression on Panter, as did his grown-out mod haircut replete with sideburns.

Jeremy David Hounsell Dammers was born in Ootacamund, southern India, on May 22, 1954. Ootacamund, or "Ooty" as it's colloquially known amongst the natives, is a municipality located high up within the Nilgiri Hills. Dammers' clergyman father, Horace, had been working in the popular hill station for several years, but some time in 1957 Dammers arrived back in England, first living in Sheffield until the age of two before then moving to Coventry. By all accounts, Dammers grew up hating living within the closeted walls of a vicarage; hating having to attend mass, sing in the church choir, and the rigidity of his weekly piano lessons with equal fervour. He was about 13 when he accrued his legendary, trademark gap-toothed expression after losing his front teeth in a cycling accident. Though begrudgingly grateful that his parents sent him for piano lessons, Dammers says the lessons themselves didn't serve him in good stead for what was to come. "I was rubbish and hated practising," he told *www.rocksgodiva.tripod.com* in August 2005. "The only thing that interested me was teaching myself blues. It was The Who, Small Faces, The Kinks which made me want to be in a band. I [also] loved soul music, Otis Redding, Sam and Dave, Tamla Motown."

Horace's status afforded his son a private education and Dammers duly attended the prestigious King Henry VIII school, where, much to his parents' consternation, he managed to accrue a solitary O level (Art). His rebellious nature saw him

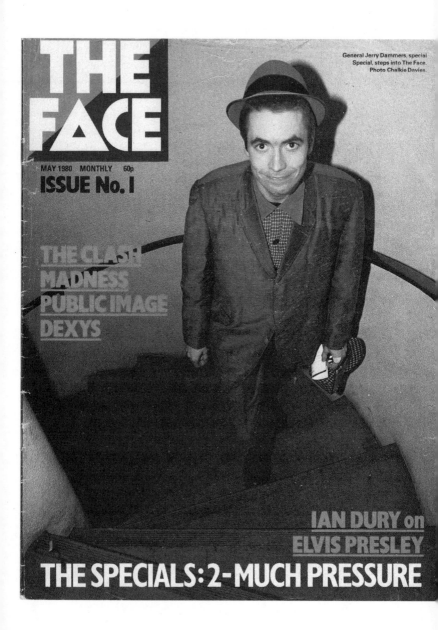

THE FACE

MAY 1980 MONTHLY 60p
ISSUE No. 1

General Jerry Dammers, special
Special, steps into The Face.
Photo Chalkie Davies.

THE CLASH
MADNESS
PUBLIC IMAGE
DEXYS

IAN DURY on
ELVIS PRESLEY
THE SPECIALS: 2-MUCH PRESSURE

abscond to a hippy commune on one of the islands situated off Ireland's west coast when he was 15. He lasted but a couple of weeks before returning home with his tail far from tucked between his legs. "When I came back I totally freaked out," he explained. "I got into this suedehead type of thing. When I was about 17, I got badly into drink and vandalism."

Dammers' "vandalism" streak consisted in the main of putting a boot through a shop window while staggering through Coventry's city centre en route home after another night's alcohol binge. While on a lads' summer jolly-up in Torquay, however, his drunken antics were to land him in court. The local magistrates took a dim view of Dammers wilfully stomping up and down on a car roof (with the terrified holidaymakers trapped within), and duly fined him £250. Had any of the family been injured during Dammers' drunken rampage the penalty would surely have proved more severe.

Dammers' anti-authoritarian streak remained firmly ingrained, but he now began channelling his energies into music and flirted with the mod scene after catching The Who performing 'My Generation' on *Ready Steady Go!* The Faces were another early influence, as were Ambrose Slade before Noddy and co. grew out their hair and went glam. But it was the ska and skinhead reggae available via Trojan Records' now legendary *Tighten Up Vol…* series that were to prove most influential. He now began thinking about making music, initially toying with the idea of being a drummer before settling on keyboards.

Having completed his foundation art course at Nottingham University, Dammers arrived at Lanchester Poly – or the "Lanch" as it was known amongst the local populace – in September 1973 with his boogie-woogie piano skills and wayward manner nicely honed.

Horace Panter was into the second year of his Fine Arts course at Lanchester Poly by the time of Dammers' arrival and had been playing bass guitar for a couple of years. He was born in Croydon, south London, in August 1953, but was raised in the sleepy East Midlands market town of Kettering, having been adopted at just six weeks old. Like Dammers, he was afforded the privileges of a private education and attended the local grammar school. Despite failing his A levels, he was accepted for a one-year foundation course at the Northampton School of Art. Whilst failing miserably on an academic level at Kettering Grammar, Panter knuckled down to playing the crappy, fire-engine red Rosetti Bass 8 he'd bought from a classmate for the princely sum of six quid.

By his own admission, the Rosetti was to remain a bedroom mirror prop for some time to come as he'd no idea how to play or tune the instrument and had little or no inclination to remedy the situation. Indeed, upon joining his first band, Möbius Trip (named after the M.C. Escher 1961 woodcut engraving, the Möbius Strip), it seemed far hipper to be known as the bass player rather than to have to prove it. Indeed, in the two years the band was in existence, Möbius Trip played only a handful of shows, one of which came opening for Mott the Hoople at a youth club in neighbouring Wellingborough.

This was long before David Bowie gifted Mott 'All the Young Dudes' to set them on the road to glam stardom, of course. Möbius Trip would only get to play three songs before the promotor decided to put the audience out of its misery by pulling the plug, but that matters not a jot to Panter. In his highly entertaining autobiography, *Ska'd for Life*, he admits to having "dined out" on his having shared a stage with the mighty Mott the Hoople for six months or so. Had he not gone on to forge a musical career with The Specials and beyond, it's likely he'd be dining out on the anecdote still.

Panter and Dammers next crossed paths some time during the autumn of 1976 on the Midlands pub and club circuit. Panter, having come away from Lanchester Poly the previous spring with a second-class Honours degree in Fine Art, was playing soul and funk standards as part of a Manhattan Transfer-esque quartet called Breaker. Dammers was plodding a similarly unrewarding furrow in The Cissy Stone Soul Band; the latter's frustrations largely stemming from Ms Stone's reluctance to allow any of his self-penned numbers into the set.

Circuit bands such as Breaker and The Cissy Stone Soul Band were little more than human jukeboxes providing twice-nightly turns either side of the bingo; there to entertain and nothing more. Panter remembers catching sight of Dammers in the crowd at one of Breaker's Monday night residency shows at the Smithfield Hotel in Coventry around this time.

Panter also remembers Breaker playing the Smithfield the same Monday night (November 29, 1976) the Sex Pistols were playing at the nearby Lanchester Poly with The Clash in support. This is the night the Pistols first performed 'No Future' (soon to be retitled 'God Save the Queen') in public. After staging an emergency meeting, the polytechnic's Students' Union announced it was withholding the Pistols' fee on the grounds they were fascists. The Clash would suffer a similar fate because of the inflammatory lyric to 'White Riot'. Incidentally, Stephen "Roadent" Connelly, who was working for The Clash and living out of the band's Chalk Farm rehearsal space, was Coventry-born and already known to Dammers and several others that were set to make their mark on the 2-Tone scene.

CHAPTER

The Pistols were just 48 hours away from their date with destiny, yet were still relatively unknown. Panter, however, had been keeping an eye on the band's exploits in the music weeklies. As soon as Breaker had finished their second set he'd packed away his bass and rushed over to the Poly in the hope of catching the tail-end of the Pistols set. His luck was to be out, however, and seeing the collective age of the kids spilling through the doors out on to the pavement left the 23-year-old rueing his decision.

Panter had assumed Dammers had simply swung by the Smithfield to check out the competition, so was taken completely by surprise when his friend contacted him a few days later asking if he might be interested in playing bass on the songs he'd written (under the nom de plume Gerald "The General" Dankey). Panter readily agreed as there'd been no mention of their forming a band, and he assumed Dammers was simply looking to work up the songs with a view to offering them to a music publisher. (By assigning the copyright to his compositions to a publishing company, the company in question would license Dammers' compositions and then look to secure commissions for films, TV, or offer them to established artists, in return for an agreed percentage of the royalties.)

Two of Dammers' compositions that would survive all the way to The Specials were 'Little Bitch', which features on the band's eponymous debut album, and 'Jaywalker', which Panter says might have made it on to *More Specials* had "stony silence and apathy" towards the song not carried the day during the recording sessions.

Dammers had called upon another of his musician friends, guitarist Lynval Golding, to assist in knocking the songs into shape. The 25-year-old Golding was born in Saint Catherine, Jamaica, before relocating to the UK when he was 13. He'd been living in Coventry for the past seven years or so. On leaving school, Golding had worked as a car mechanic, and had entertained the idea of being an engineer, but such jobs were simply a means of putting food on the table for his wife and three-year-old daughter, as playing guitar was his overriding passion.

As strange as it seems, given what 2-Tone would go on to signify, Panter says he'd never met a black person until Dammers introduced him to Golding. "Please remember this was 1976," he says by way of explanation. "I had grown up in an East Midlands market town, gone to grammar school, then to college. I had never talked with anyone outside of my race, other than a couple of Asian guys at art school."

CHAPTER SEVEN

WHERE THE LIVING IS HARDER

"Being musically competent didn't matter so much as whether you looked good. Quite a few youngsters in Coventry learnt two-and-a-half chords, wrote songs which included the word 'bored' in the title and became legends in their own sixth-form common rooms. In real terms this meant there was an awful lot of very awful punk rock being played. Coventry suffered from this as much as anywhere else, but, as happens in these sort of situations, the good stuff generally rises to the top."

HORACE PANTER

1 976, of course, was to bring about a seismic shift in Britain's musical landscape. Panter's preferred musical tastes ran to blues/rock, as played by Led Zeppelin, Cream and the Peter Green-era Fleetwood Mac. He was familiar with reggae (and indeed ska) from listening to the pirate radio stations in his teens. Yet though he was laying down a funk/soul groove with Breaker, Dammers' funk/reggae offerings left Panter somewhat bemused. It's the bass line in reggae that gets people dancing, and as such, the feeling behind the lilting rhythm is just as important as the notes being played. Thankfully, however, the amiable Golding was on hand to provide guidance. "I eventually got it," says Panter, "[but] in retrospect it would have been easier to have dragged me along to a blues dance, given me a big spliff and stood me in front of one of the walls of 18-inch cabinets."

And it was Golding, of course, who was to bestow upon Panter his enduring nickname, "Sir Horace Gentleman", supposedly because of his plummy, garden party vowels.

With Panter following Golding's lead, things quickly began to click into place. There was still no mention of anyone putting a band together, but to work up the songs into structured arrangements it was obvious they were going to need to bring in a drummer at some stage. As it happened, Dammers and Golding already had someone in mind.

Panter cites the Barbados-born Silverton Hutchinson as being the "funkiest drummer" he ever played with. Though quick to temper, the mercurial Hutchinson's laidback beat provided the added dynamic they were looking for. Dammers and Golding knew Hutchinson from their having played together in a soul outfit called Pharaoh's Kingdom.

According to an ancient Chinese proverb, when the wind of change blows, some people build walls, others build windmills. The musical wind of change that had first started stirring in February 1976, when the Sex Pistols' antics at the Marquee Club while supporting Eddie and The Hot Rods saw them steal the headliners' thunder, was now raging following the Pistols' teatime tête-à-tête with Bill Grundy on Thames TV's magazine news programme, *Today*. While the UK's staid music industry hid behind their walls pretending it was business as usual, others did indeed begin erecting windmills.

Panter realised a revolution was in the offing and recognised the opportunities to be had. "Experimenting was a prerequisite, emotion was preferable over technique. It didn't seem to matter whether the music was good, so long as it was new."

Panter felt the music he, Dammers, Golding and Hutchinson were making ticked both boxes as it was as good as it was new. As such, maybe it was time to acknowledge the elephant that had been sitting patiently within the corner of Dammers' living room where the quartet would gather to work on the latter's songs; that they were a band in all but name and a singer. Having toyed with calling themselves "The Jaywalkers", before settling on "The Hybrids", the quartet approached Tim Strickland, a James Dean wannabe with a predilection for Lou Reed, with a view to his trying out as singer.

According to *The Sun*, and the other UK tabloids, the defining diktats of punk rock was that it was no longer essential that the musicians be able to play their instruments, or the singer be able to sing. The truth, of course, was somewhat different – as those who bought into such fallacies would soon find out. Strickland had attained a degree in Social Science at Lanchester Poly and was now working out of the recently opened Coventry branch of Virgin Records. He was the first to admit that he'd need a holdall to carry a tune, yet his ego was such that he readily accepted.

CHAPTER

The Hybrids made their live debut at the Heath Hotel, a well-known live music venue situated within walking distance of Coventry's city centre. They were supporting The Shapes, a Rezillos-esque punk outfit from neighbouring Leamington Spa fronted by the quixotic-sounding Seymour Bybuss. The five-piece would achieve a modicum of success, releasing an EP on their own Sofa Records label before being picked up by Terry Hooley's Good Vibrations, while Bybuss (born Ben Browton) would go on to achieve celebrity of sorts playing the cycling art critic nun "Sister Bendy" on *Eurotrash*.

Whatever his vocal shortcomings, Strickland was totally unnerved at finding himself the band's focal point in his Lou Reed ensemble of winkle-picker boots, black drainpipe trousers and motorcycle jacket; snarling out the lyrics to 'Do the Dog', 'Little Bitch', 'Dawning of a New Era' and an embryonic version of 'Too Much Too Soon' amongst others, holding on to the mic stand with an air of measured affectation.

Dammers took to the stage in the Crombie overcoat he was rarely ever seen out of, while Golding and Hutchinson played in the loud checker jackets they wore whenever out about town, the mere thought of dressing down being complete anathema to the pair. Panter, however, was sporting a look that would come to be synonymous with the 2-Tone sound: Doc Martens boots, combat trousers, Ben Sherman shirt and Harrington jacket.

As with every other city across the UK, a punk scene had soon established itself in Coventry, with bands seemingly forming on a near-weekly basis and The Hybrids returning to the Heath Hotel a fortnight or so later with fellow hopefuls Urban Blight. The Heath's air of faded glory proved intoxicating for The Hybrids; so much so, they began rehearsing there.

Imbued with the thrill of making it through these shows unscathed, the band approached the pub's management with a view to starting a fortnightly residency. What set The Hybrids apart from the bands on the scene was their musicianship.

Indeed, the only similarity being Strickland's tuneless raving.

But not for long...

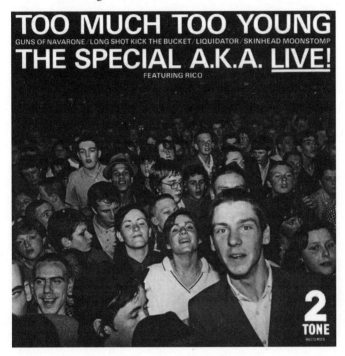

Again, as with every other city across the UK, those bands
that had hurriedly thrown themselves together after hearing
'Anarchy in the UK' soon fell by the wayside, leaving the path
clear for the ones that actually had something to offer. By far
and away the most interesting punk band within the Coventry
scene was Squad. The four-piece have since been described as
being "lunatic, loud and loveable [and] out for a good time as
their audiences inevitably were". This acclamation, however,
would only come into being following the departure of their
somewhat sullen singer, a one-time apprentice hairdresser
called Terry Hall.

Panter remembers Dammers calling him late one evening from some club or other in Birmingham to rave about Hall. He didn't pay too much heed to Dammers' slurred insistence that they poach Hall from Squad, but come the next rehearsal it was with the shy yet charismatic 18-year-old standing in front of the mic. Hall barely opened his mouth other than to run through a couple of songs, but his simply turning up was evidence enough that he wanted in. And as he was there at the band's invitation, nothing much needed to be said. Tim Strickland's time with The Hybrids was at an end. He was said to be "pissed off" on being given the news, but supposedly understood the band's position. One of the more enduring maxims in rock 'n' roll is that any band is only as good as its drummer, but a dodgy singer will hamstring a band's expectations just as surely.

Hall's arrival in the band meant The Hybrids finally had someone in the line-up that was Coventry born. His being several years younger also meant that he was the perfect age to connect with the punk zeitgeist. Whereas Panter might stop and analyse whether bands such as the Pistols and Clash would measure up to the Stones or The Who, Hall was simply enjoying being part of it all with Squad. Having said that, his preference was for the American punk bands, notably Richard Hell and The Voidoids: "Hell did vocals with sweets in his mouth because he didn't really want to be understood. He's got an amazing nervous cough, which might have something to do with the sweets."

Somewhat amazingly, while Malcolm McLaren and Vivienne Westwood have come to be recognised as the doyens of punk fashion, Hall took the view that the SEX/Seditionaries clothing made everyone look too styled: "In The Voidoids, somebody would be bald, and somebody would have long hair. It didn't matter. With Richard Hell I imagined that he couldn't really do anything else, whereas I could imagine the bass player in The Damned fixing my plumbing."

Music had been something of a constant during Hall's formative years. "I come from a gypsy-spirited family and everyone used to sing in pubs whether you liked it or not," he told *The Guardian* in March 2009. "I didn't want to be that sort of singer." He remembers his dad only ever owning two records. One was *The Legendary Edith Piaf* (the other being Leo Sayer's 'The Show Must Go On'). "He played Edith Piaf every Sunday, it was my first memory of a record going on a deck. Dad is from an Irish background, and on Sunday afternoons he would sing along – not in French – completely pissed."

Hall's inherited gypsy spirit might explain his flitting from job to job after walking away from school shortly before his fifteenth birthday. He'd already tried his hand at office work – bricklaying, quantity surveying and hairdressing – by the time of his joining The Hybrids. As with many players on the burgeoning punk scene, Hall, for a time at least, fell under the influence of a certain singer from Bromley. "When I was 16, [*Young Americans*] gave me a look, a sound, and a way of holding yourself. Apparently, all his clothes were from Wal-Mart at this time. He put a blond streak in his hair and we would do the same. Then you would go to football and get punched in the face. It was very important, really. Everything Bowie did at this time was dead cool, unlike all that *Spiders from Mars* shit."

Bowie and punk rock weren't Hall's only musical influences around this time: "My sisters were skinheads and they would listen to ska, while our gang listened to reggae. Don Letts said he played reggae in punk clubs because they were the only records he had, but it caught on in Coventry. In the mid-Seventies there was a wonderful time in which the clubs played strange reggae records. They tend to ramble on incoherently, and the music felt free."

It was undoubtedly The Hybrids' punk/funk/reggae fusion that had attracted Hall's attention; either that or the rumour his bandmates in Squad were thinking of giving him the elbow. No matter, Hall's morose technique was perfectly suited for The Hybrids' own style, and the rest, as they say, was set to become history...

Hall's debut with The Hybrids came – according to the *Coventry Telegraph*'s Tiffany's retrospective – towards the end of January 1978 supporting a pre-Midge Ure Ultravox at Coventry's premiere nightspot, Tiffany's Ballroom. Panter cites the show as being The Hybrids' first "big gig", but although Ultravox would go on to become something of a perennial fixture in the UK singles chart following Ure's replacing John Foxx in March 1979, at the time the five-piece electro-rockers were struggling to live up to the promise that had led to Island Records signing the band in 1976.

This is perhaps reflected in Panter's assessment of it being a poor turnout on the night. All that was of concern to Panter was that The Hybrids had held their own on "the big stage, in the big room, with the big sound".

Dammers, however, came away from Tiffany's feeling something missing from the "big sound", and just as he had with Silverton Hutchinson, he knew exactly where to turn.

Roddy "Radiation" Byers was already a permanent fixture on the Coventry punk scene when Dammers made his approach. He'd kicked about playing guitar in several ad hoc local outfits before forming The Wild Boys during the summer of 1975. "I grew up in a small coal mining village just outside of Coventry called Keresley End. There was only the one council house street, all the rest were pit houses owned by the local colliery. I come from a musical background. My father, Stan, played the trumpet in Jimmy Powell and The Dimensions and various other soul bands up and down the country, while my grandfather played trombone in dance bands such as the Newcastle Orchestra. I actually started out on the trombone because of my grandfather. I was about 11 at the time, but then switched to the guitar a couple of years after that. I was into stuff like The Monkees as a kid, but as I got older I moved on to Stones, The Kinks, Jimi Hendrix and all the rock and pop stuff of the late Sixties and early Seventies. The first band that I ever saw live was The Troggs.

"Men from all over the country came to work at the pit. Most brought their families with them, and some of those families were rough and ready. When I was in my teens the skinhead fashion was at its height and most of the pit family lads were skinheads. Me and my mates were always getting into fights with them. I couldn't wait to leave!"

After falling out with his father, Byers moved into Coventry central. He slept on a friend's sofa for several months before he and his girlfriend got a flat in Hillfields, close to Coventry City's Highfield Road ground. "We lived there for three years. This was where I started The Wild Boys. We were playing a mixture of old rock 'n' roll standards and glam rock stuff, so when punk came along a year or so later it wasn't too great a stretch to change our style to fit."

Panter maintains that the "Radiation" tag came from Byers' getting "beer flush" when he'd had one too many, but Byers said: "Actually, my brother Chris called me "Roddy Radiation" as a joke when I was into Ziggy Stardust in the early Seventies. When punk came along I decided to adopt it as a stage name. But actually, I do get flushed when I drink too much.

"I'd started writing my own songs by the time I formed The Wild Boys. My writing style was heavily influenced by the likes of Bowie, Bolan and Lou Reed. One of the first songs I wrote was called '1980s Teddy Boy'. It was all about my experiences growing up in Keresley End and living in Hillfields. It was later reworked into 'Concrete Jungle' once I joined The Specials."

There is some confusion as to whether The Hybrids had already undergone a name change to The Automatics, but either way Byers was already familiar with them: "I was friends with Tim because he was a James Dean fan like myself. He was also a fan of Lou Reed, and was doing a sort of Lou Reed voice when he played with The Hybrids. And I already knew Jerry as it turned out, as we'd jammed together a few years before while he was learning to play the drums. It was while I was playing with a band called The Dread Rissoles. Needless to say, he didn't get the gig. Then Tim got the sack, of course, and was replaced by Terry. I knew Terry well enough from when he was in Squad. They supported us a few times in fact.

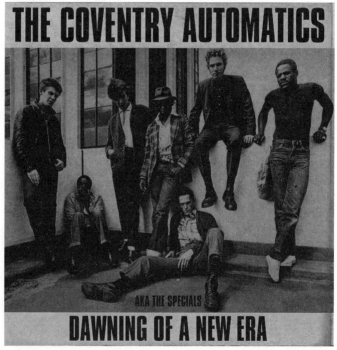

THE COVENTRY AUTOMATICS

AKA THE SPECIALS

DAWNING OF A NEW ERA

"The Wild Boys split up around the same time as Terry joining, and hearing that I was at a loose end Jerry asked me if I wanted to join. I have it in my head they were already calling themselves The Automatics by then, but I could be wrong. We were in some club or other having a late-night drink. Jerry said they had some studio time booked in London and asked if I fancied playing lead guitar on the songs. I said yes straight away as I'd recently got into reggae and dub music. I was already pretty pissed so didn't take in too many of the details. I was working for the local council as a painter and decorator.

"Me and my girlfriend had recently moved in with her family. We were looking to buy our own place and get married. The next morning there was a hammering on the door. When I looked out of the window I saw Jerry standing at the door and the rest of the guys waiting in the taxi. I got dressed, grabbed up my guitar, and headed out the door. Like I say, I was at a loose end and had nothing else lined up. I was looking forward to seeing if Jerry and I could write music together."

It's funny how those who share the same experiences will come to remember them differently, even when the experiences are noteworthy. Allowances have to be made for the passing of time, but alcohol and other recreational substances no doubt play their respective parts. For example, Byers remembers his being wrenched from a drunken slumber by a waiting taxi, whereas Panter's version of events has the demo session coming after Neville Staple's arrival on to the scene.

Neville Eugenton Staple had already achieved near-legendary status in and around Coventry by the time he entered The Automatics' orbit. Though only 22, stories of his escapades tended to precede him wherever he went. He was born in Christiana, a rural settlement within the Parish of Manchester,

Jamaica. His father, Euton, had relocated to London in search of work shortly after he was born, leaving young Neville, his younger brother and twin sisters in the care of their grandparents. Staple senior's search for steady employment took him to Coventry, and then Rugby, in neighbouring Warwickshire. In 1961, Euton felt secure enough in his surroundings to send for Neville and his siblings.

Leaving behind the life he knew meant saying goodbye to "Auntie Katherine", who was in fact his mother. It would be 20 years before he would see her again, by which time, of course, he was in The Specials.

The picture Staple paints of his life after being reunited with his father in his brutally honest, yet highly entertaining autobiography, *Original Rude Boy: From Borstal to The Specials*, is one of extreme hardship. Said hardship not so much stemming from his father's struggle to feed and clothe his new family, but rather the beatings Staple and his brother could expect for the slightest of infractions; Euton Staple's having set up home with his common-law wife, providing the prerequisite "wicked stepmother" to the grimmest of fairy tales.

Staple says he had no qualms about moving to Britain. To his mind, Jamaica, while only a year or so away from gaining its independence, was under British rule, and many of the places he was familiar with back in Christiana were named after British towns and cities. What would have come as a surprise, of course, was how the local populace reacted to the colour of his skin. Though successive governments had actively encouraged the peoples of Afro-Caribbean countries to start a new life in Britain (starting with the much-vaunted "Windrush generation", many of those that took up the offer were to endure extreme prejudice. Indeed, race relations within the West Midlands grew so toxic that in the run-up to the 1964 general election, the Ku Klux Klan formed its first UK branch in Birmingham.

Staple believes the put-downs and humiliations his father had suffered in the workplace and elsewhere since arriving in the mother country played no small part in the beatings he and Franklyn had to endure. He, however, had no intention of suffering a similar torment, and woe betide anyone foolish enough to hurl insults.

Aged 15, after yet another murderous row betwixt father and son, Staple found himself out on the street. Luckily, a cousin living close by took him in. He left school soon thereafter, with little fuss, and even less in the way of qualifications. He got a job as an apprentice TV engineer, but soon gave that up to go and work in an abattoir. With regular cash to splash he was able to indulge his interest in fashion, music and girls. At weekends he would venture to the clubs in nearby Coventry; his febrile imagination captivated by the bright lights and urban sprawl.

The jewel in the Coventry club scene crown around this time was the Locarno Ballroom (later Tiffany's). Saturday mornings were given over to matinee discos with up-and-coming local DJ, Pete Waterman. Waterman was in his early twenties at the time, and aside from his residency at the Locarno, ran his own record shop. According to Staple, the "Soul Hole", as the shop was called, was as much a local hangout as it was a record shop and he and his two closest associates – future Specials roadies Rex Griffiths and Trevor Evans – looked upon it as a home from home.

Waterman's passion for reggae was as keen as Staple's; so much so, the two soon became firm friends (Waterman would pen the intro to Staple's book). Though obliged to play sugary chart hits at the Locarno matinees, Waterman would slip the latest Desmond Dekker or Upsetters record on to the turntable, which served as the cue for Staple and his posse to take over the dance floor. Waterman would also invite Staple up on to the stage to "toast" to the records, little suspecting his future self would be up there doing the very same thing with The Specials.

CHAPTER

Staple was now living in Coventry, having accepted Evans' father's offer of the spare bedroom of a house he'd bought in the Hillfields area. Though yet to reach voting age, Staple had fathered two children with two different girls; his cavalier approach to contraception might have proved the inspiration for 'Too Much Too Young' had Dammers not already written the song.

Unlike the fictional protagonist in 'Too Much Too Young', Staple was too occupied with making a name for himself within Coventry's criminal underbelly to be a stay-at-home dad. Hanging around illicit gambling dens and shebeens undoubtedly gave him and his crew certain kudos, but inevitably also led them into a life of crime, seamlessly gravitating from shoplifting to robbing public phone boxes to house-breaking. By his own admission, Staple participated in anywhere between 50 and 60 robberies before his luck finally ran out. Following what he describes as a "tour of England's remand centres", Staple arrived at Hewell Grange youth detention centre in Tardebigge, Worcestershire, where he would spend the next twelve months rueing the error of his ways.

Following his release from Hewell Grange, Staple threw himself into Coventry's burgeoning sound system scene. He and his crew set themselves up as the "Jah Baddies", operating out of the newly opened Holyhead Youth Club. The club was soon thriving, with kids throughout the West Midlands and sometimes further afield descending en masse to drink, smoke and dance the night away. Due to growing complaints from local residents it wasn't long before the police began sniffing around; the tell-tale pungent aroma of cannabis soon confirming their suspicions. With the club being council run, the inevitable wasn't long in coming.

Staple was operating out of a bedsit further along Holywell Road, and would occasionally pop into the club, if only to check on the sound system stored away under lock and key in the cellar. The club was still available for hire as a rehearsal space, and as Staple made his way down the stairwell his interest was piqued by the punky reggae party emanating from behind the door. Never having been one to stand on ceremony he simply barged through the door, whereupon he recognised the drummer as being an ex-boyfriend of his long-suffering girlfriend's sister serving as an entree into The Automatics' world.

Within no time, Staple was accompanying The Automatics to gigs serving as an ad hoc roadie to avoid paying admission. During soundchecks he'd occasionally take over one of the mics; his off-the-cuff toasting serving to plant a seed in Dammers' mind.

The Automatics were steadily enhancing their reputation playing a Monday night residency at Mr. George's, a run-of-the-mill, red-flock wallpaper, chicken-in-a-basket nightspot located within the Lower Precinct shopping centre that had quickly become the venue of choice within the Coventry punk scene. Back in December, the Sex Pistols had played there on their Never Mind the Bans Tour. Legend has it that Jerry Dammers made his way back stage, where he fruitlessly petitioned Roadent and Pistols "minder" Steve English to moot the possibility of The Automatics providing support.

Neville Staple's raving about The Automatics was enough to tempt him to check them out for himself at one of the band's Mr. George's residency shows. Waterman was impressed by what he saw. Having boasted about the contacts he'd made in London, he reportedly paid for the band to spend a day at Berwick Street Studios.

Despite certain misgivings over Waterman's show of altruism, the chance to record in a top London studio was one they couldn't refuse. With Dammers borrowing an organ worthy of such an undertaking, they climbed into Golding's transit van and headed for the M1. "Yeah, I've heard the story of how Pete claims to have 'discovered' The Specials," says Byers. "Pete's involvement came from his being friends with Neville, but there were other people on the scene looking at ways to help us out. I remember Jerry bringing people along to rehearsals that were big on promises as to what they could do for us."

The three songs recorded at Berwick Street that day were 'Too Much Too Young', 'Concrete Jungle' and 'Jay Walker'. Staple remembers Waterman waxing lyrical over the end results: "Pete became our loudest advocate and would often bring his record industry contacts to see us, but the sound wasn't getting through to them. He thought we were brilliant. Eventually, sick of banging his head against the wall, Pete ran up the white flag of surrender. He met with Jerry and explained that industry know-nothings were saying that 'punk-reggae' would never catch on."

How wrong they were…

CHAPTER

EIGHT

BERNIE RHODES KNOWS

"Bernie would ramble on about this and that at times, but he was The Clash's manager. I was very impressed by that because I was a fan of The Clash. Bernie wasn't with us all that long in the scheme of things so I'm not sure if he influenced us all that much. I remember him saying something about how we didn't look united, didn't look like a band. So maybe that's where Jerry got the idea to have us wear tonic suits and pork pie hats because Paul Simonon was wearing stuff like that at the time."

RODDY BYERS

CHAPTER

The average time a signed act will spend in the studio recording a single is anything up to a week, often longer. Demos are therefore intended for limited circulation or reference use, and only really become of interest if the act or artist in question goes on to achieve success. As with countless other hopefuls down through the years, The Automatics were left somewhat underwhelmed with the end product. The band had given their all, but Berwick Street's in-house engineer was hearing the songs for the first time and wasn't expecting to hear them ever again. The Automatics might have been making waves in the West Midlands, but they were just another bunch of scruffy hopefuls coming to London and chasing an unrealistic dream. Much to the band's consternation, these fabled "lost demos" would surface on a Receiver Records compilation: *Coventry Automatics AKA The Specials: Dawning of a New Era.*

Within weeks, The Automatics were bombing down the M1 again to record another set of demos, this time at the behest of Chris Gilby, the manager of The Saints, the pioneering Aussie punksters who had made a name for themselves by releasing 'I'm Stranded' on their own Fatal Records label in September 1976, a full month before The Damned's 'New Rose'.

As with the Berwick Street recordings, the new demos failed to engender any reaction of note, but at least they had a chance to prove themselves in front of a London audience as Gilby had invited them to support The Saints at the Marquee Club on Wardour Street.

Treading the same boards as the Stones, Led Zeppelin, The Who, the Sex Pistols et al should have proved another highlight, but a pitiful turnout on the night meant there was no money left over for The Automatics, who were left having to borrow a tenner from Gilby for the petrol to get them back to Coventry. Further insult came when Gilby called Dammers one evening to say he was no longer interested in taking the band under his wing because, to his mind, they had "missed the boat". In his inimitable fashion, Dammers responded by saying "We are the boat, mate!" before hanging up.

The Automatics remained undaunted and simply knuckled down doing what they did best: playing live – thanks to the auspices of Mike Horseman, a known "face" on the Birmingham scene who was working as a rep for MCP (Midland Concert Promotions).

Horseman's first undertaking on their behalf was to secure The Automatics a residency at the Golden Eagle. Though long-since demolished, the Eagle has earned a lasting place in Brum folklore, if only for the apocryphal tale of the night Noddy Holder and Robert Plant watched an underage Stevie Winwood fronting what would become The Spencer Davis Group. Another tale that has since taken on mythical proportions (as revealed by Panter) is of Guy Stevens deciding to sign Mott the Hoople after watching them struggle up the three-flight spiral staircase leading to the club's concert room with Verden Allen's Hammond organ. If Panter was hoping a musical maverick in the Guy Stevens vein would emerge from the shadows while they were engaged in a similar tussle with Dammers' church organ, he was left sorely disappointed.

The Clash had supposedly paved the way for white punk-related acts to play reggae, yet when The Automatics took to the Birmingham Top Rank stage supporting the second city's very own Steel Pulse they were to suffer the ultimate indignity. "The crowd was predominantly black, and they just cut us dead," says Byers. "Steel Pulse were from Handsworth, and I suppose we were on a hiding to nothing.

It wouldn't have been so bad if they'd booed us off the stage. That I could understand, but they just stood there. There was no applause, each song greeted with stony silence. I don't think anyone even coughed. I suppose you had to be there to understand just how bad it was. I couldn't wait to get out of the place."

Horseman had also arranged a support slot for The Clash at Barbarella's, also in Birmingham. Dammers, Byers and Panter were all card-carrying Clash aficionados and arrived at the much-vaunted "Marquee of the Midlands" with an added spring in their collective step. For one reason or another The Clash didn't turn up, but as they were now the last prong of punk's unholy triumvirate they could be forgiven anything. The last-minute no-show left The Automatics facing something of a dilemma: in order to receive their fee, they would still have to play. Doing so, of course, meant running the risk of being given the same cold shoulder treatment they'd endured at the hands of the Top Rank crowd on their last foray into Birmingham.

The disgruntled Brummie punks proved amenable to the club management's offer of honouring the Clash tickets while allowing them in for free to at least check out the support act. A support act they'd most likely never heard of – and one from Coventry of all places! To everyone's surprise, not least the band's, they went down a storm. With the rite of passage successfully navigated, The Automatics were heartily welcomed on to the Barbarella's stage at the rescheduled Clash date a fortnight later.

Despite them all holding down day jobs, there was little doubt in anyone's mind that The Automatics were ready to step off the hamster wheel that was the West Midlands' live circuit. There was only one problem, however. Mike Horseman wasn't living up to his initial promise. On top of that he'd started acting very weird of late. While the band were ignorant as to how many of

Horseman's fingers were knuckle-deep in pies at any given time, they heard on the grapevine that he'd fallen foul of some local gangsters and had taken to recording all his telephone conversations. Anyone feel a song coming on?

Horseman's parting gift to The Automatics was to introduce the band to The Clash's road manager, Dave "Corkie" Cork. The Clash had spent much of the year holed up in Basing Street Studios recording their second album, the woefully underrated *Give 'Em Enough Rope*, and were about to hit the road in support of their latest single, '(White Man) in Hammersmith Palais'. The Clash on Parole Tour was a tongue-in-cheek reference to The Clash's recent brush with the law. Taking a break from working up the songs slated for the new album at their Chalk Farm base, Topper Headon and Paul Simonon had gone up on to the roof to try out a couple of air guns Headon was thinking of buying.

Rather than shoot at tin cans, the duo decided to take pot shots at some pigeons. A stray shot hit the window of a passing train, the railway police duly reported the incident, and before you could say "Guns on the Roof" an anti-terrorist squad stormed the building. To add to what was already a farcical situation, the pigeons Headon and Simonon had targeted were in fact prized racing pigeons. The duo were hauled off to Brixton Prison and subsequently fined £750.

Suicide, a New York-based avant-garde synth duo, were lined up as the official support act on the three-week tour that was set to get underway at Friars in Aylesbury on June 28. Owing to some long-standing commitments of their own, Suicide wouldn't be joining the tour until several dates in. Upon hearing this, The Automatics offered to serve as a temporary stand-in.

"Our being invited on to the Clash on Parole Tour came about because of what happened with the Barbarella's show," says Byers. "Jerry played his part talking us on to the tour, and The Clash were into reggae, so they liked what we were doing. Another Clash connection came with my being friends with Roadent."

According to Specials folklore, Jerry Dammers headed down to London around this time armed with a cassette tape of the demos The Automatics had recorded in the capital, hoping to tempt John Lydon into fronting the band. He got as far as hooking up with Roadent, and who agreed to pass the tape on to Lydon. This scenario seems preposterous given that Dammers had been instrumental in poaching Hall from Squad, and yet Roddy Byers remembers Dammers mooting the idea: "Jerry did talk about wanting John to front the band, but whether he said it in jest or was serious who knows?"

Lydon had already unveiled Public Image Limited to the waiting world by this juncture, but even if he had still been pondering his post-Pistols options, his antipathy towards bands such as The Clash for playing "white man reggae" meant the likelihood of his joining a ska-influenced band would have been remote in the extreme. Roadent remembers the occasion of Dammers' visit, but for different reasons: "I don't remember Jerry handing me any cassette tape for John. I'm not denying it, only that I don't remember it happening. I knew Jerry of old, of course, so I suppose it made sense for him to sound me out. I did introduce him to Bernie, however. So, despite what you've read elsewhere, I'm the one who actually discovered The Specials. Just one of my 'fifteen minutes' of fame, I suppose..."

Regardless of how The Automatics got on to the tour, or how many dates they were set to play, that they would be opening for The Clash on a national UK tour was the stuff of dreams; the dreams that had made Dammers, Panter, Byers et al first pick up a musical instrument. As the Friars date loomed ever nearer, the excitement was near palpable.

So, alas, was the sound of six chins collectively hitting the rehearsal room floor when a solicitor's letter arrived representing a band called Automatics who had recently signed with Island Records and were about to release their debut single, 'When the Tanks Roll Over Poland Again'. In short, they could expect all the legal severity the Island dollar might afford should they persist in calling themselves The Automatics. Thankfully, the invitation on to the Clash tour came after the promo artwork had gone to press, but the solicitor's letter left the band in something of a predicament nonetheless.

Choosing a band name is no easy matter – especially with the clock ticking. Said name needs to roll off the tongue, as well as look good visually. And if it conjures up a readily identifiable logo then so much the better. Panter remembers the band huddled in the back of Golding's van, everyone offering up names in the hope one might catch the imagination. None did. At some point during the brainstorming someone hit upon the idea of "The Specials", if only because of the obvious self-deprecation with the band as yet virtually unknown outside of their home city environs. This was expanded to "The Special AKA (Also Known As The Automatics)", before being truncated to the snappier-sounding "Special AKA".

It was during the soundcheck at Friars that the rest of the newly incorporated Special AKA came face to face with Bernard Rhodes. History would have us believe that Rhodes was the Sancho Panza to Malcolm McLaren's Don Quixote, but this is simply not the case. It was he that had spotted the surly, soon-to-be-rechristened Johnny Rotten making a nuisance of himself on the King's Road during the summer of 1975, and it was under his tutelage that the fledgling Sex Pistols first stretched their wings. He'd been under no illusion that McLaren would renege on his co-management offer, but had walked away from the Pistols safe in the knowledge that the "Finsbury Park bomb with the thousand-yard stare that I planted under Malcolm's chair would fuck him over at some point". He'd encountered Mick Jones and

Tony James at the Nashville Rooms one Saturday in early August 1975, and upon hearing about their band, the fabled "London SS", had begun a careful tutelage of Mick that would ultimately bring about The Clash.

The original idea behind the £100,000 advance CBS London's CEO, Maurice Oberstein, handed over when signing The Clash in January 1977 was in fact for Rhodes and McLaren to set up their own label, with CBS providing the all-important distribution. As with the Pistols, McLaren couldn't bring himself to share so Rhodes had renegotiated the deal. He'd been nurturing Subway Sect for going on two years by the summer of 1978, and had recently added soul outfit The Black Arabs to his roster. Upon meeting Dammers, he had deemed The Special AKA worthy of his attention.

It must have appeared to Dammers and co. that the planets were aligning specially for them, but behind the scenes all was far from well within the Clash camp. Or to put it more succinctly, Mick Jones had decided Rhodes' days as their manager were numbered.

Rhodes' dictatorial approach to band management had all but eroded his and Jones' working relationship, but his stubborn refusal to meet Headon and Simonon's bail following their arrest over the pigeon-shooting fiasco had finally tipped Jones over the edge. The ill feeling was mutual, however. When ex-Sex Pistol Steve Jones turned up out of the blue in Blackburn, where The Clash were set to play King George's Hall (a late addition to the tour), it was assumed it was because he was passing through en route to London and The Clash invited him to join them on stage for the encore. When Jones began turning up at other venues, Mick challenged his namesake for an explanation and was somewhat taken aback when the guileless Steve owned up to Rhodes' scheme.

"We didn't know anything about Bernie's scheme to replace Mick Jones with Steve Jones from the Pistols," says Byers.

"Bernie thought of musicians as though they were football players that he could put together in any team. There was a story doing the rounds that he wanted to put Terry with The Black Arabs. Not sure how that would have worked with Terry being white."

Panter remembers Dave Cork dipping into the Clash tour kitty to secure them a couple of rooms in a cheap boarding house on occasion, but mostly they were left to their own devices.

"They were travelling in a big, beat-up Dormobile," says The Clash's tour manager, Johnny Green. "[They] also slept in it because they couldn't afford hotels. So, we had given them a big boy scout-style tent. When we pulled into a town for a gig, we all kept a lookout for The Specials' encampment on the outskirts."

When Suicide did finally join the tour, they were to suffer a similar fate to that which befell Richard Hell and The Voidoids on the Get out of Control Tour the previous autumn. While speaking with *The Guardian* years later, Dammers singled out the On Parole date in Bracknell, Berkshire, where Suicide's Alan Vega was set upon by a gang of skinheads, as providing the catalyst for his concept of what The Specials would become. (The show Dammers refers to was actually the one at Crawley Sports Centre on July 8.)

"I idealistically thought, 'We *have* to get through to these people.' It was obvious that a mod and skinhead revival was coming, and I was trying to find a way to make sure it didn't go the way of the National Front and the British Movement. I saw punk as a piss-take of rock music committing suicide. It was great and really funny, but I couldn't believe people took it as a serious musical genre which they then had to copy. It seemed to be more healthy to have an integrated kind of British music, rather than white people playing rock and black people playing their music. Ska was an integration of the two."

It was a different story where The Special AKA were concerned, however, as their reggae-tinged numbers were in perfect sync with what the crowd could expect from the headliners.   Of course, this didn't mean to say, certain sections of the audiences were left bewildered by what they were seeing on stage.

The On Parole Tour climaxed with four nights at the Music Machine in Camden Town (now Koko). And it was here that six became seven. The Specials were on stage performing 'Don't Try to Love Me', and Staple, sensing the London crowd wasn't getting into the ska-derived sound emanating from the stage, leapt across and grabbed one of the mics. "Without a second thought I took one bound and found myself next to Terry. There was no going back now. Straight away I was on the mic and to song after song, I belted out my toasting. Then I'd leap about – a perfect foil to Terry's static performance. I bounded around like a mad man and I didn't stop 'til I could feel the audience warming up. They loved it."

Seeing the reaction from the crowd, Rhodes suggested Staple be invited to join the band. He thought the rough and ready Staple's introduction would influence the rest of the band into adopting his rude boy style. He also thought it worth pointing out that if The Special AKA were all about promoting black and white harmony, it made sense to have black and white vocalists on stage. Seeing as this was something Dammers had already been contemplating, The Special AKA headed back up the M1 as a seven-piece.

"Neville and his two mates, Rex [Griffiths] and Trevor [Evans] were a part of the band already as roadies anyway," says Byers. "Jerry for one definitely wanted Neville on stage, and I guess most of us were too scared of Neville to say otherwise."

EIGHT

Touring with The Clash had given The Special AKA a national exposure of sorts. They had made a few connections that might prove beneficial and had even managed to get the odd write-up in the music press. They imagined being invited out on the road with other named acts, hopefully as the main support, but as the weeks began slipping by with nary a call, self-doubt and despondency soon set in. Rhodes' offer still held, of course. It would mean giving up their day jobs and relocating to London, but that had to be better than being left to wither on the bough in Coventry. It was time to take a leap of faith in their own ability.

The Camden Market of today is one of London's "must-see" locations, with thousands of tourists flocking to marvel over such artisan creativity on any given day. Many of those same tourists seek out the iconic stairwell that once led up to "Rehearsal Rehearsals", as The Clash had playfully named their HQ. When The Special AKA took up residence there during the autumn of 1978, however, it was a dilapidated two-storey end-of-terrace railway storage shed; many of its soot-encrusted windows broken and stuffed with scrunched-up newspaper to keep out the chill. There was a toilet and sink, but no hot water. Aside from the one-bar electric heater, upon which Paul Simonon famously cooked the leftover flour and water paste from one of The Clash's fly-posting forays, there was no form of heating.

"It was a shithole, but it was The Clash's shithole," says Roadent with typical candour. "I was looking at having to doss on the streets when I arrived in London, so any port in a storm and all that. But I can imagine it coming as something of a shock to Jerry and a couple of the others…"

Indeed, it was. However, as they had all signed on the dole before leaving Coventry, their returning to collect their giros at least allowed them the chance to spend a couple of days luxuriating in the everyday creature comforts they'd once taken for granted. "Rehearsals was very basic," Byers confirms. "There was nowhere to sleep bed-wise, there was the legendary electric fire and a sink, which I remember as having hot water, but my memory could be playing tricks after all these years. I couldn't have cared one way or the other. We were young, and it was all an adventure."

Rehearsals were located within walking distance of both Dingwalls and the Roundhouse, but more often than not The Special AKA could be found stretching out a pint at The Clash's preferred Camden watering hole, the long-since closed down Carnarvon Castle on Chalk Farm Road, bemoaning their lot and questioning Rhodes' motives. The Clash's operating within such squat-like confines had undoubtedly given their eponymous debut album added dynamic, but their being expected to exist without even the basic amenities was beginning to grate. "Bernie would pop in occasionally and give us enough money to buy fish and chips," Byers adds. "We sometimes toasted slices of bread on the electric fire. I remember a rat running over Silverton's chest one night while he was sleeping in the rehearsal space. Most of us slept on the floor in the upstairs office."

The Specials (AKA, or otherwise) have always been keen to stress that Rhodes was never their manager. Negotiations would get as far as having a contract drawn up, but as with The Clash's contract, the legalese couched within the small print weighed heavily in Rhodes' favour. However, it's worth remembering that while the band were on an upward trajectory, they were an unsigned act. There were no A&R teams beating a path to their door, and the money they'd made from playing live had proved sufficient to keep them in their respective day jobs. Rhodes was schooled enough to recognise there was "nothing new under the sun" when it came to rock 'n' roll. He readily boasts being able to source any riff or melody anyone might care to play. The Sex Pistols and Clash hadn't reinvented the wheel, they had merely given it a fresh and exciting spin.

Panter had found operating within the "rarefied atmosphere" of The Clash's world during the On Parole Tour totally intoxicating and desperately wanted to be a part of it. By the time he and the rest of The Special AKA had set up home at Rehearsals, of course, Rhodes was no longer managing The Clash; his aloof attitude, coupled with his ongoing feud with Mick Jones, having brought about an acrimonious parting of the ways.

Roddy Byers says Rhodes somehow managed to keep the news of his dismissal from the band – for a time at least. "This was all long before mobile phones and social media. We didn't have the money to buy music papers, and no one from the music press knew who we were so they'd have no reason to tell us. Micky Foote would have known, of course, but he would have been under orders not to say anything."

CHAPTER

NINE

TIME TO STRAIGHTEN RIGHT OUT

"By now, everybody in The Specials was basically on the dole. We were all equally poor and the only way was up. After a few weeks in the [Rehearsals] boot camp, we began to ask Bernie when he was going to release us into the big wide world. We couldn't just rot there forever after all. So he decided the best place to showcase his new talent was France."

NEVILLE STAPLE

B ernard Rhodes' being sacked by The Clash left The Special
AKA in something of a quandary. It was the kudos that
came with being stablemates with The Clash that had led
their relocating to Camden Town, and being stablemates with
Subway Sect and The Black Arabs didn't have quite the same
zing. Rhodes was going to need a new monkey if he was to
continue playing the organ-grinder, and whether to pick up
the tin cup was causing divisions within the band. "I'm not
sure where the others stood," says Byers, "but me and Lynval
wanted to sign. We were all on the dole, and the money Bernie
was offering was more than we were getting for signing on.
Luckily, Jerry said no, or we would have been on a meagre
wage forever."

Rhodes must have sensed the in-house wavering, and as a
means of bringing the dissenters in line he arranged for The
Special AKA to play a five-night residency at Le Gibus in Paris,
commencing Tuesday, November 14. The band were obviously
thrilled at the thought of heading over to Paris, and yet the
prospect of spending a week there didn't prove sufficient an
enticement to push them into putting pen to paper.

The Paris trip would rapidly descend into a folly worthy of an
Ealing comedy. It would also see The Special AKA come close
to breaking point, and yet in hindsight it was to prove one of
the defining weeks of their career as it provided the inspiration
for the lyric to 'Gangsters', the song that gave rise to the
2-Tone movement.

Speaking with *thespecials2.com*, Golding said Rhodes arranged
the Paris trip to get the band out of London "cos he thought
we weren't right yet". Rhodes' penchant for residencies would
evidence itself during his second stint managing The Clash –
most notably the Bonds NYC residency of June 1981 when
The Clash famously "took over New York". There was little
likelihood of The Special AKA bringing the streets around Le
Gibus to a standstill, of course, and one has to wonder why

Rhodes would think to book an unknown band to play five nights at the same Paris venue instead of booking shows in five European capitals. But as a certain song goes, "Bernie Rhodes knows, so don't argue…"

The Special AKA were set to depart for Paris on Monday, November 13, but by then things had started to unravel. The band's designated driver, Gordon Reaney, had shied away from the trip, supposedly because his van needed a new engine. Panter, however, hints that the real reason behind the former Breaker guitarist's reticence stemmed from his being "pretty pissed off with the Rhodes organisation". Given the "tour de farce" that was to follow, the "Rhodes organisation" was surely a contradiction in terms.

On the Sunday before departure, the hometown replacement driver (Dennis) who had been drafted in was cajoled by Rhodes into ferrying Subway Sect up to Manchester as their van had supposedly broken down. While in Manchester, Dennis got into an argument with Rhodes' ever-faithful factotum, Micky Foote, the result of which saw him withdraw his services, though he agreed to pick The Special AKA up as arranged and ferry them to London. "It all seemed really exciting at the time, but it turned into a nightmare pretty quickly," says Byers. "Dennis wanted cash up front which was fair enough, but Bernie refused to pay him, so he cleared off home after dropping us in London."

When the band arrived at Rehearsals sometime on the Monday they were informed by an irate Rhodes that they wouldn't be leaving till the morrow. This meant a day in London with limited funds, a cold night on a hard floor, and a dressing down from Rhodes for his careful planning having been wrecked owing to their friends refusing to take them to Paris as arranged. Come the Tuesday, however, there's still no van and departure time has been pushed back till the following day. This meant another day in London with even more limited funds and another restless night at Rehearsals. More importantly, two of the five shows would have to be cancelled. Dammers vented his frustrations by trashing a door and the payphone at Rehearsals, an act which, though understandable, was hardly likely to have endeared him to the frugal-fisted Rhodes.

Micky Foote was already set to accompany the band to Paris, but Golding says he was under the impression that Rhodes would also be accompanying them on the trip. When they arrived at Dover, however, Rhodes ordered them to unload the gear on to trolleys, before handing Foote a wad of cash and driving off in the van. "We were under the impression that Bernie would be coming with us," says Byers. "That's how the trip was sold to us, that he'd be coming with us. When we arrived at Dover he told us to unload the gear and get it on to the ferry as another van would be meeting us at Calais. As soon as we got the gear out of the back Bernie shouted something that sounded like 'good luck' before driving off."

If the band thought their problems were behind them they were in for a rude awakening when they arrived at Calais. Foote had taken care of the carnet needed to get the band's equipment through customs, but owing to all the hullabaloo over the van, no one had bothered to check whether the band's documentation was in order. Silverton's Barbados passport had proved sufficient to get him through customs back in Dover, but he would require a visa to enter France. The French officials remained unmoved, however; though it wasn't entirely clear to the rest of the band whether it was the passport's validity or the colour of Hutchinson's skin that was the issue. Hutchinson was already bemoaning his lot. He hadn't joined the band to sleep in dank, disused railway sheds or live on Rhodes' sporadic handouts and hadn't been shy in letting the others know his feelings. With the French officials having moved on to the passengers, the disgruntled drummer had no option but to retrace his steps back to London to get the necessary documentation.

The mood amongst the rest of the band was hardly improved on discovering the van Rhodes had sorted out to ferry them the 175 miles or so to Paris was a Volkswagen Camper. It was immediately obvious to all that six musicians, a sound engineer and the band's gear —backline and instruments — wasn't going to fit into the Volkswagen's cramped confines. With the backline and equipment taking priority, it was left to the band to decide amongst themselves which two would be accompanying Foote in the van.

Given Hutchinson's treatment there really wasn't much to discuss, and so Staple and Golding clambered in beside Foote. Hall, Dammers, Byers and Panter headed into the port's lorry terminal, hoping to find a driver sympathetic to their plight.

Their search was cut short by the port police, but their luck was about to change, as Byers explains: "It was getting on for midnight when a Rolls-Royce pulled up. The driver was a Welsh guy that had picked the Roller up at the port and was delivering it to his boss. The guy wasn't going all the way to Paris unfortunately, and dropped us off at a motorway services about fifty miles from Paris. We had to hang about the services for a while before finding a driver that was making for Paris. He would only take two of us though, so me and Jerry jumped in the van. We only had the address of the club we were playing. It was still dark when we got to Club Gibus. I remember Terry and Horace getting there about an hour or so after we did. We were all exhausted by now, but with no way of getting hold of Micky we wandered around the streets for a bit.

"Someone, Jerry, I think, went back to the club to await Micky, Neville and Lynval. The rest of us settled down on some park benches to try and get some sleep. Not an easy thing in November. It was starting to get dark again when we headed back to the club. An Australian girl – a friend of Micky's that was living in Paris – showed up to take us to the hotel where we were booked to stay."

The trials and tribulations of the previous 24 hours would have tested the patience of Saint Monica herself, yet The Special AKA remained unbowed and put in solid enough performances later that night. Byers is of the opinion that the Paris trip would "make a good movie as things just went from bad to worse".

Indeed, they did…

Firstly, the band were deemed responsible for the hotel's plate-glass doors being smashed. Someone from the hotel had burst into Foote's room and demanded 500 Francs as payment for the doors. The band quite rightly pleaded their innocence and ignorance in equal measure, but the hotel's proprietress was having none of it. Panter's recollections saw her bursting into the room he was sharing with Dammers (brandishing a Coca-Cola bottle) and dragging an unsuspecting Dammers from the shower. In the interim, two "heavies" had arrived and confiscated Golding's and Byers' guitars in lieu of payment for the shattered doors.

Foote had managed to get hold of the Gibus' manager and have him come to the hotel to try and interpret some sense out of the unfolding farce. Unbeknown to the band, Rhodes had booked them into the same hotel The Damned had stayed at while playing the Gibus the week before. Sensible and co. had apparently run amok (as was their wont) before absconding without paying the bill. Deciding one English band was the same as any other, the proprietress announced the 500 Francs was to cover The Damned's outstanding bill, while the guitars would cover The Special AKA's stay and the damaged doors. The couplet "Can't interrupt while I'm talking, or they'll confiscate all your guitars" in 'Gangsters' relates to the standoff betwixt band and proprietress. "Everything in 'Gangsters' was about that trip," Staple reflected. "And it was a brilliant trip in the end because it gave us our first hit record – can't complain about that."

At the time, however, Staple was rather less philosophical and might well have tested the French heavies' mettle had it not been for the police's timely intervention. The cops proved as biased towards Jamaicans and English musicians as their Calais counterparts. Fortunately, the Gibus' cigar-chomping owner arrived soon thereafter, and a settlement of sorts was eventually thrashed out. According to Panter, said arrangement had Foote, having obviously been given the nod by Rhodes back in London, agreeing to hand over half the money the proprietress was holding out for, with the Gibus' owner paying the rest.

The Paris jaunt would indeed provide The Special AKA with their first hit record, but the man responsible for sending them to the French capital wouldn't be around to share in the celebrations. "I think we'd had enough of Mr Rhodes by then," says Byers. "He was right about our disjointed sound and stage look, but it just wasn't going to work after Paris."

Staple was more succinct in his appraisal. "Bernie was toast. Nobody in The Specials wanted to continue this relationship – he had put us through hell."

Though they had been in awe of Rhodes for being the guy who'd "put The Clash on the map" and were thankful for his giving them a sense of purpose, The Special AKA felt it time to move on.

When approached for his reflections on his relationship with
The Specials, Bernard requested that his response be printed in
full:

"Jerry Dammers approached me, it must have been around
the late 1970s; said he had a group from the Midlands
called The Coventry Automatics. We discussed music, etc.
Jerry was enthralled with my deep knowledge of blue beat,
ska and reggae. He also respected my street style, punk
commitment, and of my early involvement in the mod
movement.

"I soon realised he was a bright kid with a rare talent,
although the name of his group wasn't right. I told him so
in that it reminded me of The Dave Clark Five; they used
to play at the Tottenham Royal when I was a youngster.
After some thought I emphasised that **'I wanted a group
to be something really special.'** The next time Jerry
contacted me the group was now called **The Specials**.

"I had The Specials rehearse and write new songs,
rearrange old ones, and make demos at my Camden
studios. This vibrant studio atmosphere, with many creative
characters passing by, inspired The Specials forward. I
offered advice, got them gigs, and had them be the support
on a forthcoming Clash tour.

"I liked most of their live sound, the Roddy Rockabilly
thing worked well with the ska stuff; however, we had
trouble with the original drummer. I believe he went off to
join a disco band.

"Then there was Neville dancing about the mixing desk
– Rasta-rapping to the music. I told him to do all that
on stage as part of the show, which would also put some
extra diversity into the group – make it more colour/
class balanced. (Two Tone). Plus, his aggressive style
strengthened the slightly wimpy vocals. From then on,

Terry thought I was trying to replace him. This insecurity stopped Terry absorbing my brilliant idea of two singers with its dynamic/entertaining value.

"It eventually led to us parting company, which is a shame because with me around The Specials would have been a more successful, interesting and adventurous combination, also a group which still included Jerry."

Bernard Rhodes, May 2018.

For all its promise, by the spring of 1979 punk was already becoming a cliched caricature of itself; its initial vibrancy long-since dissipated and assimilated into the music mainstream as "new wave". However, with Britain still in the grip of the wintry discontent that was set to sweep Margaret Thatcher into 10 Downing Street on the back of a landslide General Election victory, another generation of disenfranchised and disaffected kids faced walking out of the school gates and straight into seemingly ever-growing dole queues.

Many of these same kids had seen first-hand how punk had given their elder siblings an exciting distraction from their otherwise humdrum existence and were actively seeking something to provide them with a similar identity and sense of belonging. But where might this new movement come from?

In *The Great Rock 'n' Roll Swindle*, Malcolm McLaren justifies his "manufacturing" of the Sex Pistols by paraphrasing Mikhail Bakunin's famous quote: "The urge to destroy is also a creative urge." Punk had indeed stripped rock back to its roots, yet the bands that would thrive beyond the scorched earth policy – namely The Clash and The Jam – did so by acknowledging the music that had stimulated them to pick up a guitar and form a band.

Dammers was a jobbing musician on the West Midlands soul scene when punk broke, but he too had tipped a nod to Bakunin when penning the songs that had given rise to The Special AKA. They had yet to follow through on Bernard Rhodes' suggestion they define their image, but bringing Staple into the line-up was at least pointing them in a certain direction.

On hearing '(Whatever Happened to) Bluebeat and Ska', the latest release by Matumbi, a seven-piece, south London reggae outfit featuring Dennis Bovey on bass guitar, Panter says he and Dammers "took it as a sign" that ska would define them – both musically and visually.

Dammers already knew where he wanted to take The Special AKA's image. As Byers says, it was Paul Simonon's penchant for "rude bwoy" chic during the On Parole Tour rather than Bernard Rhodes' suggestions per se that had truly formed Byers' mind.

The term 'rude boys' was coined to denote the street-wise gangs of unemployed, yet dapperly dressed youths who had all but terrorised Kingston during the mid-to-late Sixties. "Rude" was Jamaican slang for "cool", and it was the concept of an immaculately dressed rebellion that had fired Dammers' febrile imagination. His enforcing the rude boy look in the band was certainly endorsed by Staple, if only because his wardrobe consisted entirely of tonic suits, Harrington jackets, Fred Perry T-shirts and Ben Sherman gear.

In 2009, reflecting on the subtle shift in musical direction that was to have such a seismic effect on the UK post-punk scene, Dammers said the "ska idea" came on hearing a long-forgotten Birmingham reggae act called Capital Letters. "They did a track called 'Smoking My Ganga', which was dub reggae but had a ska-like rhythm. I was already wearing a shiny blue mod suit and it suddenly all clicked."

Hutchinson and Golding, however, proved reticent to the move. Ska was what their parents had grown up listening to, and both viewed playing "old man music" as a backward step. Golding eventually came round to the idea, but Hutchinson wasn't for turning. He'd tolerated living hand to mouth in abject squalor at Rehearsals, had even put up with vermin making midnight runs across his chest, but the opportunity to introduce a part of his musical heritage to a new generation went against the grain. He quit showing up at rehearsals, then quit the band altogether when Coventry's self-styled answer to Geno Washington, Ray King, stepped in and offered him £40 per week to join his soul band.

Drummers were ten-a-penny on the pub and club circuit, but good drummers were worth their weight in gold. Though traditional ska has a straightforward 4/4 beat, the rhythms The Special AKA were looking to incorporate into their songs would need to keep the reggae swing that Hutchinson had effortlessly put down.

Seb Shelton would go on to play with Secret Affair and achieve mainstream success with 'Come on Eileen'-era Dexys Midnight Runners, but during the spring of 1979 he was playing with The Young Bucks, a Newcastle-based quartet formed some four years earlier by future EMI and BPI CEO, Tony Wadsworth. The quartet were signed to their home city label, Bluebeat Records, but the future that had seemed so promising when *Sounds* proclaimed their 1978 debut offering, 'Get Your Feet Back on the Ground', their "Single of the Week" would fail to materialise.

When Dammers got wind of Shelton's disenchantment with his lot, he and Panter headed down to London to catch The Young Bucks play the Nashville Rooms in West Kensington. They were impressed enough by what they saw that night to offer Shelton the gig, but Shelton either failed to be impressed by their spiel or was already being courted by ex-New Hearts duo Ian Page and David Cairns for their new band, Secret Affair.

The irony surely wasn't lost on Dammers that he schlepped all the way to Nashville to check out Seb Shelton when the guy that was to occupy The Specials' drum stool through the band's heady heyday and beyond was already known to him and living under the same roof as part of some music collective for one-time art students.

Born in February 1953, John "Brad" Bradbury had lived his whole life in Coventry. He'd been playing the drums since the age of eight, driving his parents, siblings and put-upon neighbours to distraction till someone suggested lining the walls of his bedroom with egg boxes as a means of absorbing the din. As with Dammers and Panter, he showed a flare for art from an early age and had graduated from Hull Art College in 1970 with a Fine Arts degree. From there he took a teaching course, and for a time taught English and art at a secondary school in Birmingham. For reasons best known to himself, he gave up teaching to work behind the counter at the local Virgin Records – the same Virgin Records store where the band's one-time frontman Tim Strickland had worked.

Bradbury was also acquainted with Terry Hall. The two lived just two streets apart, but they'd come to know each other from Hall's not-infrequent forays to Virgin. Dammers would subsequently claim to have been unaware that Bradbury played the drums, but it beggars belief that he'd remained ignorant to Bradbury's currently working with their mutual friend – and future Selecter mainstay – Neol Davies in Transposed Men, an ad hoc outfit who were touting an acetate of a trombone-led ska/reggae instrumental called 'Kingston Affair' (the tune that would soon be renamed 'The Selecter' in time to feature as the flipside to 'Gangsters'). Dammers had borrowed Davis' Revox tape recorder while experimenting with the funk/soul hybrid tunes he would subsequently present to Panter, so again it stands to reason that Davis would have kept

Dammers abreast of his own musical experimentations with Bradbury. Yet even when this was made known to him, he took some convincing that his housemate's style was right for The Special AKA.

There's only one thing worse than having a disheartened drummer, and that's having no drummer at all – especially given The Special AKA were desperate to see how their material might sound with a ska-tinged beat. It soon became apparent that Bradbury "had chops", as the saying goes. Panter goes so far as to put Bradbury alongside UB40's Jim Brown in his authentic playing style. "He [Bradbury] had the reggae groove down. He didn't just play reggae, he could change tempo seamlessly from a 'one-drop' reggae beat to 'four-on-the-floor' rock. Rehearsals began with a new enthusiasm as we learnt old ska numbers like 'Monkey Man' and 'You're Wondering Now' and adapted our old material with our new ska feel."

Staple was another quick to appreciate Bradbury's talents. He'd felt that with Hutchinson the band's momentum could get a "bit slow and ponderous", and Bradbury's up-tempo style gave him something to move on. "The way he played was a hundred per cent reggae, always hitting the third beat, and his no-nonsense underpinning of the band's sound was a real asset. Pretty soon he'd earned the nickname 'Prince Rimshot'."

Bradbury's inclusion meant The Special AKA were now sounding just as Dammers and Panter had imagined. Not only was it time to get out and road test the new ska-tinged rhythms, it was time to make a record. The record industry "know-nothings" Pete Waterman had despaired about were still showing little interest in the band, but while Dammers had regarded punk as a "piss-take", it had nonetheless shown that making your own records was no longer an unobtainable flight of fancy.

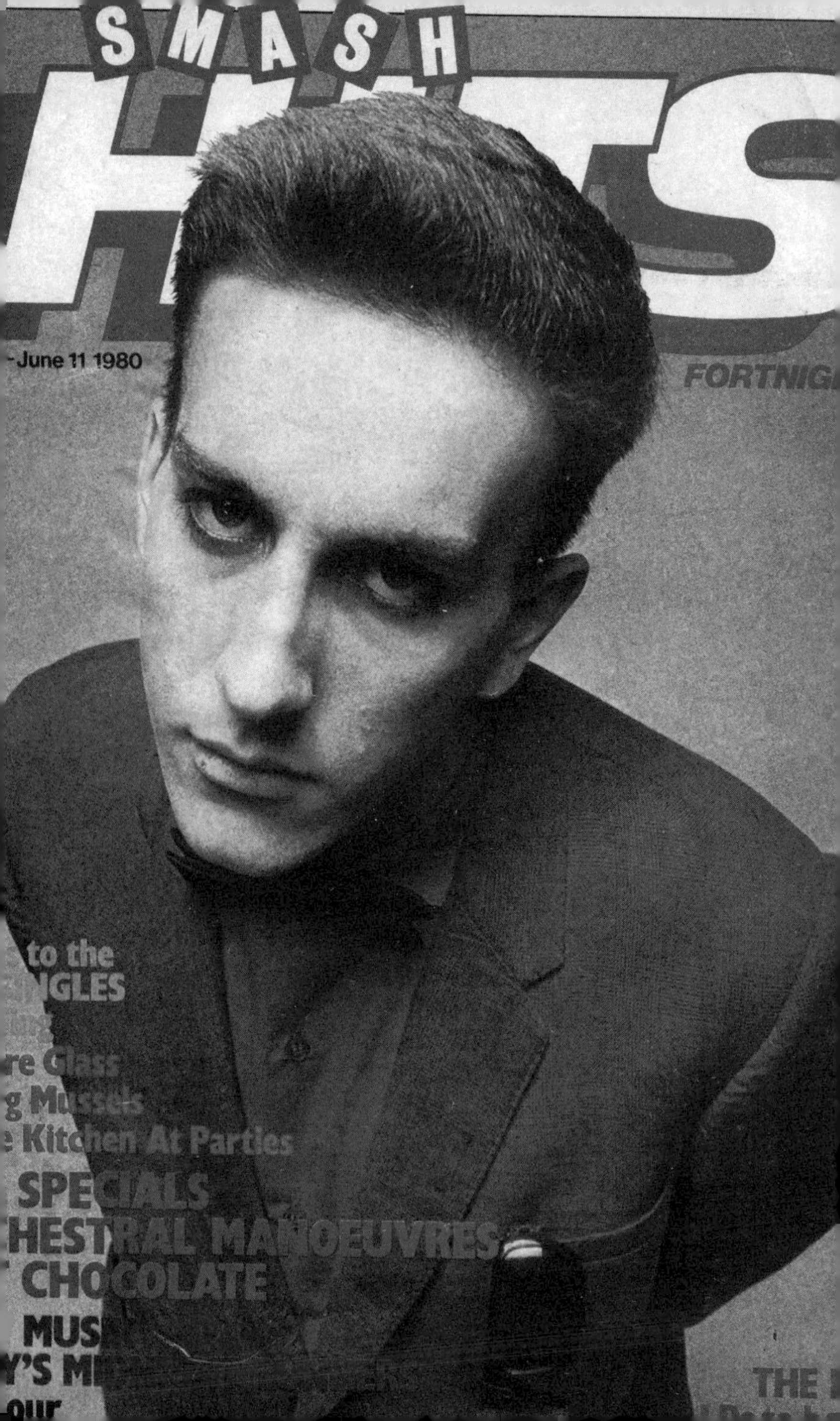

SMASH
HITS

– June 11 1980

FORTNIG

to the
NGLES

re Glass
g Mussels
e Kitchen At Parties

SPECIALS
HESTRAL MANOEUVRES
CHOCOLATE

MUSK
Y'S MI
our

THE

CHAPTER

TEN

LIVING IN GANGSTER TIME

"We didn't even realise we were playing 'ska'
— we grew up in a heavily Jamaican populated
area, and we were referencing music we grew
up with. We once played a gig to skinheads
and found our audience by accident. We did
venture down to London, but none of the record
companies were interested. They didn't know
who we were, so we formed our own label in
Coventry."

TERRY HALL

CHAPTER

P unk's whole DIY ethos was about getting up and doing things yourself, and this was typified by Buzzcocks releasing their four-track EP, 'Spiral Scratch', on their own New Hormones label in January 1977; the singular event now cited as the catalyst for independent record labels becoming something of a norm and ultimately giving rise to "indie" as a music genre. Not a bad return for the £500 Buzzcocks borrowed from friends and family to pay for the recording session and 1,000 records plus picture sleeves.

Instead of going through the rigmarole of hiring a van and driving up to London, The Special AKA opted to book themselves into Horizon Studios, located on the top floor of a three-storey warehouse situated within the shadow of Coventry's main train station. According to Panter, a well-to-do local car dealer-cum-property developer had purchased the space with the intention of converting it into a studio for the city's independent station. When Mercia Sound grabbed the franchise from under his nose, the developer instead installed two state-of-the-art recording studios, or at least state-of-the-art as far as the musicians of Coventry were concerned.

In early January 1979, The Special AKA set up home in Horizon's Studio One to record versions of 'Too Much Too Young', 'Nite Klub' and the recently penned 'Gangsters'. The £700 cost of the recording session and the 1,500 copies of their intended vinyl debut was met by James "Jimbo" O'Boyle, a local businessman of questionable repute who Dammers, Golding and Byers had encountered at Domino, a late-night drinking emporium adjoining the Mr. George's nightclub. O'Boyle wasn't helping them out of the goodness of his heart, of course. He was anticipating a sizeable percentage of the profits from the sale of the single in return for his largess. And O'Boyle's ever-present minder – a man-mountain called Frasier, around whom even Staple warily trod – would ensure the undisclosed percentage would be paid on time and in full.

TEN

Whereas Buzzcocks had future Factory whizz kid Martin Hannett manning the mixing desk at Indigo Sound Studios, the £700 The Special AKA handed over for their time at Horizon didn't extend to a producer. As such, Dammers would assume responsibility for mixing and producing the tracks. While the band could call upon their previous studio experiences – screening off certain instruments, leaving Panter's bass open to create a distinct "wall of bass", having Hall record "angry" and "bored" vocals, etc. – they were nonetheless entrusting the whole enterprise to Dammers' enthusiasm.

Of the three finished songs, only 'Gangsters' was deemed worthy of being consigned to vinyl. "It wasn't that 'Nite Klub' or 'Too Much Too Young' weren't good enough in themselves," says Byers. "We'd nailed 'Gangsters' in a couple of takes, but the other tracks were taking longer, and we ran out of studio time."

Approaching "Shady" O'Boyle for more cash to book a second day at Horizon wasn't really a road the band wanted to go down, so if they were going to release a record they needed to find something suitable for the B-side. One option was to remix 'Gangsters' as an instrumental. It wasn't uncommon for reggae artists to place what was known as "versions" on the flip side, but these were generally by other reggae acts. It was then that someone remembered the 'Kingston Affair' instrumental that Bradbury had recorded with Neol Davies (as Transposed Men). Davies was naturally open to the proposal, and at Dammers' behest dusted off the eighteen-month-old tape and added a ska guitar part to bring the instrumental into keeping with 'Gangsters'.

"There wasn't anything behind our using Neol and Brad's track other than we didn't want to have to borrow more money," Byers adds. "It really was as simple as that."

By the time the single came to be pressed the instrumental had been renamed 'The Selecter' and it would be issued on Dammers' newly incorporated 2-Tone Records as a double A-side – again in traditional Jamaican style – as The Special AKA vs The Selecter.

Dammers had hit upon the name "2-Tone" for the band's record label from two-tone being the colloquial term for the tonic suits The Special AKA had incorporated into their look. Panter remembers "Satik" and "Underworld" being bandied about as potential names, but 2-Tone did what it said on the tin; complimenting the band's new ska sound and image. More importantly, it sounded fresh and exciting.

Having settled on the name, Dammers and Panter put their art school heads together to come up with an eye-catching logo. Panter takes credit for placing the "Tone" underneath the "2", but says the rest was all Dammers: "I designed the 2-Tone label based on the black and white sticky tape I used to decorate my bike [with] when I was a mini mod," Dammers told *House of Fun: The Story of Madness* author John Reed. "[I also used] a tracing of Peter Tosh of The Wailers, in the early days when they were trying to The Impressions. I named this "2-Tone" man "Walt Jabsco" after a bowling shirt that I bought in Tunisia when I was in Nite Trane with Neol Davies."

The "Sillitoe Tartan" black and white checkerboard motif Dammers refers to is one of the most readily identifiable motifs in the world, if only because of it being adopted by UK police forces. "Walt Jabsco", the monochromatic rude boy dressed in black suit, white shirt, black tie, white socks, black loafers, pork-pie hat and shades set within a black/white checkerboard grid, would soon be adopted by the band's ever-burgeoning legion of followers. Indeed, for a time it was the most identifiable cartoon silhouette next to Felix the Cat. Those kids adopting the Walt Jabsco wardrobe would also have their own dance – "skanking" – a.k.a the "2-Tone twist".

Ska dancing was extremely vigorous, using a forward-leaning position, almost a crouch, whereby the bent knees served as springs bobbing up and down, while the arms pump up and down in front alternately. Dancers would frequently move to another spot (room allowing, of course), using a little jump to make the seamless transition, and would be facing another direction – or their dancing partner – while continuing to dance.

The Special AKA's first show with Bradbury in the line-up came at the University of Birmingham in Edgbaston. The band put in a solid performance, but only a handful of people were there to bear witness. One positive that came from the night, however, was a one-time Coventry Art College lecturer friend of Dammers called Alan Harrison mentioning he was acquainted with The Damned's current manager, Rick Rogers.

Rogers had been serving as press officer at Stiff Records at the time the fledgling label added The Damned to their roster in September 1976. He'd accompanied the hapless Damned on the Sex Pistols' ill-fated Anarchy Tour in the December of that year. Punk's perennial pranksters had undergone the first of countless splits in 1977 following the dismal showing of their second Stiff album, *Music for Pleasure*, but had reunited in early 1979 (albeit without founding guitarist Brian James). On taking over the managerial helm, Rogers secured The Damned a recording contract with Chiswick, and the resulting album, *Machine Gun Etiquette*, had proved a stunning return to form.

Rogers was operating his own PR company, Trigger, from a room above Ted Carroll's now-legendary Rock On record store in Camden Town at the time. Despite Camden and The Damned having both left an unsavoury taste in his mouth, Dammers visited Rogers and successfully petitioned him to come and see The Special AKA play a forthcoming show at Warwick

University. It was to prove a wise choice as Warwick Uni was on the band's home turf and Coventry's punk contingent descended on the university en masse. Imbued by such partisan support, The Special AKA played out of their skins. Rogers had been impressed by the songs on the demo tape Dammers had left with him, and on hearing the songs live he knew he had to be involved. It would mean scaling down his involvement with The Damned, but the strain of dealing with Captain Sensible and co. was already starting to show.

Before leaving Coventry, having spent the night sleeping off a heavy drink on Panter's sofa, Rogers had agreed to manage The Special AKA, but only on the proviso they operate on a handshake basis until a recording deal had been secured.

Upon taking receipt of the 1,500 copies of their debut single, Panter and Hall set about imprinting the cardboard covers Bradbury had "appropriated" from the store room at Virgin Records with "The Special AKA: Gangsters" and "vs The Selecter" stamps Panter had made up specially to make the packaging more visually appealing. Armed with a handful of copies, Dammers and Panter ventured up to Rough Trade Records in London's Ladbroke Grove to speak with the owner, Geoff Travis. The Special AKA's reputation had preceded them, as Travis was aware of the band from their supporting The Clash on the On Parole Tour and readily agreed to stock the single.

The Special AKA were ska influenced yet were anything but ska revivalists. In turn, while the tune to 'Gangsters' was woven around the riff to Prince Buster's 'Al Capone', Dammers' treble-heavy piano, coupled with Byers' punk-infused reggae licks, over which Hall's laconic tone reflected the modern-day mood of a recession-hit, dystopian Britain. Travis was soon asking for more copies, and when the initial 1,500 ran out he stepped in to have Rough Trade take over the pressing.

Dammers wasn't envisioning 2-Tone to be a one-off showcase label, as New Hormones had proved in helping Buzzcocks secure a deal with United Artists. He saw himself as the Berry Gordy Jr. of the West Midlands, imagining 2-Tone signing other acts of a similar ilk to The Special AKA, and coming to signify its own specific sound, the same as Stax, Blue Beat or Tamla-Motown. "To make a 'label-sound' was our dream," says Panter. "To hear a tune and immediately be able to say, 'That's a 2-Tone record/band.' Punk had an overall image, [but] all the punk bands had their own agendas by now, and it was never a 'movement' in a unified sense. So, we sat up in Coventry thinking ourselves the UK's Tamla-Motown."

Byers remembers sitting in on the idea-trading sessions from which 2-Tone was born.

"Jerry wanted a record label, so he could sign bands and start a musical movement. The rest of us would have been happy with just a record deal, but Jerry had bigger plans."

Rick Rogers was now fully committed to the cause, and the band were getting more and more reputable gigs via Oak, the Birmingham-based booking agency run by one-time Brent Ford and The Nylons frontman John Mostyn. But the soon-to-be truncated "Specials'" meteoric rise and equally spectacular crash to Earth truly took off thanks to a certain Radio 1 DJ giving 'Gangsters' a spin on his late-night show. "He [John Peel] played 'Gangsters' one Wednesday night," says Panter. "He played it again on the Thursday. He played it every night for the next fortnight, as often as not at the beginning of the show. He was as responsible as anyone for getting The Specials known

outside of Coventry. I loved him. I felt like I'd lost a
favourite uncle when I heard the news of his death." (Peel
succumbed to a massive heart attack while holidaying in
Cusco, Peru, in October 2004. He was 65.)

John Peel's show of patronage put The Special AKA in the
enviable position which had A&R (Artists & Repertoire)
reps showing up at their shows. Dammers wasn't looking
to tie the band to a conventional deal, but he wasn't yet in
a position where he could go it alone. But the help he was
looking for wasn't long in coming.

On Wednesday, May 2, 1979, the eve of Margaret
Thatcher's general election victory, The Special AKA played
the Moonlight Club, a sweat and spit-pit located within the
basement of The Railway Hotel in West Hampstead. Thanks
to some opportune entrepreneurialism by someone within
the Decca Records organisation, a bootleg of the Moonlight
Club show was in circulation within a matter of weeks.
Decca Studios (now the English National Opera Gardens)
was situated next door to The Railway Hotel, and given that
The Special AKA were still an unknown quantity, it stands
to reason that whichever of Decca's staff was responsible for
setting up the illicit audio feed did so more in anticipation
than expectation.

Though the band would have frowned on such nefarious
activities, the bootleg at least serves as a testament how
much The Special AKA had come on musically in recent
months. Hall's opening comment about his not having "much
to say" about the outcome of the morrow's general election,
and that it was up to everyone to make their vote count,
also shows that he was already being viewed as a contender
for "spokesman of his generation" in the John Lydon/Joe
Strummer mould. The bootleg appeared in the run-up to the

release of *The Specials*, and such was its continued popularity that in 1992 2-Tone was moved to issue an official live album: *The Specials: Live at the Moonlight Club*.

Dammers was making his way off stage when he was approached by Chrysalis Records' A&R head, Roy Eldridge. The one-time *Melody Maker* scribe was convinced The Special AKA were the "most exciting band he'd ever seen", and he was determined to snap them up.

Chrysalis being an independent label had obviously got Rogers' blessing, and with Eldridge happy to meet all of the demands Dammers put before him, a deal was soon struck. The Special AKA signed with Chrysalis for £20,000, half of which was paid upon signing, with the remainder to be paid upon the label taking receipt of the band's debut album. Said album, and all other Special AKA records, would be released via the 2-Tone label but be distributed and marketed through Chrysalis.

Dammers' dream of the band having their own record label had come to fruition as the Chrysalis contract contained a clause allowing 2-Tone to release up to ten singles by other 2-Tone acts per year, with a £1,000 budget allotted to each project.

Where to find these acts wasn't going to be as easy as it seemed. As Oscar Wilde so succinctly put it, "Imitation is the sincerest form of flattery that mediocrity can repay to greatness." A classic example of Wilde's maxim is the plethora of punk bands that wilfully copied the Sex Pistols in the hope of gaining an audience. Those bands who were inspired by the Pistols – The Clash, Buzzcocks, The Damned, Siouxsie and The Banshees,

Chrysalis RECORDS

Generation X et al – all enjoyed careers that lasted into the 1980s and beyond. Those bands that fell for the "learn three chords and form a band" mantra rarely lasted beyond the fag-end of 1977.

The Special AKA had taken certain elements of punk and assimilated them into the music they wanted to make. First with reggae, and now with ska. As soon as word got out that a Coventry-based band had carte blanche to offer a single deal, and have it marketed and distributed by Chrysalis, those bands wearily ploughing a forlorn furrow on the jaded punk circuit would have switched styles overnight before beating a path to Dammers' door. However, with the Chrysalis clause stipulating "up to" ten singles per annum, there was no question of 2-Tone being under pressure to deliver.

What the Chrysalis deal meant to The Special AKA, of course, was that after two long years of seemingly never-ending hardship and hard slog, they could finally consider themselves a professional outfit. The £10,000 advance put an end to cramped Transit vans, and stretching giros to cover the cost of drumskins, guitar strings and other sundries essential to keeping a band on the road, while still making ends meet. Griffiths and

Evans were already receiving an equal share of the band's fees, but their being put on to the payroll meant they could at last give up their day jobs.

The Special AKA signed with Chrysalis on Friday, June 8, 1979. To mark the occasion, as well as allow the Chrysalis hierarchy to see their latest acquisition on stage, later that day the band played the Nashville Rooms in West Kensington. The Nashville date was to prove momentous in more ways than one, for sharing the stage with The Special AKA that night was a certain sextet operating out of Kentish Town.

CHAPTER

ELEVEN

THEY CALL IT MADNESS...

*"I think it was my idea to do 'One Step
Beyond', the track. It was one of the old Prince
Buster records we used to play on the pub
jukebox. Chas Smash came up with the intro:
'Hey you, don't watch that, watch this.
This is the heavy, heavy monster sound.' It was
inspired by the shouty, slightly preposterous, 'I
am the magnificent' intros you got on
Jamaican records."*

SUGGS

CHAPTER

It would be grossly unfair to suggest Madness owed their career to The Specials, but there can be no denying it was the latter act's munificence in dropping Madness' name into the conversation during interviews that gave them a baggy-trousered leg up. What's surprising, given that several of the guys in Madness were Clash fans, was that none of them had attended any of the three On Parole shows at the Music Machine the previous July. The much-anticipated meeting of the 2-Tone twain came on Saturday, May 5, 1979, when The Special AKA were invited on to the bill for a Rock Against Racism concert being staged at the Hope and Anchor in Islington.

The Hope and Anchor has since become synonymous with the pub-rock scene of the mid-Seventies following its taking over from the Tally Ho in Kentish Town as north London's "go to" place for live music. It was also responsible for opening its doors to the nascent punk scene, however. Indeed, it was where The Damned filmed the promo video for 'New Rose'.

The guys in Madness were vaguely aware of some Coventry-based act claiming the honour of reintroducing ska to appreciative audiences. With the Hope and Anchor being their preferred watering hole, it was only natural that they would check out the competition – even if their curiosity didn't extend to buying tickets. "We hadn't heard of them really, but they were similar to us," Suggs (aka Graham McPherson) later recalled. "Funnily enough, the first thing I had heard about them was a half-page article in the *Melody Maker*. I could see they dressed the same as us, in a way."

Suggs goes on to say how he and the rest of the guys in the band were more or less using the Hope and Anchor as their HQ. They'd monopolised the jukebox to the point where it was weighted with obscure ska and Blue Beat tracks. The Special AKA's coming on to their turf could have been construed as a gauntlet being thrown down, but there was to be none of the petty rivalries that had riven punk asunder. Indeed, the bonhomie extended to Suggs inviting Dammers to kip on his mum's sofa after the show. It was to prove a pivotal moment in the history of British subculture. "He [Dammers] explained he was going to start his own label," Suggs continues. "We talked long into the night about pop music and his vision and future that was to be 2-Tone. Pretty momentous. I didn't think at that point it would ever happen."

Before taking his leave the following morning, Dammers told Suggs that should Madness be interested in making a record, he would be happy to release it via 2-Tone. Arrangements were also made for the two bands to do something the next time The Specials had cause to visit the capital.

When Dammers, with Neol Davies in tow, made another of his visits to Geoff Travis at Rough Trade, he'd been "intrigued" by the graffiti daubed on the buildings around Euston Station; his intrigue no doubt stemming from why the "North London Invaders" (whose membership included "Chalky", "Toks" and "Bird's Egg") would see the need to invade one of north London's best-known landmarks and leave their tag? He would also subsequently recall seeing "Chalky n Suggs ov Chelsea" etched into toilet doors and walls during another sojourn to London. The mystery was solved following Dammers subsequently being invited to see Madness play the Hope and Anchor towards the end of May. "They had apparently hit on the idea of doing ska themselves," Dammers reflected. "They had a dance which consisted of head-butting each other! They were ropey as hell, still virtually a school band. Obviously, they had to be snapped up for our fledgling label. My idea was that, instead of competing, we should work together with like-minded bands."

Suggs' claim that he hadn't expected anything to come of Dammers' dreams of starting his own record label in the near future didn't stop Madness recording a rough demo of 'The Prince' and handing the tape to Dammers at the Hope and Anchor show. "The demo they gave me was really, really bad," Dammers goes on. "There was no record company going to sign them at the time in their career except 2-Tone. I did see the potential…"

The potential Dammers saw in Madness, both at the Hope and Anchor and on cassette, had been evolving for some three years. As Dammers was to discover, the "North London Invaders" weren't a gang of disorientated football hooligans, but rather the embryonic acorn from which Madness would grow. They had also been inspired by punk, but unlike The Hybrids hadn't allowed their inspiration to extend beyond the "anyone can do it" attitude. Speaking with Pete Frame for the latter's "Madness Family Tree", founding keyboardist Mike "Monsieur Barso" Barson admitted to sensing the opportunities that might arise from punk's anti-musicianship stance. The Sex Pistols espousing being into chaos rather than the music was enough to put a smile on his face, but the clarion call of 'Anarchy in the UK' had left him unmoved. He'd been enrolled at the Hornsea College of Art around the time the Pistols started getting notices in the music weeklies.

One of Barson's fellow foundation course students at Hornsea, Eric Watson, who would subsequently photograph Madness in their pomp, remembers tipping his friend the nod about the Pistols after catching one of the band's Nashville Room dates in April 1976. "Their attitude was good," Barson said of the Pistols, "but I don't think any of us liked their music." (Coincidently, Barson's older brother,

Ben, was playing with rock 'n' roll revivalists Bazooka Joe, the band the Pistols made their live debut supporting at St. Martin's College of Art & Design on November 6, 1975.)

Madness' long-serving saxophonist, Lee "Kix" Thompson, was left equally unmoved by the punk explosion. "The original idea of our nutty sound was to keep the music fun and humorous, almost as a rebellion against the punk thing," he explained. "We wanted to keep the music away from politics. Music should be fun and, above all, loving. I was never a punk for that reason. I wouldn't give it an inch because of the way they looked, the aggressiveness."

Thompson's upbringing was wayward to say the least. His father, Frederick, has gone down in north London folklore as being one of the top safe-breakers in Soho. Being good at his nefarious profession didn't keep him from being apprehended with embarrassing regularity, however. Indeed, he seems to have spent more time behind bars than not. Unsurprisingly, by the time Thompson junior reached secondary school he was more interested in robbing than any of the "three R's". His raids were more of an opportunist nature to those of his father. On his fourteenth birthday, having bunked off school, he wandered into one of the local hospitals and came away with £130 that he'd happened upon in one of the staff lockers. He was soon apprehended and was sentenced to two years at Chafford Approved School for boys in Harwich, Kent. Indeed, Thompson would later cite his meeting and befriending Mike Barson and Christopher "Chrissy Boy" Foreman – the third of the "cheeky chappy" triumvirate that would form the nucleus of Madness – as being the only reason he didn't go the same way as his father.

It was Barson's tickling the ivories at family gatherings and such that proved the inspiration for Foreman, the eldest of the three, to purchase a guitar. His folk singer father, John, had tried teaching him the rudiments of the instrument years earlier, but Foreman readily admits to lacking both inclination and interest. The guitar, a "Waltone", was a cheap and cheerful semi-acoustic, barely worth the £20 he paid for it in one of Camden's backstreet second-hand shops. "I just used to play the notes one string at a time," he recalled during an interview. "I wasn't very interested in it. Then I started playing chords and that started me off." His being left-handed was to prove a handicap initially, but discovering Jimi Hendrix was left-handed yet always played right-handed guitars saw him persevere.

Foreman had recently done the "honourable thing" in marrying his childhood sweetheart to save her blushes. On losing his job as a painter and decorator, rather than look for another job he became a stay-at-home father, playing along to Dr. Feelgood albums betwixt feedings and nappy changes. Reflecting on this period of his life on the Friends Reunited website, he spoke of spending "some most excellent quality time looking after my young son whilst on the dole and also trying to learn how to play the guitar".

Despite being both a husband and father, Foreman would accompany Barson and Thompson to the Aldenham Boys Club on Highgate Road. Thompson was also in a long-term relationship with his future wife, Debbie, who was also playing her part in keeping him on the straight and narrow. It was while kicking about the boys club that Thompson encountered Cathal Smyth. "When I first met Lee, he was so cool," Smyth told *Later* magazine. We were all going against the grain – that was what was exciting. We did things like painting our boots before anyone else, wearing baseball jackets from America and mixing up different cultures. We were developing our own thing, not that we were conscious of it at the time. This was from 1975 onwards."

ELEVEN

Smyth was born into a loving extended Irish family, but his father (also called Cathal) working as an engineer in the petrochemical industry brought plenty of upheaval during his childhood and formative years; his itinerant upbringing, which took the family to far-flung places in Iran, Iraq and Africa, meant forming any sort of lasting friendship was all but impossible. One of Cathal senior's postings was to County Derry in Northern Ireland circa 1971. The "Bloody Sunday Massacre" of January 1972 still lay in the future, but the mounting tensions that would see soldiers from the 1st Battalion, Parachute Regiment open fire on civilians during a march in protest again internment, resulting in fourteen deaths, meant for an uncomfortable time for anyone speaking with an English accent.

His education was also to suffer during this period. While in County Derry he attended the Dominican College, a grammar school in Portstewart. "It was pretty horrible," he would recount for *Nut Inc*. "I was beaten up every day for three weeks, so I stopped going to school and missed a year's education."

Upon returning to north London, Smyth made the decision to shorten his name to Carl, if only to minimise attention to his Irish background during his schooling. Having been punched from pillar to post during his brief tenure at Dominican College for being English, being targeted for his Irish ancestry would have proved beyond the pale. He had intended staying on at Finchley Catholic Grammar School to study in the sixth form, but his headstrong nature put paid to that. Following yet another dressing down in the headmaster's study, at the end of which he was informed to pull his finger out or be asked to leave the school, Smyth announced he'd save them the trouble and walked out the gates for good. Thanks to his wily father, however, he landed a position at a London-based petrochemical company, and by all accounts was soon earning more than his teachers.

Through Thompson, Smyth was introduced to Barson and Foreman. He hadn't shown any interest in learning a musical instrument or joining a band, but if learning the bass guitar meant being part of something for the first time in his life, then so be it. He duly bought himself a second-hand bass, and, possibly as a result of reading about The Clash's Paul Simonon having done something similar, placed stickers on the frets as markers for his fingers.

There are several versions as to how the boys acquired the services of their first drummer, John Hasler, but the one that tends to get told most often is that Smyth had befriended Hasler in the pubs in and around Hampstead. Hasler's skills proved to be as rudimentary as Smyth's, but they were willing to persevere as a mistimed beat here and there was better than no beat at all.

Foreman's parental duties began taking up more and more of his spare time, but when he did make rehearsals the five set about putting a set together from their favourite songs. It would prove an eclectic mix, and anyone wandering in off the street would surely have been left bewildered seeing five rough and ready-looking teenagers fumbling their way through Elvis' 'Jailhouse Rock', The Temptations' 'Just My Imagination', Stevie Wonder's 'For Once in My Life', Carole King's 'It's Too Late' and Kilburn and The High Roads' 'The Roadette Song'.

Barson and co. hadn't thought to set a date for when they might be ready to look at playing a gig. Indeed, they might well have been content to while away a few hours working up arrangements for their favourite songs had Smyth's one-time housemate, Simon Birdsall, not invited them to play at a party he was throwing at his parents' place, located but a pickled onion's throw from the Hope and Anchor. The landmark date was Friday, June 30, 1977.

Barson didn't feel confident enough to sing, and with Thompson playing sax and Foreman, Smyth and Hasler incapable of singing and playing at the same time, a budding actor of Armenian descent called Dikron Tulane, whom they knew solely as being the friend of a friend, was cajoled into helping out.

The 21-year-old Tulane would go on to appear in *Henry VI*, as part of BBC Television Shakespeare in 1983, as well as breaking into films following his relocating to the US in the early Nineties. Learning the words to the songs the band would be performing at the party was to prove too taxing, however, and so he scribbled the lyrics down on a notepad. Unfortunately for him, Birdsall had decided to have the band set up in the garden. This wouldn't have proved too much of a problem given it was the height of the summer, but by the time the boys started playing, the sun had slipped too far over the yard arm. "It was too dark for him [Tulane] to read," Smyth told Pete Frame, "so we told him to get lost and converted our set to an instrumental session."

The boys could now consider themselves active, but with Tulane having only agreed to help out at Birdsall's party, they would need a singer before they could think about taking bookings. The search was on.

As luck would have it, they didn't really have to search hard as one of the few party-goers who had bothered to step out into the garden to watch the "live entertainment" was 26-year-old Suggs McPherson.

McPherson was already aware of Barson and the others from having seen them kicking about various north London locales such as the annual Hampstead Fair; their snappy dress sense making them stand out from the flared loons and permed mullet brigade. "They were pretty cool-looking blokes," Suggs later recalled. "They seemed more interested in style than the average person. There was a real 'scene' there [Hampstead]; parties and pub discos that they all used to go over to from Highgate and Kentish Town."

McPherson's itinerant upbringing wasn't too dissimilar to that of Cathal Smyth owing to his mother, Edie, having to keep one step ahead of the rent man following his father's fleeing the marital home while he was but a toddler. Edie had a passable singing voice by all accounts, but her flitting from one city to another in search of work on the club circuit meant young Graham grew up without having any place to call home till Edie arrived in London some time around 1968. Edie got occasional singing work in the pubs and clubs of Soho, but more often than not the closest she got to the stage came with collecting the empty glasses from the tables at closing time. Try as she might, Edie wasn't always able to make her barmaid's wage stretch to putting two plates on the table, and for a time he was farmed out to live with his auntie in Pembrokeshire.

Mother and son wouldn't be reunited permanently until the latter was approaching secondary school age. Even then, life was less than idyllic as he was constantly picked on by the other boys at Quintin Kynaston Comprehensive in Swiss Cottage. Suggs has since claimed the torment he endured at the school stemmed from his being the only kid there of Scottish ancestry, but Edie's insisting the fancy school uniform his auntie had bought for the school he was set to attend in Haverfordwest would have proved reason enough for any bully. Again, in a move that echoed the one Smyth would make upon his own return to London, Graham decided on a name change in the hope his peevish-minded peers might view his adopted persona more favourably.

Blindly opening the pages of an encyclopaedia of jazz musicians that he'd happened upon in Edie's bedroom, McPherson hastily stuck a pin into one of the falling pages. On opening his eyes, he found the pin lodged beside the name of Pete Suggs, a Kentucky-born jazz drummer who had enjoyed a steady if unspectacular career from the 1930s through to the 1960s. And so was born one of British pop's more enduring alter egos.

Suggs would later say his invitation to audition for the, as yet still unnamed, band came after Barson or one of the others heard him caterwauling at the top of his voice after emerging from one of the local cinemas. Whether Suggs was in his cups on that occasion he neglects to say, but he was certainly the worse for wear when he turned up at the appointed hour and slurred his way through Bill Haley's 'See You Later, Alligator'. To his astonishment, however, he was given the gig.

Suggs had no sooner got acquainted with his new bandmates when Smyth up and quit following a dispute with Barson over – of all things – a promised lift home that never materialised. Barson's being the only one in the band with transport meant he was often put upon to give the others a lift home after rehearsals, and ferrying the others to their respective homes soon began to grate. "I was feeling quite used," Barson said by way of explanation while speaking with *Later* magazine. "Everyone was just like, 'Drive me home', and I was just the mug driving them. These may be petty things, but we didn't communicate very well in those days."

Smyth's replacement on bass was Gavin Rodgers, whom Barson knew from dating his sister, Kirsten.

With Suggs (and Gavin Rodgers, to a certain extent) completing the line-up, it was time to start thinking of an appropriate band name. Barson had been approached by a female acquaintance who wanted the boys to play at her forthcoming birthday party at Hampstead Town Hall, and as they'd be playing on a proper stage they didn't want the DJ or whoever introducing them as "Evelyn's friends". Barson suggested they call themselves "The Invaders", after the ropey late Sixties US TV series of the same name.

ELEVEN

The Hampstead Town Hall birthday bash was to prove a memorable night for all the wrong reasons. Evelyn's Teddy boy friends were up jiving to 'See You Later, Alligator', but The Gladiators' 'Feeling So Fine' and other ska and reggae numbers the boys had worked into the set weren't as warmly received; their steadfast refusal to dip into the rock 'n' roll songbook for another Haley, Elvis or Little Richard classic prompting a barrage of abuse and beer cans – not all of which were empty.

The Invaders had come about more by accident than design. Whereas Barson and Foreman remained totally focused, the commitment of others was often found wanting. Suggs' passion for his Chelsea FC knew no bounds; so much so that choosing between taking his place in The Shed or going to rehearsals on a Saturday afternoon was no choice at all. Instead of giving the errant Suggs an ultimatum, however, Barson placed a "singer wanted" ad in the *Melody Maker* classifieds, along with his telephone number – a number the bemused Suggs readily identified while reading the issue in question. On ringing Barson for an explanation (as if one was needed), Suggs was informed he was "out" as the band was intent on "getting a bit more professional".

Barson was clearly putting the band above personalities, but criticising Thompson's sax playing a tad more forcefully than was perhaps necessary resulted in the latter storming off in a huff. Thompson's replacement was Lucinda Garland, the sister of one of Foreman's old school friends. Garland, however, was merely killing time before going off to university, so it was perhaps inevitable that fences would be mended, and Thompson would be back occupying his customary spot (this, in spite of his having relocated to Luton in the interim).

Suggs' absence was even briefer. Hasler had volunteered to take on the added responsibility, but his singing voice left much to be desired – too much as it transpired – and Suggs was back behind the mic when The Invaders played the City & East London College in Hoxton in February 1978 – the band's first fee-paying gig.

After months of flitting from church hall to garage, to bedroom, and back to church hall, the band secured a permanent rehearsal space – the cellar of a vacant property on

Finchley Road owned by the father of another of Barson's lady friends. It was time to start looking at penning their own material, but who amongst them was willing to take on the mantel?

Somewhat surprisingly, it was Hasler who got things moving with the "here today/gone tomorrow" offerings 'Rich Girls' and 'Sunshine Voice', the latter of which was dutifully recreated in the 1981 Madness opus, *Take It or Leave It*, owing to its significance in the band's story.

Fee-paying gigs had given The Invaders an air of professionalism, but the prospect of earning some easy extra cash wasn't enough to tempt Suggs away from Stamford Bridge whenever Chelsea were playing at home and resulted in a second parting of the ways. Thompson found the commute to and from Luton three times a week both a drag and a drain on meagre finances, and he began spending more and more time playing with a band closer to home who were in need of a sax player for the Bruce Springsteen songs they featured in their shows.

The to-ing's and fro-ing's would see Rodgers serve notice. He couldn't see The Invaders amounting to anything, and thought he'd try his luck elsewhere. The latest reshuffle saw Hasler again standing in for Suggs (his singing having obviously been deemed to have improved), while an old school friend of his called Gary Dovey filled in on drums. And it just so happened that Dovey knew a bass player living in nearby Holloway who was currently in between bands.

Mark "Bedders" Bedford was born in Islington in August 1961. According to an interview his mum gave to *Smash Hits* once Madness were in their pomp, Bedford had shown an early aptitude for all things musical. Motown was his preferred music, but like many other boys, his interests became many and varied. Indeed, had a relative not thought to buy him a record player for his fourteenth birthday, his career path might well have turned out somewhat different. By fifteen, he was fumbling his way through the Beatles songbook in the first of several William Ellis School bands, honing his skills with each band in turn.

Bedford had no real musical pedigree to speak of, and yet the boys went to some lengths to secure his services. Rather than audition Bedford at the Finchley Road cellar and risk losing their prospective bassist at the first hurdle, they instead picked him up from his flat in Holloway and ferried him to the swanky rehearsal space belonging to a local band they were on speaking terms with called Split Rivett, where – with Hasler singing – they tore through The Miracles' 1960 US hit 'Shop Around'.

There were initial reservations on both sides regarding age. Barson thought Bedford too young, while Bedford found playing with guys who were all several years older yet bouncing around like "complete idiots" somewhat unnerving. Bedford's first gig with The Invaders came on July 3 with his end-of-term school disco.

It wasn't long after Bedford's induction into The Invaders that the on-going Suggs saga took another twist. Suggs had attended both shows the band had played with Hasler on vocals (the second coming at the 3C's Club in Cumberland Square, off Warren Street); his determination to get back into Barson's good graces had even seen his filling in for Dovey at a rehearsal. When Barson called upon him for a temporary return to duty for a show Bedford had organised to celebrate his boss' birthday at the Camden Lock roller blind factory where he was now employed while Hasler was away holidaying in France, Suggs readily agreed, secretly hoping that his reinstatement would prove more lasting.

And so it was to prove, for Barson and Foreman hadn't been able to convince the other as to Hasler's singing, and upon his return from France they offered him the role of manager.

Suggs' latest coming in from the cold wasn't the only change to The Invaders' line-up in Hasler's absence. Kix Thompson had ended his self-imposed exile in darkest Bedfordshire, but an argument betwixt him and Dovey during rehearsals had resulted in the drummer's departure. It seemed for every forward step the band took they ended up at least one place behind where they started. Indeed, such was their luck that a black drummer they auditioned turned them down for playing too much reggae in their set.

The vast majority of the audience when The Invaders played the William Ellis school-leavers party back in July had been 16 or under, but Bedford's drummer pal, Daniel Woodgate, had dropped by in a show of support. He'd been impressed by how much Bedford's bass playing had come on in recent months, but came away questioning his friend's sanity in joining The Invaders. He'd thought them "terrible in most respects", yet the more he thought about it the more he came to realise they had that indefinable something. Upon learning of Dovey's departure following his fracas with Thompson, he'd tongue-in-cheekily called Bedford saying he'd heard on the grapevine how The Invaders were looking to offer him the drum stool. The ruse was enough to fool Bedford into inviting him along to a rehearsal.

Barson had already apparently paid for another ad in the *Melody Maker* classifieds so was reluctant to give Woodward either 'yeah' or 'nay' following his audition. His shoulder-length locks and disinterest in reggae also weighed heavily against him. However, his friendship and familiarity with Bedford's style of play ultimately won the day. The hair still had to go, though.

The aforementioned "meeting of minds" at the Nashville Rooms in early August 1975 between Mick Jones and Bernard Rhodes, which in turn begat The Clash, came at a Deaf School showcase gig. Rhodes had been standing unobtrusively at the rear of the Nashville when Jones and sidekick Tony James came and stood nearby. Upon noticing the mole-like individual was cramping Jones' style in sporting the same "You're Gonna Wake Up One Morning…" T-shirt, James had sidled across, telling Rhodes to "sling his hook", to which Rhodes indignantly retorted: "You two sling your hooks, I designed the fuckin' shirt!"

Between 1976 and '78, the Liverpool-based art-rocking Deaf School released three albums via Warner Bros., yet while having since been lauded as the second most important band to come out of Liverpool after The Beatles, commercial success was to evade them, and the band went their separate ways to pursue other avenues. By the summer of 1979, guitarist "Cliff Hanger", aka Clive Langer, was fronting The Boxes, which included his old school friend Ben Barson, elder brother of Mike. The band were signed to Jake Riviera's Radar Records and were set to release their debut five-song EP, 'I Want the Whole World'.

At Barson elder's urging, Langer agreed to check out Madness, most likely at their Friday night Dublin Castle residency show of June 8, the same night they'd played with The Special AKA at the Nashville earlier in the evening.

Langer had caught the final Invaders show before the name change to Madness (circa February 1979) at Acklam Hall – situated underneath the Westway flyover of Clash folklore just off the Portobello Road in west London – the previous November. But he already knew Barson and co. from his playing days. "It all started when Deaf School were playing the Roundhouse in 1978," he told *M* magazine in August 2016. "There was this gang of kids by the side of the stage and I knew them vaguely, because I knew Mike Barson's older brother, Ben. After the gig they told me they'd started a band."

Langer was impressed by what he saw that balmy Camden night and agreed to swing by the band's rehearsal space. "I said I'd go to their rehearsals and have a listen to what they were doing," he continues. "They played the song 'My Girl', which, at that time, Mike was singing. I was really impressed. I told them to get £200 together to go into the studio and I'd produce them. Not thinking I was a producer, but just that I could help them record. Then Jerry Dammers heard it, put it out on 2-Tone and it was a hit. So that was that."

Well, not quite, of course. Recounting that fateful afternoon with *Uncut* magazine, Langer said he immediately saw the potential. Woodgate and Barson stood out, but while the rest of the band were "a bit rough around the edges", they were close to being where they needed to be in terms of recording a demo worthy of garnering interest within the industry.

Langer had remained on close terms with Rob Dickins, who'd been head of publishing at Warner Bros. during Deaf School's tenure with the label but was now International Vice-President of Warner Music. Langer called Dickins and announced he'd found a band worthy of his friend's attention. With The Specials being the hottest A&R ticket in town, Dickins was aware of Madness from their being name-checked in various bits and pieces in the music papers. Dickins was initially wary as the majority of said name-checks dismissed Madness as little more than a Specials rip-off. Langer's enthusiasm was enough to win him over, however.

On June 16, 1979, Madness were holed up with Langer at Pathway Studios, a compact eight-track facility located in Newington Green, north London. The songs recorded that day were 'The Prince', 'Madness' (a 1963 hit for Prince Buster which had been recently incorporated into the band's set) and an Invaders original called 'My Girl', with Barson taking on the lead vocal. Barson had penned 'My Girl' (originally called 'New Song') as something of an open letter to Kerstin Rodgers. "We had quite a difficult relation," Rodgers explained to John Reed. "Mike was quite uncommunicative, not emotionally very open. He's the talent, and like many talented people, he's got some issues." (The two would soldier on for a few months more before Rodgers called time on the relationship over Barson's wilful philandering.)

The issue facing Langer regarding 'My Girl' was the catchy pop vignette having "hit" written all over it, only not with Barson singing. Rob Dickins shared Langer's concern that 'My Girl' would be wasted if Barson was allowed to sing it – regardless of the song's inspiration. He was also somewhat bemused at the band recording 'Madness'. He'd been promised three original compositions, not two originals and a cover of an obscure Prince Buster song that had obviously provided the inspiration behind the change in name, his bemusement in part stemming from his having had to fund the session owing to Woodgate (who'd decided to follow the band's van on his motorbike) taking a wrong turn en route to Pathway on the day of the scheduled recording session.

One listen to the finished version of 'The Prince', however, was enough to convince Dickins that his money had been far from wasted.

When the boys met with Dickins the following day they explained the single deal Dammers was offering. Dickins, while appreciative of the waves The Specials were making, didn't see much sense Madness wanting to play second fiddle to anyone – let alone a band that already had the ska revival angle sewn up. As far as he was concerned, both 'My Girl' and 'The Prince' were potential hits. He was confident his opinion held enough sway to convince one of the majors to sign Madness.

Much to his dismay, however, his overtures went unheeded. Many of those same labels had lost one or two fingers in the feeding frenzy that had seen the majors snapping up any act with punk connotations, and so were proving reluctant to dip their toes into the unchartered waters of a ska revival. Dickins gave the boys his blessing to take the Pathway demos to 2-Tone. What Dickins hadn't stopped to consider when sounding out the majors was what Dammers' reaction might be when he discovered Madness were viewing 2-Tone as a fall-back option.

Dammers was shrewd enough to recognise Dickins only had Madness' interests at heart and was happy to sign them to 2-Tone for the proposed single deal, however. And it wasn't as if Dammers had anything to lose in taking Madness. It wasn't his money he'd be investing into 'The Prince', and if the single tanked, his arrangement with Chrysalis meant he still had nine lives remaining. With a deal quickly being thrashed out, Madness put pen to paper over halloumi and Heineken at a Greek-Cypriot restaurant in Camden, the deal allowing Hasler to take up temporary residence at Rick Rogers' Kentish Town office.

On July 9, the boys returned to Pathway with Clive Langer to remix the versions of 'The Prince' and 'Madness', primarily to remove the hum on Thompson's sax.

'The Prince' (b/w 'Madness') was released via 2-Tone on August 10, 1979. The boys didn't need telling they were leaving themselves open to a mauling at the hands of the music press. Bands name-checking their influences was nothing new, but it would only take one review dismissing the single as a homage to Prince Buster and the soon-to-be-renamed Madness' career might have been dead in the water.

We are, of course, viewing these events with the benefit of hindsight, and there was nothing to suggest the leading music weeklies would review the single simply because Jerry Dammers deemed Madness worthy of putting on to vinyl. Any writer worth their salt at the leading music weeklies all had contacts working at the major labels so as to get the inside scoop on what was happening in any given week. Dickins peddling Madness' demo tape about town without success would have been common knowledge by the time promo copies of 'The Prince' arrived at the *NME*, *Melody Maker*, *Sounds* and all the rest.

Dickins might have been off the mark in his reasoning about Madness being snapped up by one of the majors, but his judgement in regard to 'The Prince' being a hit proved sound enough when the single subsequently broke into the Top 20 (peaking at #16).

Scoring a Top 20 hit at the fist attempt would have proved sufficient to have the music weeklies beating a path to any band or solo artist's management's office door, but Madness' connection with The Specials' 2-Tone label had only heightened the interest. Such interest was to prove a double-edged sword, however. The positive comments far outweighed the negatives, but remarks about Madness being a "rude boy ska band" soon began to vex. It wasn't so much the ska revivalist tag, but rather their being categorised at all.

"We were upfront in realising the 2-Tone thing was going off like a packet of crackers and we were in that mode stylistically," Suggs told *Uncut* magazine in 2008. "We certainly put more ska into our set and we'd been lucky to meet Jerry. Earlier than God intended, we were suddenly the thing." He then went on say that while there were certain similarities between Madness and The Specials, he was keen to stress that whereas Dammers and co. were writing songs with a political bent, Madness' gang mentality – which, aside from Chas Smash' one-man nutty dance to the "heavy, heavy monster sound" – had their mates serving as ad hoc roadies who were encouraged to get up and help out with the backing vocals. "Madness were the leaders of the little bit of north London we lived in and led colourful lives, which fed into our songs," Suggs continued. "I was the idiot savant – well, certainly an idiot. I was just happy to be there."

But it wasn't only the Specials-inspired ska revival Madness were anxious to separate themselves from. A mod revival was gathering apace with Secret Affair, Purple Hearts, The Lambrettas and Merton Parkas playing punk-tinged rhythm and blues a la The Jam. The irony being, of course, that punk was deemed to have consigned all that had gone before to the musical scrapheap.

By the time 'The Prince' was released, Madness had welcomed back another of its prodigal sons. Cathal Smyth, or "Chas Smash" as Kix Thompson had rechristened his friend during his self-imposed two-year exile, hadn't proved able to walk away completely. He'd started turning up at Madness shows, occasionally jumping up on to the stage; his quirky – or "nutty" – dance moves providing an added dynamic. Seeing the crowd's reaction whenever Smash got up and did his thing, Thompson had invited him to introduce the band on stage.

It was to prove an inspired move on Thompson's part, as Smash's on-stage antics were enough to get the most reticent of crowds moving in tandem with the music – or the "nutty sound" as it soon became known. From there, it was perhaps inevitable Smyth/Smash's reinstatement would be made official.

It's doubtful Madness would have accepted the offer of a 2-Tone follow-up Madness single had Dammers made the offer, but with Sire and Virgin having now joined what had initially appeared a two-horse race betwixt Charisma Records' Tony Stratton-Smith and Roy Eldridge of Chrysalis for the band's signatures, the boys found themselves in the enviable position of being able to pick and choose. There was to be a late entry in the unfolding Dutch auction, however.

CHAPTER

Stiff Records boss, Dave Robinson, invited Madness to play his wedding bash at the Clarendon Ballrooms in Hammersmith on August 17. Performing in front of their hero Ian Dury (who was also singing for his supper on the night) was a surreal experience in itself, but little did the boys know there was more to the invite than met the eye.

Robinson had been tipped the wink about Madness being Stiff material, but sorting out a wedding on top of running the label single-handedly in the wake of Jake Riviera's departure was eating up his days and preventing him from checking out the band. "I heard that Chrysalis were interested in signing them," Robinson explained. "I was getting married and I needed a band, so I thought I'll have two birds with one stone."

Robinson enjoyed the performance, recognising two potential singles in the mix. "I asked them about the instrumental they did, a short thing with a rant at the front, and that was 'One Step Beyond'."

Thinking 'One Step Beyond' would make a great name for an album, Robinson arranged to meet the boys the following week.

In the days leading up to the meeting, Robinson put out feelers in the hope of gauging the levels of interest in Madness at Virgin, Chrysalis et al. The general feedback was that while none of the competition was showing signs of backing out, none had yet thought to make a definite move. At the meeting (in a pub conveniently located next door to Stiff's offices on Alexander Street in Bayswater), Robinson grabbed the metaphorical bull by the horns and asked the band straight out what they wanted to do. The response was candid. The boys wanted to make an album, and they felt they had enough good songs to justify their wont. They also wanted Clive Langer to produce the album. (Langer's working with Madness wasn't to be the band's only link to Deaf School as Suggs would subsequently end up dating – and marrying – the band's singer, Anne Martin, who was enjoying moderate success as a solo artist under her stage name, Bette Bright.)

Robinson sensed he might not get another opportunity. In between plying the boys with pints, Robinson nipped back to the office, block-booked Eden Studios in Chiswick for Monday week, and spoke with Langer. The boys were blissfully unaware of Robinson's shenanigans, but were impressed with his flying-by-the-seat-of-his-pants manner – impressed enough to become Stiff's latest acquisition; the £10,000 advance they received upon signing proving sufficient for those in the band who had day jobs to hand in their notice. Sire Records weren't far behind in picking up the option for North America.

Madness would remain a Stiff act for the next five years, releasing five albums and 18 singles during that time. They could have held out and got a better deal in financial terms elsewhere, but Stiff being as nonconformist as themselves meant the creativity flowed free of corporate restraints.

Though recognising they might never have found themselves in a position where they could cherry-pick from several suiters had it not been for Dammers' signing them to 2-Tone, the band have come to recognise their good fortune. "[Stiff] was just the perfect place for Madness," Suggs reflected. "It couldn't have been anywhere else. We could stay at 2-Tone and falsely remain as a ska band, which we weren't entirely, or go to Stiff, which was equally independent and maverick and free."

Madness might have lived up to their name on stage, but the no-nonsense approach the band adopted at Eden meant the 14 songs were recorded with minimum fuss. Indeed, the only distraction came with who was to sing 'My Girl'. Rob Dickins would liken Barson's vocal style as being akin to that of *Carry On* star Bernard Bresslaw. Barson's taking over the mic to sing his ode to Kerstin Rodgers during live performances provided Vaudeville-esque schtick, and while it was admirable that the rest of the band were happy to let him lay down the vocal at Eden, Dickins knew 'My Girl' could never be the hit single it so patently was. He decided he could hold his tongue no longer.

The band had relocated to TW Studios by now, and try as Dickins might, Suggs refused to get drawn into the debate. As far as Suggs was concerned, 'My Girl' was Barson's song, and if Barson wanted to sing it then so be it. Langer could see Dickins' argument made sense, but was reluctant to broach the subject with Barson. In the end it was left to Dickins to break the news to Barson as diplomatically as he could over a bite to eat in the burger bar next door to the studios.

There was to be a final twist in the *One Step Beyond* recording process, however. Dave Robinson's inability to refrain from tweaking the final mixes of his acts' albums was well known, and the band had made his promise to keep away from the studio. It wasn't until the band and Langer (along with co-producer/engineer Alan Winstanley) were mixing the album at Genetic Studios in Streatley, Berkshire, that Robinson was allowed to hear the results. Though impressed with the album, Robinson was perplexed as to why the title track was missing. He suspected he was being set up, but seven straight faces told him otherwise.

The band's collective thinking was that the Prince Buster instrumental (the B-side to 'Al Capone') was nothing more than a playful means to get an audience going. They didn't even play the whole tune, usually coming to a halt after 30 seconds or so. There'd never been any thought of incorporating it fully into the set, so Robinson's viewing it as a single – the album's lead single – came completely out of leftfield. It was their turn to await the punchline, but Robinson was deadly serious. So serious, in fact, that he kept at the boys into the early hours until they finally acquiesced. Robinson's persistence would be justified, with 'One Step Beyond' giving Madness their first Top 10 UK hit.

CHAPTER

TWELVE

NO GIMME NO MORE PICKNI...

"We covered all the bases. The rhythm section was ska and reggae, which is the sexiest music ever. You could dance to it. You didn't just jump up and down to it. But it was played with the aggressive energy of punk. It looked fantastic to watch at a show."

HORACE PANTER

CHAPTER

C hrysalis were naturally keen to get The Specials out on the road as part of the label's strategy to build the band's profile – both in the music media, as well as on the street – in time for the debut album, which was slated for an autumn release in time for the highly lucrative Christmas market. The band were now living the dream Dammers had envisioned while penning the lyrics to the songs betwixt Cissy Stone Soul Band dates. Headlining shows was second nature to The Specials by now, but it was only natural they would headline dates they'd organised themselves. The Moonlight Club show had been organised by Rogers, yet it was nonetheless just another foray on to the London pub circuit, with each member (along with Griffiths and Evans) coming away with £15 (if they were lucky) after the usual deductions had been taken care of – primarily van hire and petrol – from the band's customary £250 fee.

Heading out on a nationwide UK tour with record company support was several sizeable base camps higher up the mountain, and the view was proving heady indeed; so intoxicating, in fact, that for those involved the tour had since melded into a series of snapshot-like memories.

Panter's personal highlights involve the band huddled around the cheap radio/cassette player – bought specially for the purpose – in Leeds listening to the session they'd recorded for John Peel on the Kid Jensen show, his discovering an old college acquaintance would be directing the promo video to 'Gangsters', and of his feigning to browse those racks closest to the counter at his local Virgin Records earwigging people asking for the single. No shame in that, Sir Horace! And there's little doubt the rest of the band did the same – especially Bradbury, who'd once worked there.

Another highlight for Panter was catching a band called The Akrylykz (pronounced "Acrylics"), fronted by future Fine Young Cannibal Roland Gift, whom Panter had encountered on the On Parole Tour.

"All of us, except Roland, were undergraduate students at the [Hull School of Art in Kingston upon Hull]," the band's one-time drummer, Wojciech "Piotr" Swiderski, later reflected. "Nick (Townend – guitar), Fred (Reynolds – bass) and Steve Pears (alto saxophone and vocals) were studying BA Fine Art (Painting), I was studying BA Fine Art (Sculpture), and Stevie B (Robottom – alto saxophone, keyboards and vocals) was studying Graphics.

"We talked about forming a band as soon as we started college in September 1978."

The majority of these "let's start a band" discussions were conducted after classes in the back room of a pub located within staggering distance of the college. "The pub was popular at the time with musicians, artists, etc. Often, our conversation was interrupted by this young black guy with blond hair and rainbow stripes across one side of his head. He kept telling us that he was good on the sax and that he had some connection with Bernie Rhodes. He told us his name was Roland. We felt we needed more 'middle' sound in the material we were writing, so we invited him to our next rehearsal."

Having bandied potential band names about, the six finally settled on The Akrylyk Vyctyms, before shortening it to The Akrylykz. The six-piece started out playing locally in and around Hull, but as the band's popularity grew they started venturing further afield to Manchester, Birmingham, Sheffield and London. Regular appearances in a punk/ska fanzine put together by several of their fans brought The Akrylykz to the attention of the local media.

In 1980, The Akrylykz signed with the York-based indie label Red Rhino Records, soon after releasing the double A-side single 'Spyderman'/'Smart Boy'. John Peel would play both sides incessantly and lauded The Akrylykz as causing "a large ripple in the music pool".

The Akrylykz would support The Specials, Madness and other 2-Tone acts, but Dammers didn't feel they were ultimately 2-Tone material. Polydor's Chris Parry, having caught the band supporting Dexys Midnight Runners at the Music Machine, thought they were good enough for his label and ended up buying Red Rhino to get them. The band's first (and only) Polydor release was 'JD (Juvenile Delinquent)' (b/w 'Ska'd for Life'). A second Polydor single was apparently recorded, but never released.

While visiting with family and friends in his native Birmingham, Gift had encountered John Mostyn, who was looking after The Special AKA at the time. When Mostyn subsequently started managing The Beat, he invited The Akrylykz to tour with his new charges. Their association with The Beat would lead to their becoming session musicians for Desmond Dekker. "The Beat were initially approached by the Stiff label to work with Dekker," Swiderski explained. "They were just about to embark on recording their first album and promotional tour. The Beat suggested to Stiff that they contact us as a talented, competent outfit to do the job. We ended up doing the recording as session musicians, as this wouldn't put us in direct conflict with Polydor.

"We recorded 'The Israelites', 'It Mek', 'Many Rivers to Cross', 'Work Out' and 'Pickney Gal'" (all of which appear on Dekker's 1981 Stiff album, *Black and Dekker*).

While The Specials were rehearsing for the impending tour, Geoff Travis met with Chrysalis to thrash out the deal which saw the latter label take over the pressing of the 'Gangsters' single once all the copies Rough Trade were still holding had been sold. In the interim, however, Chrysalis would throw their not-inconsiderable weight behind helping Rough Trade promote the record in the UK, as well as begin work on a European marketing campaign.

Chrysalis' promo campaign involved both the tabloids and the music media. The *NME* and *Sounds* had been monitoring The Specials' rise from a distance, whereas *Melody Maker*, which was unfairly perceived to be staid and outmoded following the advent of punk, had featured a live shot of the band on its front cover (the shot – showing Panter, Byers and Staple – was from their support slot on the Gang of Four's Lyceum Ballroom show towards the end of May). The band also featured on the cover of *Smash Hits*, the twice-monthly magazine aimed at the UK's teen music market. Instead of in-depth interviews or live reviews, *Smash Hits* reproduced the lyrics to songs by artists considered hip and happening (not always accurately, it has to be said), while regaling its readership with nonsensical titbits and factoids about the artists.

The Sun, employing the same scaremongering tactics it had used to unnerve its readership about the "punk rock cult" some three years earlier, was careful to mark The Specials' card by proclaiming the band to have been "adopted as the musical representatives of the Rude Boys... that special brand of aggressive youngsters who are a cross between Mods and Skinheads."

By the time the club date tour was over, 'Gangsters' had entered *Sounds'* own "Alternative Chart" at #4, claiming the top spot soon thereafter. The record was also making an impressive showing on the all-important BMRB (British Market Research Bureau) chart, ultimately peaking at #8. This not only saw daytime Radio One DJs add 'Gangsters' to their playlists, but also provided the band with the first of many appearances on *Top of the Pops*.

Byers has special occasion to remember the band's inaugural appearance on BBC's then-flagship music show: "Some of us in the band liked to party a bit too hard in those days, and at the BBC you were expected to respect their rules. Some producer or other pushed in front of me at the bar, and I said something like, 'I suppose you're with *Top of the Pops?*' When I complained, the guy went and told the security to throw me out. I think Brad had similar problems as he got chucked out as well.

"I also have vague recollections of some of the club dates. But with everything that happened following the signing with Chrysalis, 'Gangsters' charting, recording the album, touring the album, the second album, more touring, etc., it all starts to blend into one after a while. I remember us doing a session for John Peel while we were out on the road. That was great fun – even if Jerry did piss the engineers off because he wasn't happy with the mix. Did I hang about the Virgin store watching people queuing up to buy 'Gangsters'? That would be telling…

"One of the major stand-out moments, I suppose, was when we played with Madness and The Selecter at the Electric Ballroom in Camden. We'd already played with Madness by then, but having The Selecter on the bill gave us a hint of what was to come on the 2-Tone tour later in the year.

"I remember Madness having a lot of skinhead friends/ fans that liked to take the piss out of us older musicians. There were already a few bands around the country that were experimenting with ska and rock steady – The Beat, Bad Manners, The Akrylykz, etc. – so it was a case of 'the more the merrier'. No one really knew who any of these bands were at the time, but Jerry was looking to sign them to 2-Tone for one-off single deals. But with Madness and Selecter we became a 2-Tone ska movement, which made the whole thing much stronger."

The Selecter, as a band, hadn't existed at the time of the 2-Tone 'Gangsters' release, of course. Indeed, the seven-piece line-up that took to the Electric Ballroom stage had only been rehearsing together a matter of weeks. When the 2-Tone issue of 'Gangsters' was first released, most of those hearing "The Selecter" being played on the John Peel show had assumed it was also written and played by The Specials. Neol Davies had been so irked on hearing Peel announce the instrumental as such that he'd felt compelled to call into the show and rectify the glaring oversight.

Once 'Gangsters' started climbing the UK singles chart (eventually reaching #6), he sensed an opportunity in the making and quietly set about recruiting from amongst his musician friends. First to be included were long-time associates Desmond Brown (Hammond organ) and Charley Anderson (bass). These were soon followed by guitarist Compton Amanor, Charley "Aitch" Bembridge on drums, and Arthur "Gaps" Hendrickson on vocals.

CHAPTER

Pauline Vickers was a 25-year-old radiographer at Walsgrave Hospital when Lynval Golding tipped her the wink that was set to change her life. She had made her first public performance during the summer of 1976 singing Bob Dylan's 'Blowin' in the Wind' (while accompanying herself on her boyfriend's Spanish guitar) to the Sunday regulars gathered in the smoke-laden back room of a Spon End pub.

Born in October 1953, Vickers grew up in Romford, Essex, around the time suburban expansion was reinforcing the market town's significance. It was also a time when black people were something of a rarity within the Borough of Havering, and Vickers' being the only black face at her junior school brought her an early education in the racial intolerance in those halcyon days of Fifties post-war Britain; her discovering she was adopted only serving to heighten her feelings of alienation. She attended Romford Technical High School, passing all eleven of the GCE "O" levels she sat. It was a different story when it came to her "A" levels, owing to boys and pop music eating into her study and revision time.

She'd harboured ambitions of becoming a doctor, but her failure to accrue the desired grades meant having to forego the place she'd been offered at Birmingham Medical School. Resitting her "A" levels meant staying on at Romford Tech for another year, but staying on anywhere in Romford was no longer palatable. She entered her grades into the UCCA (Universities Central Council on Admissions) clearing-house system and was offered a place at Lanchester Polytechnic. Following her interview with the Polytechnic's head of science she was duly offered a place on the Combined Science BSc course. And so another of the main players in the 2-Tone story was on her way to Coventry.

By the end of 1977, Vickers was being paid to sing folk songs while others ate their suppers. "I led a double life," she reflected in *Black by Design: A 2-Tone Memoir*. "By day I was mild-mannered

Pauline, the hospital radiographer, in a fetching white uniform
and matching clogs, and by night I was Pauline the singer/
guitarist, clad in a yellow linen shirt and brown corduroy
dungarees, performing at any folk club that gave me a
gig. I didn't try too hard to be anything very much. I just
enjoyed myself."

Vickers made her semi-professional debut playing for £1 a song
at a folk club operating out of the Golden Cup pub (now The
Beer Engine) on Far Gosford Street, believed to be one of the
city's oldest public houses. She'd been packing away her guitar
when she was approached by Lawton Brown, a "bespectacled,
clean-cut black man bearing a strong resemblance to Malcolm
X" who was studying politics at Warwick University. Through
Brown's sensimilla-tinged tutorage, Vickers underwent what
she describes as "an immediate black music education". She
and Brown began writing songs together in keeping with her
musical enlightenment: Third World's *96 Degrees in the Shade*,
Bunny Wailer's *Blackheart Man*, Culture's *Two Sevens Clash*, and
the Last Poets song 'Wake Up Niggers'. "Aitch" Bembridge was
sharing a house with Brown at the time, and occasionally sat in
with them.

Slowly but surely, a band began to coalesce around Vickers
and Brown's song-writing. Silverton Hutchinson came in
on drums, followed soon thereafter by Brown's namesake,
Desmond. It was during one of the quartet's impromptu
rehearsals circa May 1979 that Golding had shown up.

Vickers was aware of The Special AKA, but only from
Hutchinson's having been in the band, and if she is to be
believed, the drummer had made no mention of having
toured with The Clash. At the end of the evening, Vickers gave
Desmond Brown and Golding a lift home. Golding had been
pretty dismissive of Lawton Brown's guitar technique, and

during the drive he'd suggested Vickers might like to meet up with some friends of his who were looking for a singer for the band they were putting together. The friends in question would be meeting up the following evening, and before taking his leave Golding slipped her an empty Rizla packet, upon which he'd scrawled an address. He also tipped her the wink that Desmond Brown and Bembridge would also be there.

Vickers arrived at the one-up, one-down terraced house in Hillfields at the appointed time and was ushered inside by Anderson. The amiable bassist's lack of surprise at finding her on the doorstep suggests Golding had either called or phoned in advance.

Anderson, who was born in Negril, Jamaica, had been living in Coventry since he was 11. He knew Golding from their having been in a band together with his brother, Winston. His first musical experiences came in DJing at Sound Systems in and around Coventry. "I was adventurous and travelled to blues parties in different cities," he reflected during a July 2009 interview with *marcoonthebass.blogspot. com*. "We didn't have night clubs in the UK, only the major cities, so we organised a night club at a house in every city where black people lived and there were blues being played."

Anderson says ska was the first music he can remember hearing whilst growing up in Negril. "We had the Fisherman's Club on the beach where sound systems would come, set up the speakers and put the tanoy speakers high up in the tree, and big sound boxes on the ground. We kids had our own dancing competition to see who could do the best shuffle to the local sound master, El Red."

Having received lessons from Lloyd Minto, the bassist in a local Coventry band called The Merrytones (which had also featured Lynval Golding and Desmond Brown in the line-up), Anderson had gone out on the road mixing for a local soul band called True Expression. "I sang and sometimes played bass," he explained. "I also learnt to play the rhythm pans with the Tropical Harmony steel band at weekends. They always had a gig and I was never out of work."

Anderson was also already acquainted with Neville Staple from their working together on the Jah Baddis sound system operating out of the Holyhead youth centre. The Merrytones were using the centre's cellar as their rehearsal space, but when they elected to chance their arm in London – including Golding – Brown decided to remain behind. "Desmond and I used to hang out a lot," Anderson continues. "He said to me one day, 'Charlie, go buy a bass guitar. I need you to play with me on the piano.'"

As soon as the two had learnt a few songs, Anderson had invited Gaps Hendrickson to join them. "[Gaps] was a very good shuffle dancer in the ska days and played guitar. He also sang but was a very shy vocalist. With a bit of a push he was up for the challenge."

Silverton Hutchinson began helping out by providing a beat, and it was through his living on the same street as Neol Davies that they came together as the short-lived Chapter 5.

Vickers was comforted to find Brown and Aitch Bembridge were already there; the two sprawled on the floor rolling spliffs. It was the tall, blond, angular-featured Neol Davies and his Elizabeth Taylor-esque wife, Jane, that captivated Vickers' immediate attention, however, if only for their being the only white faces in the room.

Davies was a familiar face on the Coventry music scene. Aside from Chapter, he'd also played in a band with Aitch Bembridge in the past, just as he had with Jerry Dammers and Lynval Golding. Anderson, Brown, Bembridge and Hendrickson were currently playing together in Hard Top 22.

There was the usual "meet-and-greet" small talk while a couple of spliffs were imbibed before they got to the business at hand. At Anderson's bidding, Davies plucked a copy of the 'Gangsters' single from his wife's handbag before walking over to the Dansette record player in the corner and slipping the record on to the spindle Selecter-side up. Vickers caught a flash of Panter's "The Special AKA Gangsters vs The Selecter" stamp on the sleeve, but says she was still unaware of either the record or The Specials. In hindsight, this can be little more than her adding to the significance of the meeting as it seems unlikely that Brown or Bembridge wouldn't have thought to mention how their mate Lynval Golding was in The Specials, the band that was fast becoming the talking point of the Coventry scene – and one that Chrysalis Records was now showing interest in. Hutchinson had left The Special AKA under his own volition, so again it seems unlikely that he wouldn't have dropped this into the conversation during one of the get-togethers with Lawton Brown.

Having given "The Selecter" a second spin, Davies explained the reason for their all being there, before then enquiring who was "in". Vickers was penning her own songs but had never contemplated being a pop singer. However, now the opportunity had presented itself she grabbed it without sparing so much as a second thought as to how chasing the chimerical dream of pop stardom might jeopardise her career as a radiographer.

The primary aim was to try and capitalise on the attention "The Selecter" was gaining thanks to John Peel, or put another way, to be perfectly placed to latch on to The Specials' coattails should they sign with Chrysalis. This, perhaps, was the principle reason Davies had mooted the idea of bringing in a female vocalist. The Specials were now established as a seven-piece, and Davies was obviously wary of the possible negative reaction to The Selecter being another Coventry-based seven-piece ska revival act at the hands of the music press. (Hammond had mooted the idea of the band calling themselves "Stryder", but this was dismissed as a non-starter.)

A rehearsal was arranged at the Binley Oak, where The Hybrids/Special AKA had also rehearsed on occasion. The rehearsal also served as an audition for Vickers, as Davies had yet to hear her for himself. Instead of deciding on a song everyone knew, Vickers announced she had a song called 'They Make Me Mad' and asked Davies and the others to jam around with the simple G/Em/Dm chord pattern while she sang. She had, of course, performed the song (which would make it on to The Selecter's debut album, *Too Much Pressure*) many times with Bembridge, Hutchinson and Brown, but under Davies' guidance they "ripped up the blueprint and fashioned it anew".

Vickers was the only one of the seven with a bona fide job and spent the next few weeks juggling her shifts at Walsgrave Hospital with rehearsals. The work paid off, as by the beginning of July they had amassed ten songs deemed worthy of going out and playing live.

The Selecter made their debut in early July at some long-forgotten club in Worcester, with Vickers' Michael Jackson circa *Off the Wall*-era Afro and pink spandex pants no doubt proving the only talking point for the handful of souls who could honestly swear they were there. With the exception of the seemingly perpetually cool Davies, the rest of the band each had their own sartorial shortcomings. Come the second show – supporting The Specials at the F Club in Leeds – a week or so later, however, the band had undergone a sartorial transformation. Hammond's safari suit, and the denim flares and garish sleeveless jumpers favoured by the others had been consigned to the skip.

As a rule, Caribbean people eschew second-hand clothing, or "dead man's threads" as such apparel is known, yet Hammond and others dutifully followed Davies' lead. Vickers took to the stage in the Sta-Prest trousers, Ben Sherman shirt and double-breasted jacket ensemble we would soon come to know, her Afro pulled up into a topknot.

Vickers says The Specials show came about from John Mostyn latching on to the buzz surrounding the 'Gangsters' single and his recognising the commercial value of having the two bands on the record playing on the same stage. This might well be the case, but a call from Davies to Dammers or Golding would have surely proved just as effective.

The Electric Ballroom show of July 21, 1979 would indeed prove something of a dress rehearsal for what was to follow. It also provided The Selecter with their first press review, courtesy of *Sounds*' Giovanni Dadomo. Dadomo had been one of three music journalists to witness The Clash's in-house unveiling at Rehearsals in August 1976, and was no doubt viewing The Specials with a similar interest. When penning his favourable review, Dadomo freely admitted to not knowing whether there was a connection betwixt the band on stage and the 'Gangsters' single but was nonetheless impressed – especially by the band's "two all-action vocalists".

It was only natural that Dadomo likened The Selecter to the headliners. Although his likening her introducing the songs in a "squeaky oop north accent somewhat reminiscent of the late 'Clitheroe Kid'" hadn't endeared him to Vickers, his signing off saying how The Selecter "conspire to make dancing the only way to walk" assuaged her somewhat. It wasn't until the *NME*'s Paul Rambali contacted Davies a couple of weeks later requesting an in-depth interview with the band that Vickers realised she was facing a dilemma. She was in line for a promotion to senior radiographer and was worried what impact her moonlighting as a pop singer might have on her securing the coveted position. "Suddenly I was scared. Everything was moving so fast. Was I prepared to destroy my career and throw away three years of training just to follow what could possibly turn out to be a damp squib?"

The worry that was eating away at her was soon dispelled, however, when Hammond suggested she change her surname. After several light-hearted suggestions from her fellow Selecterites, Vickers finally settled on calling herself "Pauline Black".

The Specials, namely Dammers, had felt confident enough to oversee production duties on 'Gangsters', but it was felt that a more experienced head be brought in to work alongside the band on *The Specials*, as the band's debut album was to be called. The experienced head was to be none other than Elvis Costello. Costello had started out on London's pub-rock circuit before coming to prominence on the UK punk scene with hits such as 'Watching the Detectives', '(I Don't Want to Go to) Chelsea', 'Radio Radio' and 'Oliver's Army'. This was to be Costello's first production credit, but he'd picked up plenty of pointers while watching his friend Nick Lowe manning the mixing desk at Eden Studios on his own albums.

It was hoped Costello's enthusiasm for The Specials would shine through on the album, engineered by Dave Jordan, who's mixing credits included the Stones' 1977 live offering, *Love You Live*. "Costello had been to a few of our early shows," says Byers. "He was a fan of the band, and was very much into ska and reggae, so seemed our best bet. But Dave Jordan being the engineer was a lucky break as he later became an important part of our live and studio sound. I think Dave was really the producer while Costello came up with some good ideas."

Ordinarily, signed acts recorded their singles and albums in their record company's studio, or one affiliated with their label. 2-Tone, of course, didn't have a studio, affiliated or otherwise. Returning to Berwick Street, or the studio in Tower Hamlets where The Special AKA had recorded demos for Chris Gilby, were never seriously considered. Costello's preference for recording at Eden would have surely come up in conversation, and it can only be the studio being unavailable that saw them look elsewhere. The Who's Ramport Studios was given a try-out, but the recording – an extended dub version of 'Too Much Too Young' suffered what Panter describes as the studio's "cavernous sterility".

No one can now remember how or why TW Studios came to be chosen. In hindsight, the most viable reason was the studio being affiliated with Chrysalis Records in some way. The basement studio was situated beneath a launderette 150 yards or so further along the Fulham Palace Road from the Fulham Greyhound, where the band had played earlier in the year – reportedly with Mick Jagger in the audience.

TW had a pedigree of sorts as The Stranglers had recorded their first three albums and many of their early singles there. It was also where Buzzcocks had recorded their tongue-in-cheek ode to male masturbation ('Orgasm Addict'), and where The Jam had recorded their first set of demos during the summer of 1975. And it was where Madness would record their own debut long-player, *One Step Beyond*.

"I don't know how we chose it, but it was obviously the studio for us," Panter revealed. "[It was] basement level, small, badly lit, and very funky. We soon gelled into our own version of a well-oiled machine, and the record was completed in what seemed like no time at all."

"I seem to remember we went for TW because Jerry preferred a basic studio over a flash one," says Byers. "It wasn't like we sat down and had discussions about which studio to use. Someone made a few phone calls, TW was available, so we booked it."

The Specials couldn't be expected to make the daily commute from Coventry, so Chrysalis set the seven musicians – along with Griffiths and Evans – into a flat in the World's End, a spit and a bondage stride along the King's Road from Sex/Seditionaries, the shoebox-sized emporium from which the UK punk scene had been spawned.

"From what I remember it was a very posh King's Road flat," says Byers. "It became party central for a while. Most of us ended up moving out and staying with friends as it soon became overrun with either friends or fans."

Nerves and occasional hiccups aside, recording a debut album is usually straightforward as the track-listing is by and large made up of the songs the artist has been playing live for some time. This was certainly true of The Specials, even if half of the tracks intended for the album were either covers or derived from covers. The opening track on side one, 'A Message to You, Rudy' (or 'Rudy, a Message to You', as the song was originally called), was released as a single in 1967 by Dandy Livingston, 'Monkey Man' had proved a minor UK hit (reaching #47) for The Maytals in 1969, 'Too Hot' was recorded by Prince Buster in 1966, 'You're Wondering Now' (penned by Coxsone Dodd) was first recorded by Andy & Joey in 1964, and 'Do the Dog' was a rearrangement of the Rufus Thomas song, while 'Stupid Marriage' was a reworking of another of Dodd's songs.

The band were so familiar with the songs making up the track-listing that the only number they had to work on was 'Dawning of a New Era'. And this was only owing to Bradbury's unfamiliarity with the song as it hadn't featured in the set list for two years or more.

To give the album added gravitas by forging a link between 2-Tone and the original ska sound of Jamaica, Rico Rodriguez was brought in to play on the album. In turn, Rodriguez brought in his sidekick, one-time Island Records engineer Dick Cuthell, to add trumpet, cornet and flugelhorn to the mix. Rodriguez had, of course, played on the original version of 'Rudy, A Message to You'.

Rodriguez had been living in Britain since 1961, playing with Georgie Fame, and as a session musician for Chris Blackwell, Sonny Roberts and Joe Mansano under varying names including Rico's Combo, Rico & The Rudies and Reco Rodriguez. He would go on to record two solo albums but would be forced to seek alternative work – including painting and decorating, and what he would later cite as a "soul-destroying" fortnight working the night shift on the Ford production line in Dagenham – to supplement the money he earned as a session musician.

By 1975, with reggae in the ascendancy following the success of Jimmy Cliff, Desmond Dekker and Bob Marley, Rodriguez's labours were about to be rewarded. Blackwell brought him in to play with Toots and The Maytals on their album *Reggae Got Soul*, and upon hearing a demo he had cut with Cuthell while the latter was still at Island, the Island supremo gave Rodriguez carte blanche to return to Jamaica to work on his third solo album, *Man from Wareika*. Working alongside Jamaica's leading rhythm section, Robbie Shakespeare and Sly Dunbar, and fellow Alpha alumnus Bobby Ellis, *Man from Wareika*, a contemplative, meditative instrumental album inspired by his Rastafarian beliefs, has come to be regarded as Rodriguez's crowning musical achievement.

By the time of Dammers' call, Rodriguez had toured with Marley on the *Exodus* tour, as well as played on other Island acts' albums, including Jim Capaldi, John Martyn,

Linton Kwesi Johnson, Burning Spear and Steel Pulse. He'd also worked with Ian Dury, having already been name-checked in Dury's 1979 hit 'Reasons to Be Cheerful, Part 3'.

By their own admission, Panter had limited knowledge of reggae and knew next to nothing about ska at the time of his teaming up with Dammers, and so was left bemused by the reaction Rodriguez's impending arrival had on Staple, Golding and Bradbury. Staple was already acquainted with Rodriguez from his Jah Baddis days.

Having trombonist Rico Rodriguez on Specials recordings added credibility

He knew that die-hard ska fans would immediately understand the significance of Rico's involvement in The Specials, but was anxious as to what the band's growing army of Walt Jabscos might think of the "old guy on the trombone".

"I knew Rico's name from the early Skatalites recordings," says Byers. "Having Rico on the recordings definitely gave us some credibility. Later on, he and Dick added a touch of class to our live shows."

Both Panter and Staple make mention of Costello not wanting Byers to appear on the album. "I wasn't told at the time," Byers continues, "but as he [Costello] had been discovering early Sixties ska, he didn't think my punk rock 'n' roll guitar fitted. But Terry was hardly Desmond Dekker, and our take on ska was still related to the punk/ new wave style of the time – not a complete revival of the original ska from Jamaica. And, of course, it's since been said that I invented ska punk. Lol."

And as for Staple's claims that Byers and Dammers didn't see eye to eye on occasion during the recording? "I don't know where Neville got that one from. Me and Jerry got on fine on the first album. It was only when we came to recording *More Specials* that we started to disagree. For example, Jerry wanted to put drum machines on 'Hey Little Rich Girl'. He also made my song 'Holiday Fortnight' into an instrumental as he thought the lyrics were about him. It was originally called 'Why Argue with Fate', a version of which – including the lyrics – can be heard on my website, *www. roddyradiation.com*.

"By the time of *More Specials*, Jerry thought we should change our sound drastically. I thought we should do another ska/punk-type album. He was getting into what I felt was jazzy-type soundtrack muzak, whereas I was rediscovering rockabilly, so we were going in different directions musically.

"What you have to remember here is there were different factions within the band in the early days – and again more recently. Not along black and white lines, but sometimes by class and education, college and public school. And there were always the ones who would side with the 'leader' for whatever reasons best suited them individually. Lynval would try to be everyone's friend and agree with whoever he was talking to at the time. The band was made up of very different people with different lifestyles and tastes in music, etc."

Reflecting on *The Specials* while penning his 2007 memoir, Panter thought the album was "very British" with a "Sixties beat group" influence. "It sounded old and new at the same time. It still sounds good."

Staple is naturally of a similar opinion. "The album didn't have a duff song on it. No fillers, no second-raters. There can't have been many albums in the history of pop that were bursting with that many hits. We were creating a new ska sound that was taking over the bedrooms of the nation's teenagers."

The Specials is now rightfully lauded as being one of the most influential albums of the 1970s (or 1980s in the US owing to its later release date). At the time of its UK release, however, the album divided the critics. The *NME* was fulsome in its praise, waxing lyrical about its ska and bluebeat rhythms wrapped within "ferocious rock 'n' roll" as being the "kind of hybrid that so many other British bands have tried to contrive but, in comparison, failed to make convincing". The paper subsequently ranked *The Specials* at #10 in its end-of-the-year Top 10 Albums of 1979.

Sounds' Dave McCullough, however, felt the album had failed to fulfil its potential, lacking the prerequisite rough edges and shock factor. He then targeted the band for having seemingly lost the "attacking, forward-thinking, forward-moving, almost militant momentum that was witnessed and promised from the beginning".

Melody Maker's in-house ska and reggae enthusiast, Viv Goldman, echoed McCullough's observations on the album's failure to match expectations, while also taking a swipe at Costello's production. Opining that while The Specials were a great band to party to, they lacked the studio nous to sustain the shock of having certain numbers being purposely slowed down in tempo. Goldman, however, did end her critique on a positive note, saying she still had "high hopes" for The Specials.

202

CHAPTER

THIRTEEN

GOING FROM TOWN TO TOWN
MAKING DISTURBANCES

*"We had a great time doing ['The Selecter'].
There was no money involved, it was just a
very creative time. Shortly after that we recorded
some demos – 'On My Radio', 'Missing
Words' and 'Washed Up and Left for Dead'.
More or less all the songs were written before
the band actually formed. I think 'Three
Minute Hero' was the only one I wrote later."*

NEOL DAVIES

CHAPTER

Paul Rambali's article on The Selecter, the punningly titled "They Still Bear the Skas", was the first occasion the music world would hear the name "Pauline Black", but the higher The Specials and Madness' stars rose, the more The Selecter's profile came into prominence. The band had been together such a short time yet were playing gigs further and further afield. Taking time off from work, coupled with arriving at Walsgrave Hospital where she was working she looked as much in need of a bed as her patients owing to the lengthy return drives to Coventry wedged in the back of a Transit van that was taking its toll. Not only that, but in the wake of Rambali's *NME* article, *Sounds*, *Melody Maker*, *Record Mirror* et al began badgering the band for interviews.

Black's work colleagues were already questioning the change in her appearance and demeanour, and she herself was getting ever more nervous of someone putting two and two together. All it would take was for one of her colleagues to attend a local Selecter show and her cover would be blown. If her bosses did find out what she was doing in her spare time and gave her an ultimatum to choose between band and career, she was no longer sure which option she'd take. To buy herself a little breathing space, she limped along to her GP with a made-up story of having hurt her knee and came walking away with a doctor's note signing her off work for six weeks.

The Specials had already given The Selecter an opportunity most bands would sell their granny for in selecting 'The Selecter' as the flip side to 'Gangsters', but Dammers' largesse extended to signing the band to 2-Tone for another of the one-off single deals, as per his agreement with Chrysalis.

Now that The Selecter were a signed act, the next logical step was to secure the services of a manager. Black says Neol Davies' decision to offer the job to 21-year-old Juliet De Vie, who at the time was working for Rick Rogers' PR company, Trigger, had as much to do with her looks and physical attributes as her management skills. Yet beneath De Vie's bottle-blonde, doe-eyed exterior lurked a "will of iron and a mind like the enigma machine at Bletchley Park", as the band would soon come to appreciate. "Our ad hoc schedule became structured thanks to Juliet," Black explained. "No longer were we running hither and thither like headless chickens looking for a gig."

De Vie continued working at Trigger, but her first endeavour upon taking up her managerial role came with booking The Selecter on to the bill of a benefit concert at the Hammersmith Palais in aid of On Parent Families. As The Specials would be headlining, De Vie reasoned the majority of the crowd would appreciate having another ska-influenced band on the bill. The Selecter were to open proceedings, but come show time they had been bumped up the billing owing to punk poet John Cooper Clarke having to withdraw.

Black was thrilled to be playing the Palais, the prestigious west London venue immortalised in song by The Clash the previous summer. She was equally excited at the prospect of seeing Linton Kwesi Johnson, as cassette tapes of the dub poet's albums, *Dread Beat & Blood* and *Forces of Victory*, were on heavy rotation in the van while travelling to and from shows. Her exuberance was soon tempered on seeing the circular bandstand stage on which the bands were expected to perform. The stage was so small that The Modettes (the four-piece all-girl band brought in as an eleventh-hour replacement for Cooper Clarke) would struggle to move about freely, so there was no hope for either The Selecter or The Specials.

Black had thought her days of running around like a headless chicken were behind her, but a rude awakening awaited as she and the other musicians were forced to pitch in erecting a larger replacement stage.

She remembers being left in awe on seeing the likes of Elvis Costello, Iggy Pop, Pretenders guitarist James Honeyman-Scott and a certain John Lydon loitering about the bar area. Lydon had no doubt come along to see his friend Linton Kwesi Johnson perform, and while Costello would have been there to see The Specials, his love of ska could well lead to opportunities for The Selecter.

One Parent Families was undoubtedly a worthy cause, but it was The Specials' headlining the event that brought the music weeklies out in force. Much of the copy was naturally dedicated to The Specials, but The Selecter's performance moved *Record Mirror*'s Peter Coyne to eulogise about the band "play[ing] harder than The Specials and their demonic, danceable sound is pleasurably akin to being whip-cracked across the skull with white-hot barbed wire".

The *NME*'s Charles Shaar Murray was also taken by The Selecter's "tightly constructed proper songs", and came away from the Palais thinking The Selecter capable of giving the headliners a "taste of serious competition in time to come". Black was understandably elated at having a writer of Shaar Murray's standing championing them – even if he did initially mistake her for a "ska-orientated Michael Jackson".

The Selecter booked into Horizon Studios. The decision to record at Horizon wasn't so much out of superstition, given that it was here Jerry Dammers had elected to go with 'Kingston Affair' for the 'Gangsters' single, but rather owing to his friend and one-time collaborator, Roger Lomas, now working out of Horizon. Lomas had helped Neol Davies record 'Kingston Affair' at the four-track studio he'd set up in his garden shed. It was a wise move on Davies' part as his relationship with Lomas ensured the latter wouldn't treat this as just another assignment.

Speaking with *The Guardian* in April 2015, Lomas reflected on his initial collaboration with Davies: "I had a four-track studio in my back garden and, in 1977, Neol turned up with a song he wanted to record called 'The Selecter' [sic]. It was different: ska with a bit of rock. John Bradbury, who later joined The Specials, and a fellow called Barry Jones was on trombone. I'd only heard trombones in the Salvation Army, so I put the same effects on it I'd use on a guitar. It sounded great, but I couldn't get any labels interested."

The Selecter would be recording the three songs they deemed the strongest from their live set: 'On My Radio', 'Too Much Pressure' and 'Street Feeling'. They would have three days (August 23 to 25) to record, arrange and mix the songs. Ordinarily, three days would prove sufficient, but while the band's musicians had all been playing for several years, only Davies understood anything about the recording process – and his know-how was limited to watching Lomas twiddle the dials in his garden shed. Black was particularly mindful of their being a "novice band on a budget", and of the £s being eaten up by the studio clock, even though it was Chrysalis' money they were spending.

This was Black's first time in a studio, and she readily admits to finding the recording process somewhat daunting. Thankfully, Lomas' relationship with Davies meant nothing was too much trouble. "Roger was incredibly patient and helpful," she explained. "He realised that I didn't know about studios and helped me double-track my vocal to give the sound depth."

"I got the vocal right on the first take," Lomas explained. "I asked her to do it again anyway and she sang it identically, so I used one vocal in the right channel and the other in the left, which gave it a really unusual sound."

It was also Lomas' idea to have Black singing the chorus response "on my radio" on the song of the same name in a falsetto voice. "This, and the odd-time signature of the bridge section, was enough to lift an ordinary song into a classic one." (in Black's eyes at least).

According to Lomas' recollections, the band hadn't intended recording 'On My Radio' as the general feeling was that it was unworthy of being released as a single as it sounded too much "like a Eurovision entry". Lomas says he'd come away from a recent Selecter show (supporting The Ruts) humming the melody to one song in particular. "One track stood out a mile: 'On My Radio'. But when we got to the studio, I asked them to run through their songs to get warmed up – and there was no sign of it. There was a stand-off. Eventually, I persuaded them to record three songs and let the record company decide on the single. They instantly picked 'On My Radio'. I was a pop and rock man, really. I never much liked ska. 'On My Radio' went on to sell over 240,000 copies. From the moment I heard it, I knew it was a hit."

One of Lomas' traits that didn't go down so well was his calling everyone "boy". Black says she accepted this as simply being one of Lomas' "conversational tics", and one certainly not meant in any way derogatory. Yet despite Davies' vouchsafing of Lomas, Brown, Bembridge and the others viewed it as a putdown; their resentment towards Lomas becoming more ingrained with each repeat. "A deep resentment was forged towards Roger, which rumbled on for months," says Black. "Later this catchphrase would lead us to make the worst decision of our short-lived career. But that was still a way off…"

Indeed, it was. Black, Davies and the others might have been bleary-eyed from lack of sleep, but they came away from the studio sensing the band's horizon had been extended. There was no time to relax, however, as the next night saw them supporting The Specials at Lanchester Polytechnic. The show was billed as The Specials' "homecoming gig" following on from their two-month club tour and time away in London recording their debut album. The event was particularly pleasing for Black, as her overriding memories of the Polytechnic's main hall prior to this were of fretting over the answers on her exam papers, but now here she was lapping up the adoration of a packed crowd. There was to be a sting in the tail, of course. With the whole of Coventry embracing The Specials, the local media coverage of the Lanchester Poly show was extensive, which meant Black's cover was finally blown – and it wasn't for being caught out bounding about a stage with a supposedly dodgy knee.

It was to prove a bittersweet experience walking into the radiography department at Walsgrave Hospital to tender her resignation. While part of her would have been yearning for the band to get to a point where she could give up her day job, she'd hoped it might have come with the security of a £10,000 advance, as it had for The Specials and Madness. One thing she was sure of as she walked away from the hospital for the last time was that she would make her chosen career path work come what may, be it with The Selecter, another band, or even as a solo artist if needs be.

The Selecter were gearing up for the up-and-coming 2-Tone tour at the time of the release of the double A-sided 'On My Radio' / 'Too Much Pressure'. Altruistic though it was, the decision to release a double A-side didn't sit well with Black. She felt they should hold on to 'Too Much Pressure' for the second single. She was also in favour of using the covers they had incorporated into their set as B-sides, so as to generate royalties for the original artists as The Specials and Madness were doing.

CHAPTER

The positive reviews within the music weeklies had given the band a natural high no amount of sensimilla could hope to match, but the euphoria dissipated into the ether at a show at Bristol's Trinity Hall towards the end of September. In truth, the mood was already soured long before the band took to the stage. The PA was late in getting to the venue, which had curtailed the soundcheck, leaving the band in a prickly disposition.

Black and Hendrickson had agreed to an interview and thought they might as well conduct it in the pub around the corner. They'd no sooner walked through the door when the landlady pronounced – albeit in couched terms – that blacks weren't allowed on the premises. The pub's close proximity to Trinity Hall should have alerted Black and Hendrickson to what the evening held in store, but the two were still reeling from what had just happened to join the dots. They returned to the venue and just settled into the interview backstage when the put-upon promoter burst in on them, threatening to pull the show unless the band went on in the next five minutes.

Tensions were mounting within the former church hall youth club owing to the sizeable gangs of mods and skinheads – who had been sizing each other up from the get-go – becoming more and more belligerent. Trouble was nothing new at 2-Tone-related shows by now, of course. In a bid to defuse such situations, the band had worked what Black herself describes as being a "splendid piece of theatricality" into their live show. Midway through 'Too Much Pressure', the band would stop playing and stage a mock fight. Though their on-stage theatrics had usually proved successful in curbing tribal and racial tensions, it quickly became apparent that tonight would be different. "A small skirmish broke out and escalated like a forest fire finding dry tinder," Black reflected. "The battle that everybody came for happened, even though the music they had just danced to had the message of unity attached to it in capital letters."

Black goes on to say that prior to the emergence of 2-Tone, such "Lord of the Flies disputes" were settled on the football terraces. There's no arguing that the National Front and other far-right extremists such as the British Movement had taken affront to Dammers' attempt to defuse mounting racial tensions through music and were now infiltrating skinhead gangs in Britain's inner cities, but violence at punk gigs had been the norm for the past two years or more.

On a more positive note, the groundswell of interest that had been steadily rising in the six months since the release of 'Gangsters' meant that, like Madness before them, The Selecter found themselves being courted by the major labels. It was obvious Chrysalis would express an interest given that it was their money that had funded the Horizon recording session, but Arista Records' MD, Clive Davis, was also keen to add The Selecter to his roster.

Black recalls the surrealism of finding Davis, together with the label's A&R head Tarquin Gotch, parked up outside Aitch Bembridge's house in Davis' Rolls-Royce. Davis and Gotch were no doubt hoping to make an impression. They did, but not the one they'd been hoping for. Coventry was renowned for its car manufacturing, but with Margaret Thatcher's economic initiatives beginning to bite hard – particularly in the West Midlands – car sales were plummeting. Indeed, Davis couldn't have got it more wrong if he'd done a loop-the-loop over the ruined shell of the city's St. Michael's Cathedral in a Heinkel bomber, his naivety more or less paving the way for Roy Eldridge. Davis' being based in New York could perhaps excuse such insensitivity, but the London-born Gotch should have known better.

Eldridge's approach was rather more laidback. The Chrysalis deal was more or less the same as the one Eldridge had offered The Specials, only without the special 2-Tone clause. Dammers certainly wasn't bearing any grudges over Madness' signing with Stiff, but rather than see The Selecter following suit he invited them to become co-directors with 2-Tone Records to help further the label's aims.

The Selecter signed with 2-Tone on October 10, 1979, the same day they recorded 'On My Radio' for appearances on *Top of the Pops* and *Multi-Coloured Swap Shop*, the BBC's Saturday morning kids show hosted by Noel Edmonds and Keith Chegwin. The following day they recorded a session for John Peel at the BBC's Maida Vale studios. The Selecter had come far in the last six months. To those looking from the outside in, it seemed the next six months would see the band scale greater heights… yet in truth the rot was already setting in.

The Selecter had based themselves on the Specials model: there were seven people in the band, they were guitar-orientated and played rock-infused ska. And as such, there were rumblings of discontent about the musical direction the band seemed to be taking. Bembridge and the other Hard Top 22 guys were for adopting a more laidback reggae feel, while Davies and Amanor (unsurprisingly) were keen to continue promoting the twin guitar attack, as favoured by The Specials.

The in-house grousing was put on hold while The Selecter got on with rehearsing for the mammoth 40-date 2-Tone Tour, which was set to get underway on October 19 with a sold-out show at the Brighton Top Rank Suite. Before that, however, there was the small matter of making their *Top of the Pops* debut alongside Suzi Quatro, Lena Martell, XTC and Buggles.

Despite all its cheesiness, and the questionable behaviour of some of the Radio One DJs presenting the show, *Top of the Pops* was the only music show that mattered at the time. With regular viewing figures anywhere up to 19 million, a single appearance could send an act's record sales through the roof.

Television, of course, is all about the magic on screen. What goes on away from the cameras is somewhat different, in this case hanging about in a windowless dressing room until it was their turn to mime along to the pre-recorded version of 'On My Radio' the band had recorded the day of the Chrysalis/2-Tone signing. Although singing a song decrying Radio One on the Beeb's flagship music show with producers and DJs watching on none the wiser would have more than made up for the interminable boredom.

Like Roddy Radiation and John Bradbury before him, Aitch Bembridge caused a bit of a ruckus in the BBC bar, or in this case outside the bar, as the jobsworth commissionaire refused to let the dreadlocked bassist through the door unless he first removed his leather cap. There was neither rhyme nor reason why Bembridge should be asked to remove his cap as Black strolled past the commissionaire in the dove-grey fedora that was to set to become her trademark with nary a word said.

Black was bemused as to Bembridge's refusal to remove his hat. She didn't know enough about Rastafarianism to question why her bassist was proving so obstinate when he had no problem whipping his dreadlocks about while on stage. Indeed, the loose-locked Bembridge strutting his stuff on stage was a sight to behold and wouldn't be repeated for five years or so until Mick Jones recruited Don Letts and Leo Williams for his post-Clash outfit, Big Audio Dynamite.

CHAPTER

FOURTEEN

2-TONE TAKING OVER

"Coventry City FC had just got a new bus, so we got their old one and it actually had things like seats with tables in it. Several times the coach would have to stop while I made calls from a roadside phone box to find out what venue we were in, in case it had been put up a size."

RICK ROGERS

CHAPTER

At first glance, The Specials releasing 'A Message to You, Rudy' as the lead single of their highly anticipated eponymous debut a week prior to the 2-Tone Tour getting underway, and the album itself on the day of the opening show in Brighton, might have seemed like a calculated marketing ploy, and yet according to Panter no one at Specials HQ thought of taking tour T-shirts, posters, or indeed any other official merchandise out on the road. Madness were to prove far more enterprising, printing up three different shirts (one of which, of course, bore the memorable "Fuck Art, Let's Dance" logo), and Dammers and co. were left to rue their short-sightedness as scores of kids at each of the designated tour stop-offs readily snapped up the shirts. However, while not specifying which band, Rick Rogers says it was "selling T-shirts and ties" that kept the tour rolling owing to The Specials' steadfast ruling that all ticket prices be fixed at £2.50. "As soon as the doors opened I had to jump across the [merchandise] table and start selling because just a swarm of people wanted to get this stuff. Initially, it was £2.50 for a ticket, the same price it would have been for a single band. It was a bit less than half of what it would cost you to buy an album.

"The only annoying part of it was trying to get that many people on a coach in the morning. Sometimes we'd be sitting there for two hours before we got everyone on, but the atmosphere at the gigs was amazing. The plan was coming together. It was new. It was happening. The tour was the beginning of what the 2-Tone movement was meant to be. It was like, 'Let's go on tour together – Madness, Selecter, The Specials – like a Motown review.' There was nothing more natural. This was more than just going to see your favourite band."

Panter likens the 2-Tone Tour to the Motown reviews and package tours of the late Fifties and early Sixties put together by legendary pop impresario Larry Parnes. It was also reminiscent of the Sex Pistols' ill-fated Anarchy Tour of December 1976, as put together by Malcolm McLaren, a self-confessed Parnes aficionado. A three-band bill with low ticket prices did indeed emulate the package tours of yesteryear, but whereas Parnes had ruthlessly exploited his acts, and McLaren exploited situations, The Specials were careful to ensure the only thing separating them from Madness or The Selecter was the order of play. The bands and their respective entourages travelled together on the one-time Coventry City FC team bus (replete with the Walt Jabsco logo adorning its rear panel), the crew would travel separately in a minibus, while the lighting and sound equipment was ferried from venue to venue via articulated truck.

Had The Specials not enjoyed a special relationship with Chrysalis, it's highly unlikely the 2-Tone Tour would have happened, as no other record label would have booked like-minded acts as support for fear of their band being upstaged. It wasn't unusual for bands like The Clash or The Damned to give over the support slot to up-and-coming punk-related acts, but punk was stripped-back 4/4 rock 'n' roll when all is said and done, whereas ska was derived from Caribbean calypso.

Three bands offering the same musical fare might have been deemed as overkill, but Dammers wouldn't have signed either Madness or The Selecter to 2-Tone had they been Specials copyists. The Selecter were as guitar-driven as The Specials but infused their style with reggae as opposed to rock, while Madness played ska with a music hall bent. Black thought the differences in vocal styles was even starker than the playing styles: "The Selecter had the surly coolness of Gaps and gender-bending me, sometimes singing lead individually with a whirlwind on-stage energy. In contrast, Suggs gave Madness a definite Ian Dury-esque flavour. Terry Hall brought The Specials an unmistakable post-punk whine flanked by a charismatic rude boy, Neville. What was not to like?" What indeed?

There had to be a pecking order, of course, but there was to be none of the usual loitering in one of the nearby pubs or the venue bar while the support acts were on. Each venue would be packed solid by the time The Selecter came on stage.

Rick Rogers would be accompanying his charges on the tour as much as possible, but the day-to-day itinerary would be overseen by Frank Murray, an inveterate road manager who had cut his teeth looking after his pals and fellow Dubliners, Thin Lizzy. Speaking with John Reed, Madness' occasional tour manager, John "Kellogs" Kalinowski, paid tribute to Murray, saying "[He] was a tough bastard – he taught me a lot."

In turn, Murray called upon former Pistols "minder", Steve English, to act as security. The Specials had first encountered English on the On Parole Tour. Panter is dismissive of English's worth on the tour, as all he remembers is him taking the piss out of them at any given opportunity. English's sense of humour might not have been to Panter's taste, but he's a born raconteur with many hilarious tales from his time accompanying the Pistols out on the road through 1977 – particularly the SPOTS Tour. His being a dyed-in-the-wool "Gooner" would also have made for entertaining on-board banter with the Chelsea-loving Suggs and others of a footballing persuasion.

"You give it a title and it will become a movement," Murray reflected for *Mojo*'s October 2016 feature on the tour. "The 2-Tone tour was an event. All three bands seemed to have this unreal energy that went through them 24 hours a day, I mean really! The Specials used to start with 'Dawning of a New Era'. I loved the excitement. It just seemed like constant motion. Lynval and Neville were always moving, and Jerry pumping away at the keyboards. Terry was a solitary individual and wouldn't say a lot. He'd join in the banter and crack a few jokes, but when you saw him walk on stage he just looked so fucking intense. Then he did that first jump and started to sing and the whole night you could see it coming out of him."

In the run-up to the tour, The Specials booked three days rehearsals at the Roundhouse in Chalk Farm, but their being in London and still flush with cash from the Chrysalis advance meant much of their stay was given over to shopping. They did, however, manage to pull themselves away from Carnaby Street long enough to film the promo video to 'A Message to You, Rudy'. The shoot was nothing more than the band (with Rodriguez and Cuthell) performing the song in front of a white backdrop, interspersed with footage of some fans and Griffiths and Evans in "rude boy" mode – simple yet effective.

Chalkie Davis had photographed everyone from the Stones to The Ramones. The 24-year-old one-time *NME* photographer was now shooting record covers (notably *The Specials*) but sensed this was an event worth capturing in his lens, and his friendship with Murray ensured him a seat on the tour bus. "There was a fabulous camaraderie on the bus, as there often is at the beginning of a tour. Because I'd moved on from the *NME*, I felt no need to take that many photos, and so I just settled in and enjoyed the atmosphere."

Davis couldn't resist taking a shot of the three bands on Brighton beach. Corralling bands into a usable shot was second nature to him by now, but never had he been faced with keeping 21 musicians (including Chas Smash) focused on the task in hand. Fortunately, he was able to get his snap before his subjects leapt up en masse to give chase to Rick Rogers, who was holding everyone's per diems."

Melody Maker thought the opening Top Rank Suite show "lacklustre", but the tour quickly established its own momentum – both on and off stage. "[We] were on top form," Panter opined. "The Selecter were learning on their feet and starting to find their own big-stage identity. Ditto Madness; one show in every four of theirs was a stunner. The Specials were just fantastic. All the experience gained over the past couple of years and especially in the last six months made us unstoppable."

The *NME*'s Mark Ellen was at the third show of the tour at Bournemouth's Stateside Centre. This was the fourth time Ellen had seen The Specials in recent months, and instead of "unstoppable", he found them "flat, drained and lifeless", with only the arrival on stage of Rodriguez and Cuthell for the final four numbers offering "fleeting salvation".

The future *Old Grey Whistle Test* presenter's signing off by saying "Skaville was a nice place to visit but he wouldn't want to live there" suggests he wasn't a fan of the genre, but he nonetheless complimented The Selecter's "bass-heavy, steam locomotive bluebeat", and Madness' "cheese-grater chords, sturdy farfisa and reckless, raucous sax".

The kids who were packing out each tour venue in turn thought "Skaville" the only place to be, and their devotion was proved with *The Specials* entering the UK albums chart at #4 and *One Step Beyond* at #16. By the time the tour rolled into Plymouth on November 6, 'A Message to You, Rudy', 'One Step Beyond' and 'On My Radio' had all charted.

The BBC were keen to show they were hip to the latest craze by inviting The Specials, Madness and The Selecter to appear "live" on that week's *Top of the Pops*. A return to London to film their respective performances would mean postponing the following evening's show in Cardiff to a later date – something none of the bands were willing to countenance. A compromise of sorts was reached, however. The Selecter

drove up to London early, recorded their performance at the Beeb's Maida Vale studios, then travelled on to the Cardiff Top Rank in time to open the show.

'On My Radio' had broken into the Top 30 at #26 before climbing five places to #21. Following this second appearance on *TotP*, the record shot up to #9, and a further place to #8 the week after. In her book, Black has 'On My Radio' peaking at #6 on the chart, but while she may be mistakenly gilding the lily, The Selecter's scoring a Top 10 hit with their debut offering was no mean feat – especially with a song the band had dismissed as a "Eurovision entry".

The Specials and Madness appeared in the *TotP* studio before continuing to the Welsh capital, The Specials via train and Madness in a specially chartered plane. Despite the hassle and added mileage, Panter cites the Cardiff Top Rank show as one of The Specials' standout performances on the tour.

Roddy Byers says his abiding memory from the tour was the "heat, sweat and mist hanging in the air like a sauna at the gigs. It was like a 2-Tone army hitting each city and town. Some of the hotels took exception to our casual regard to smoking weed in the rooms. We also had kids joining the tour wherever we went, sometimes leaving their schools, families and jobs behind."

Madness would decamp from the tour midway through November to play some US shows at the behest of Sire Records. Staple would have the world believe that Madness' leaving the tour after the final Scottish date in Aberdeen was a "bombshell" that "caused some irritation on our side".

While reflecting on the departure for his own book, Panter pronounced that Madness' show of "rock 'n' roll one-upmanship" had no direct bearing on either The Specials or the tour, yet both had to have known what was occurring as the music weeklies knew of Madness' intentions well in advance. "I don't remember reading anything in the music press about Madness already being booked to go to America, but they're leaving the 2-Tone Tour took me by surprise," says Byers. "I can only think they thought they had bigger fish to fry. They got to New York before us. I'm not sure whether they're going to America was a management idea or not. Dexys came on to the tour as replacements, but there wasn't much interaction as they kept to themselves most of the time."

No one in The Selecter camp was mourning the Nutty Boys' departure as it meant they were elevated in the rankings. Madness' replacement for the remaining dates was Dexys Midnight Runners, a Birmingham-based soul outfit fronted by former Killjoys frontman Kevin Rowland. The irascible Rowland ran Dexys like a platoon leader – they dressed, ate and slept as one. They were currently being managed by Bernard Rhodes and were signed to the latter's oddball label. There was never any intention on Dammers' part to sign Dexys to 2-Tone, but his bringing them on to the tour paved the way to their securing a deal with EMI.

Madness' absconding to America did at least serve to reduce the skinhead presence on the remaining dates. Despite the Nutty Boys' distancing themselves from the racist skinhead elements who were turning up determined to cause trouble, veiled mutterings continued as to their lacking the conviction to stand shoulder to shoulder with The Specials and The Selecter in challenging the media's perception of the 2-Tone movement being "racist". Though Chas Smash's ill-considered comments during a band interview with the *NME* about his not caring if their fans had National Front affiliations so long as they were having a good time didn't endear him to certain of his fellow 2-Toners. "Madness didn't seem to have the stomach for controversy like the rest of us," Black reflected. "Their jaunty, boyish image was in danger of being sullied with political fallout."

Staple didn't hold any grudges; if anything, he felt Madness had got the shitty end of the stick. "There was a growing subculture which had adopted the skinhead look and NF politics. As a multi-racial band there was no way they were going to follow us, so, sadly they tacked on to Madness."

With extra dates being tagged on here and there, the bands had been out on the road for two months by the time the 2-Tone charabanc rolled into London for three shows; the first coming at the Lewisham Odeon, and the others at the Lyceum Ballroom. This was followed up with two Coventry dates in the run-up to Christmas.

Reviewing the first of the "triumphant homecoming" shows, *Melody Maker*'s Simon Frith acknowledged Dexys as being "more a nod to 2-Tone's soul club past than an addition to [its] vibrant present", yet lauded them for setting the mood. The Selecter's playing with "buoyant precision" was also commented on, but Frith saved his eulogising for the headliners. "They played better than ever – crisper, more professional, and above all, with new power and arrogance. They're the best dance band there is."

A new decade was dawning, and those in the know were predicting 2-Tone's going from strength to strength. The December 22, 1979 issue of *Sounds* proclaimed the success that had already seen 2-Tone Records become the "top new label of 1979" was set to continue. The Specials (reverting back to The Special AKA) were set to release the 'Too Much Too Young' EP featuring live recordings of the title track and The Skatalites' 'Guns of Navarone' from the first Lyceum show, along with a medley of ska standards: 'Long Shot Kick de Bucket' (The Pioneers), 'The Liquidator' (Harry J Allstars) and 'Skinhead Moonstomp' (Symarip), which made up the band's "take no prisoners" encore, from the opening Tiffany's homecoming

CHARTS

TOP 50 SINGLES

...AL FLAME	Bangles/CBS
...ON YOUR HEART	Kylie Minogue/PWL
...DON'T KNOW ME BY NOW	Simply Red/Elektra
...I DON'T CARE	Transvision Vamp/MCA
...S IN THE HOUSE	Beatmasters with Merlin/Rhythm King
...Y THING	Fine Young Cannibals/London
...EM	London Boys/WEA
...BY	The Cure/Fiction
...CAMOS	Holly Johnson/MCA
...ARE BURNING	Midnight Oil/Sprint
...NOBODY BETTER	Inner City/10
...ESTING DRUG	Morrissey/HMV
...YOU LIKE CRAZY	Natalie Cole/EMI America
...YOUR PARDON	Kon Kan/Atlantic
...E HAS ALL THE LOVE GONE?	Yazz/Big Life
...G ME EDELWEISS	Edelweiss/WEA
...	Metallica/Vertigo
...MAMA DON'T DANCE	Poison/Enigma
...S YOUR LAND	Simple Minds/Virgin
...SELF AND I	De La Soul/Big Life
...LOVE COMES TO TOWN	U2 with B.B. King/Island
...E THERE FOR YOU	Bon Jovi/Vertigo
...RIC YOUTH	Debbie Gibson/Atlantic
...GHT UP	Paula Abdul/Siren
...ON MY MIND	Swing Out Sister/Fontana
...FY	INXS/Mercury
...O KEEP ON	Cookie Crew/London
...PRAYER	Madonna/Sire
...NU BELIEVE IN SHAME	Duran Duran/EMI
...OOK	Roxette/EMI
...ANY BROKEN HEARTS	Jason Donovan/PWL
...LOVE	Jody Watley/MCA
...IME I KNOW IT'S FOR REAL	Donna Summer/WEA
...E CLOSER	Tom Jones/Jive
...ON MOVIN'	Soul II Soul featuring Caron Wheeler/10
...TERY WOMAN	Chaka Khan/WEA
...OU HELP ME	Deon Estus/Mika
...MY BODY ROCK (FEEL IT)	Jomanda/RCA
...S YOUR LIFE	Blow Monkeys/RCA
...E HOLD ON	Coldcut featuring Lisa Stansfield/Ahead Of Our Time
...RRILL HAS GONE	Texas/Mercury
...UPJ SUCKER	Pop Will Eat Itself/RCA
...OISE CITY	Guns 'N' Roses/Geffen
...EN'T STOPPED DANCING YET	Pat & Mick/PWL
...WORLD	Kirsty MacColl/Virgin
...URSE I'M LYING	Yello/Mercury
...UGH THE STORM	Aretha Franklin & Elton John/Arista
...SEE CLEARLY NOW	Johnny Nash/Epic
...S ON FIRE	Stevie Nicks/EMI
...E INSIDE (THEME FROM PRISONER: CELL BLOCK H)	Lynn Hamilton/A.I.

TOP 30 ALBUMS

...	Holly Johnson/MCA
...LARE	Simply Red/Elektra
...NING FOR YOU	Gloria Estefan & The Miami Sound Machine/Epic
...THE WORLD KNOWS YOUR NAME	Deacon Blue/CBS
...W AND THE COOKED	Fine Young Cannibals/London
...PRAYER	Madonna/Sire
...CLASSICS VOL. ONE	Soul II Soul/10
...THING	INXS/Mercury
...TTLE	The Pixies/4AD
...HAT'S WHAT I CALL MUSIC 14	Various Artists/EMI/Virgin/Polygram
...TE FOR DESTRUCTION	Guns 'N' Roses/Geffen
...	Transvision Vamp/MCA
...Y IT'S THE MONKEES GREATEST HITS	The Monkees/K-Tel
...HEAT: THE SECOND BURN	Various Artists/Telstar
...BE CRUEL	Bobby Brown/MCA
...SIDE	Texas/Mercury
...FOR YOUR GIRL	Paula Abdul/Siren
...RY GIRL	Roy Orbison/Virgin
...TEMPLE	The Cult/Beggars Banquet
...RY KINGS	The Gipsy Kings/Telstar
...S THAT NOISE	Coldcut/Ahead Of Our Time
...REGULAR ADVENTURES OF THE STYLE COUNCIL – GREATEST	
...OLUME 1	The Style Council/Polydor
...HIS WAY!	Cookie Crew/London
...	Kylie Minogue/PWL
...TO CHEEK	Various Artists/CBS
...	The Bee Gees/WEA
...NT HEART	Tanita Tikaram/WEA
...1989	Lloyd Cole & The Commotions/Polydor
...RESENT	Clannad/RCA

HOLLY JOHNSON BLASTS OFF

WIRE EAR TODAY

TOM PETTY HITS FEVER-PITCH

INDIE SINGLES

1	(2)	WHO'S IN THE HOUSE?	Beatmasters
2	(3)	ME MYSELF AND I	
3	(—)	HAND ON YOUR HEART	
4	(1)	HOLLOW HEART	
5	(6)	WHERE HAS ALL THE LOVE GONE	
6	(1)	MONKEY GONE TO HEAVEN	
7	(7)	PEOPLE HOLD ON	Coldcut featuring Lisa Stansfield
8	(12)	TRAINSURFING EP	
9	(5)	WHITE KNUCKLE RIDE	
10	(11)	THE HAIRSTYLE OF THE DEVIL	
11	(10)	VOODOO RAY	A Guy Called Gerald
12	(14)	LOLA	
13	(8)	I HAVEN'T STOPPED DANCING YET	
14	(9)	NEVER STOP	
15	(—)	EAR DRUM BUZZ	
16	(13)	ROUND AND ROUND	
17	(—)	TIMERIDER	
18	(14)	MADE OF STONE	
19	(20)	SWEET JANE	Cowboy
20	(—)	LANDSLIDE	

INDIE ALBUMS

1	(1)	DOOLITTLE	
2	(10)	SURFER ROSA	
3	(3)	FEET HIGH AND RISING	
4	(4)	WHAT'S THAT NOISE?	Coldcut
5	(14)	COME ON PILGRIM	
6	(6)	LOVE AGENDA	
7	(8)	TRINITY SESSION	Cowboy
8	(—)	HEADACHE RHETORIC	
9	(5)	ONE HAND CLAPPING	
10	(—)	SILVERTOWN	The New They
11	(9)	TECHNIQUE	
12	(16)	KYLIE	
13	(12)	HOUSE OF LOVE	
14	(5)	VINI REILLY	
15	(11)	ORIGINAL SOUNDTRACK	
16	(7)	BUG	
17	(20)	SYMPHONY NO. 6	
18	(15)	SUPERFUZZBIGMUFF	
19	(—)	PRIDE OF THE INDEPENDENTS	Various
20	(13)	THE ENRAGED WILL INHERIT THE EARTH	

US SINGLES

1	(1)	LIKE A PRAYER	
2	(2)	I'LL BE THERE FOR YOU	
3	(4)	FOREVER YOUR GIRL	
4	(6)	REAL LOVE	
5	(10)	ROCK ON	Michael Damian
6	(7)	SECOND CHANCE	
7	(—)	THINKING OF YOU	
8	(—)	SOLDIER OF LOVE	
9	(8)	SHE DRIVES ME CRAZY	Fine Young Cannibals
10	(—)	ELECTRIC YOUTH	

US ALBUMS

1	(—)	FULL MOON FEVER	
2	(5)	VOICES OF BABYLON	
3	(3)	SONIC TEMPLE	
4	(5)	THE TRAVELLING WILBURYS	The Travelling Wilburys
5	(7)	TWICE SHY	
6	(2)	MR JORDAN	
7	(4)	GREEN	
8	(10)	SARAYA	
9	(9)	NICK OF TIME	
10	(—)	VIVID	

THE HIT LIST

EVERETT TRUE

BEAT HAPPENING: "TV Girl" (from the forthcoming LP "...Candy")

THE SNEETCHES: "Another Shitty Day" (from the LP "Sometimes That's All We Have")

THE KINKS: "Waterloo Sunset" (from the BR Music "Kinks Greatest Hits")

DINOSAUR JR: "Just Like Heaven" (Blast First single)

SNAPPER: "Buddy" (Flying Nun single)

PUSH

DE LA SOUL: "Ghetto Thang" (from the Big Life "...And Rising")

MARTHA'S VINEYARD: "Unravelling" (from the compilation LP "Young Blood")

JUST-ICE: "No Touch Da Just" (from the Sleeping Bag "...Desolate One")

CARTER - THE UNSTOPPABLE SEX MACHINE: (from the forthcoming Big Cat LP "1001 Damn Nights")

JIVE TURKEY: "Beautiful Way To Die" (Chapter)

show. There was some uncertainty as to how the live EP would fare in the charts, but it was deemed preferable to taking another track from *The Specials*.

The decision to release a live EP was down to Dammers, as Byers explains. "I think the EP was just a case of Jerry wanting to emulate what bands did back in the Sixties. The idea to release it as a live EP was because no matter how hard we tried, we could never capture the frantic sound we got playing live in the studio."

The Selecter were set to release 'Three Minute Hero' as their follow-up to 'On My Radio', before heading back into Horizon Studios to record their debut album, *Too Much Pressure*. A headline UK tour was being lined up – with the recently formed all-girl outfit The Bodysnatchers in support – to promote the album.

The *Sounds* feature also revealed how The Specials were set to be the focus of BBC2's long-running documentary series *Arena*, but it was 2-Tone's latest acquisition, The Beat, recently scoring a UK Top 10 hit with their debut double A-side single, 'Tears of a Clown' / 'Ranking Full Stop', and giving the label its fifth straight Top 10 hit (a feat unmatched by any other UK label at the time) that caught the eye. Dammers' Midas touch had struck gold again.

The Beat's Dave Wakeling, guitarist Andy Cox, and classically trained bassist David Steele, had started out in 1978 playing punk-edged rock before the arrival of West Indian-born drummer, Everett Morton, added a reggae flavour to their sound. The Beat were still a quartet when they made their live debut in their native Birmingham in March 1979; the same weekend as the Three Mile Island nuclear incident, after which they were introduced on stage as the "hottest thing since the Pennsylvania meltdown".

"Ranking Roger" Charlery was the drummer in the headline act, but his joining The Beat on stage and toasting over the songs proved an irresistible combination. "When I first met The Beat, I was in a punk band called The Dum Dum Boys," he subsequently recounted. "This band called The Beat wanted to open for us at a gig at a place called the Matador in the Bull Ring [a Birmingham city centre shopping mall]. They came to a rehearsal, played 'Twist and Crawl' and 'Mirror in the Bathroom'. I thought, 'We've got some work to do.' We did the gig, they came on and the place went mad. We knew then that The Beat had won the day."

The Beat were keen for Ranking Roger to come and check them out at one of their own headline shows. When he got to the club, however, there were only a handful of punters in there. "I said, 'Do you want me to get some people,' and they were like, 'Yeah, we're on in half an hour,'" he continues, picking up the tale. "I ran down a quarter of a mile to the Crown pub, where all the punks hung out. It was a Wednesday night and some of them were bored out of their heads, some were sniffing glue, and some of them were just drunk."

Having succeeded in wrenching the Crown clientele from their collective torpor, Ranking Roger led his punk posse back up the road to the club, where his new friends were playing. The Beat were understandably elated, but they'd no sooner started playing when Roger found himself being pushed up on to the stage. He instinctively grabbed Wakeling's mic and started toasting over the songs as Neville Staple would do at The Special AKA's show at the Music Machine supporting The Clash. "They [the crowd] all started going mad. I came off, and about two numbers later they pushed me back on and the band didn't mind."

Following a conversation with Wakeling, Ranking Roger quit The Dum Dum Boys and joined The Beat; an added bonus coming with his giving up living in a hostel and moving in with Wakeling at the latter's flat.

On signing The Beat to 2-Tone, Dammers had wanted to release one of the band's own compositions, 'Mirror in the Bathroom'. "I remember we were very excited by the opportunity," Wakeling reflected. "He [Dammers] said, "Mirror in the Bathroom', eh?' And I said, 'Yeah, that's the star of the show so far.'"

Unfortunately for Wakeling and co., Chrysalis had started flexing their muscles behind the scenes. If The Beat released 'Mirror in the Bathroom' they would be expected to relinquish all rights to the song for five years, something the band were far from happy about. "We were like, 'Get lost, then,' Wakeling continued. "We haven't even made an LP yet, and they already wanna rip us off, y'know? Thought we were meant to make a record first, and *then* you rip us off."

Horace Panter remembers hearing a pre-Saxa version of 'Mirror in the Bathroom' on a cassette tape during the 2-Tone tour. "[It] had us Specials definitely rocking. Rockers' drums played at Motörhead speed, sinewy bass and weedy punk-thrash Velvet Underground guitars. Fantastic tune, and this Irie Irie toasting over the top of it, all from this kid who apparently was only 16. The Beat – what a great name."

What made 'Mirror in the Bathroom' stand out was Steele's revolutionary 2/2 bassline. "It seems like the same thing, but it's not quite; it gives it an edge, especially when mixed with the off-beats from the reggae. That made it stand out from the crowd, really."

Wakeling was working as a labourer on a construction site at the time, and the song's lyric came to him while giving himself a pep talk in the bathroom mirror. "I started talking to myself in the mirror and said, 'Dave, we don't have to do this, mate. We don't have to do this.' In the mirror behind me, the door had a tiny latch, and I said to myself, 'The door's locked. There's only me and you. Just me and you here. We don't have to do this.' And of course, we did, because we needed money for Guinness that night."

While making his way to work on his motorbike, Wakeling kept running the line "The door is locked, just you and me" through his mind. It had a nice feel to it – especially when coupled with the title. While shovelling sand into the concrete mixer he began adding to the couplet, without thinking in terms of writing a song. It wasn't until he heard Steele's bassline that he realised the lyrics "fit like a glove".

The argument went back and forth. Dammers was holding out for 'Mirror in the Bathroom', but with Chrysalis proving equally obstinate and The Beat stuck in the middle there seemed no way of breaking the stalemate. "We were like, 'Fine, just get Chrysalis to stop being stupid.' You can't take a band's best song and not allow them to use it on their own record. That's nuts."

Indeed, it was. Rather than risk Dammers losing interest because of the impasse, the band told him about how their ska-twisted version of Smokey Robinson's 'Tears of a Clown' was wowing audiences wherever they played. "[We said,] 'Doesn't matter whether it's punks or grannies or Rastas, it always goes down great. If you want a single, that's it, and you can argue with Smokey Robinson about whose song it is.'"

Wakeling grew up in the Balsall Heath area of Birmingham. He had a passion for ska and reggae, and would pluck away on the cheap, second-hand acoustic guitar his dad had bought on a whim, without giving any serious consideration to either forming or joining a band. It wasn't until hearing the as-yet-unsigned UB40 rehearsing in a recreation centre in neighbouring Highgate that he reconsidered his options. "[It] really surprised me when I walked into the recreation centre. It wasn't all Jamaicans playing reggae, yet they sounded so good."

Jamaican-born saxophonist Saxa (born Lionel Augustus Martin) was initially brought in to help with recording 'Tears of a Clown'. Before relocating to Britain in 1960 he'd played with Prince Buster, Desmond Dekker, Laurel Aitken and many other ska pioneers. Saxa's playing on 'Tears of a Clown' had transformed Smokey Robinson's classic to another level. Recognising how much his playing complimented the band's style, he was persuaded to join on a permanent basis.

Rather than follow The Selecter's lead in signing with Chrysalis, The Beat set up their own label, Go Feet (a subsidiary of Arista Records), via which they would release all future recordings. "We were on 2-Tone and we had about ten record companies wanting to sign us up," Ranking Roger revealed. "[They were like], 'Anything you want, guys – the cheque is blank!' We went for Arista, who were offering us less money, but the most freedom we wanted. So, it wasn't about money for The Beat, it was about having your own say within that crooked business and people who'd actually listen to you. Because someone could offer you a million pounds and just put you on the shelf. But the guys at Arista said, 'Listen, whatever we do, whoever you sign with, it doesn't matter. But if you sign with us, we're gonna break this band and make sure [you] get the recognition.' And they did."

The Beat subsequently signed with Sire Records in the US, but a California surf band's already laying claim to the name saw them marketed stateside as "The English Beat".

The follow-up singles, 'Hands Off... She's Mine' (b/w 'Twist and Crawl') and 'Mirror in the Bathroom' (b/w 'Jackpot'; the first-ever digitally recoded single released in the UK), gave the band their second and third successive UK Top 10 hits. Their debut album, *I Just Can't Stop It*, was released in May 1980 and served to further entrench The Beat's identity as a ska band, yet their skilful melding of reggae and R&B helped give them a distinct sound all of their own.

Though largely dismissive of the 2-Tone ska revival, *Rolling Stone* lauded *I Just Can't Stop It* as a "rambunctious cluster of singles held together by tenor saxophonist Saxa's winning, authoritative blowing and a rhythm section that cared more about adventure than duplicating antique reggae".

"The thing with The Beat is we were very experimental without realising we actually were," says Ranking Roger. "We were these six guys who got together and basically jammed and these tunes came up, or 'grooves' as I call them. And for me, it was all about the groove. 'Mirror in the Bathroom' was originally a punkish, faster song. We told Everett it was a punk song, and we told him to play punk. To him, that was punk – hitting the [drums] hard. That groove came, and it was worked with that bassline and it was just 'click'. It was like, 'No, don't change nothing. I don't care what it is, that is the way forward.'"

The Selecter were now a band in demand. John Peel and his fellow Radio One DJ, Mike Read, were requesting radio sessions. Their popularity had spread to the continent, and immediately on the back of the 2-Tone Tour the band headed over to Europe for a string of headlining dates in Norway, Sweden, Holland, Belgium, Italy and West Germany. Black remembers being taken aback at kids arriving at the European shows decked out head-to-toe in Walt Jabsco black and white. "Their English was practically non-existent, but they had memorised our songs' words. They were tuned into that youthful musical sixth sense that can detect meaningful youth subcultures inside their radar range. Slowly but surely, we stealth-bombed Europe with the 2-Tone message."

Following the festive break, The Selecter convened at Horizon Studios on New Year's Day 1980 with producer Errol Ross to begin work on their debut album. Rico Rodriguez and Dick Cuthell had been borrowed from The Specials to provide horns on 'Carry Go Bring Home' and 'Black and Blue'. Of the 14 songs slated for the album, nine were band compositions; the others being The Pioneers' 'Time Hard', Leon & Owen's 'Murder', Justin Hinds' 'Carry Go Bring Home', Aitch Bembridge's ganja-paean take of Millie Small's 'My Boy Lollipop', which he'd renamed 'My Collie (Not a Dog)', and Monty Norman's readily identifiable James Bond theme, all of which were taken from their live set.

Davies' wanting Roger Lomas to produce the album had caused considerable unrest amongst the others, if only because of the still-lingering resentment over his "Alright, boy" catchphrase. Bembridge also thought they should be looking at named producers from the reggae world rather than the relatively unknown Lomas. Jamaican-born DJ and singer/songwriter Mikey Dread (aka Michael Campbell) and Matumbi's bassist/producer Dennis Bovell were approached, but for reasons known only to themselves, neither chose to accept the commission.

Black's disappointment at losing out on Dread and Bovell soon turned to despair at Ross' appointment. Though she had supported Bembridge over his wanting a "name" reggae producer, she'd disliked Ross on sight; his "unctuous demeanour coupled with his hustler mentality" failing to impress. Ross had accompanied the band on their European travels, and his playing devil's advocate in suggesting the hotels they were staying in were unworthy of a band of their status had caused querulous rumblings within the band.

As Black rightly points out in her book, the first album should be the easiest to realise in the recording studio. The Selecter had only been together seven months, but they had nonetheless packed in plenty of stage time honing their set to perfection. None of the band were seasoned professionals, but they knew their way around a studio – particularly Horizon – and yet Ross treated them like first-time novices. If anything, Ross was the novice as *Too Much Pressure* would be the one-time bass player-cum-sound engineer's first production credit. Black's opinion of Ross hasn't mellowed with the passage of time, and she still blames him for single-handedly ruining the sound, if not the songs themselves. "They were too good and couldn't be harmed, but his production skills were minor at best and majorly ruinous at worst."

Choosing to record at Horizon was also proving problematic as the studio's in-house engineer Kim Holmes' bearing allegiance to Lomas, coupled with Ross' overegging his technical knowhow, meant for a less than harmonious ambience, while his seemingly effortless ability to rub up people the wrong way made him persona non grata at Chrysalis' Stratford Place offices.

The Selecter had yet to sign a publishing deal. It was on the "to do" list, but with everything else going on they had yet to get round to it. It was only once they were ensconced at Horizon that they realised their naivety in leaving the publishing simmering on the backburner heading into the studio. Davies believed his having penned most of the original compositions set for inclusion on the album entitled him to a larger slice of the publishing pie, whereas Bembridge thought the publishing moneys should be split equally between the seven; his argument being those bands that split the publishing moneys equally tended to stay together longer than those that don't.

Somewhat amazingly, Bembridge got his way, but it failed to end the discord. "Unfortunately, the pot of resentments had been heated to boiling point. Even though it had cooled somewhat, it still simmered. Collectively, we may have been a 'melting pot', but the black/white divide had asserted itself. It was as if Neol was perceived as the 'greedy white man', while the rest of us played 'needy black folks'. And some were more needy than others."

The camaraderie that had carried The Selecter thus far was long gone and the constant sniping and backbiting was eroding the band from within. Black had more pressing things to worry about, however. She was pregnant. Aside from the pregnancy causing havoc with the band's touring and recording schedule as she neared her term, she was unsure as to whether her long-standing partner Terry was the father.

While traversing Europe she'd enjoyed a fling with a Swedish photographer called Hatte Stiwenius, to alleviate the boredom of hotel rooms as much as anything, but a one-night stand with one of her fellow 2-Toners during the tour threw another potential father into the mix. Her decision to have an abortion had been far from easy, but in hindsight she views it as the only sensible option open to her at the time.

Too Much Pressure was originally intended for a St. Valentine's Day release, only to be put back a week or so to February 23. The lead single, 'Three Minute Hero', had stalled at a rather desultory #16 on the UK chart, but the album itself would reach #4, receiving a BPI Gold certification for sales in excess of 100,000 in the process. The album also fared well at the hands of the critics, with *Sounds'* Gary Bushell giving it a five-star rating. Robert Christgau, the renowned rock scribe, waxed lyrical about The Selecter honouring "their undercapitalised roots by emulating the two-track sound of the cult hits they love", while singling out Davies' ability to "recapture the ska spirit without pretending it's 1965" and signing off by advising his *Village Voice* readership to play the album "loud".

The Selecter's 30-date UK 2 One 2 Tour in support of *Too Much Pressure* largely consisted of the same venues from the 2-Tone Tour, only with themselves as headliners. As announced in *Sounds'* December 22 article, The Bodysnatchers, a London-based, seven-piece all-girl ska outfit recently signed to 2-Tone, would be providing support. They had made their live debut just months earlier at the Windsor Castle pub in Maida Vale, supporting a pre-Pogues Shane MacGowan's band, The Nips.

The driving force behind The Bodysnatchers was Nicky Summers. The one-time fruit and veg seller had caught The Specials' Moonlight Club show and came away determined to form a band. It would seem Summers was as interested in the personalities of those who responded to her "Rude Girls Wanted" ad as she was their musicality. Having started out as a four-piece, the line-up was soon augmented to a seven-piece, and the girls set about working up rocksteady numbers to incorporate into a set (reportedly opting for rocksteady after finding ska's uptempo rhythms too taxing for their undeveloped musicianship). They were fronted by 20-year-old Rhoda Dakar, a lithesome, beehive-haired beauty whose idiosyncratic voice was perfectly suited to the band's shambolic sound.

The girls had impressed when supporting The Selecter on what was only their second live outing. So much so, in fact, that Black and co. had mooted the possibility of their being 2-Tone material. The suggestion hadn't met with universal approval within the 2-Tone camp owing to their lack of experience, but fortunately for The Bodysnatchers Dammers was happy to give them a chance. Ironically, when the girls headed into the studio to record Dandy Livingston's 'Let's Do Rock Steady' and their own composition, 'Ruder than You', they did so with Roger Lomas producing. The single would reach a respectable #16 on the UK chart, earning them an appearance on *Top of the Pops*.

Further TV outings came on *Today*, the very same magazine show that had inadvertently catapulted the Sex Pistols into enduring notoriety, and *Tiswas*, ITV's long-running madcap Saturday morning kids show that was just as much aimed at the parents.

Aside from The Bodysnatchers, the all-girl American band, Holly and The Italians were also booked to play support. The 24-year-old Holly Beth Vincent (born Holly Cernuto) had played in a variety of bands on the LA punk scene before forming Holly and The Italians and relocating to London in 1978. The band was soon snapped up by Virgin Records, and their debut single, 'Tell that Girl to Shut Up', was receiving plenty of radio airplay.

It was thought the American band's pop/punk would prove a welcoming respite from the ska off-beat onslaught. What sounds good in theory doesn't always transmute to practice, though, and so it would prove with the hapless Holly and The Italians. The Bodysnatchers were warmly received by The Selecter's burgeoning fan base, whereas Holly and her Italians were barracked, booed and, on a couple of occasions, bottled into submission. It was hoped the band would weather the storm, but with the crowd's reaction growing ever-more hostile it was decided to put the American girls out of their misery.

Holly and The Italians' replacements for the remainder of the tour were soon-to-be 2-Tone signees The Swinging Cats.

The Swinging Cats had only been playing for three months or so when the invitation came. They'd won a local Battle of the Bands competition, which earned them two days at Woodbine Studios in neighbouring Leamington Spa. The band's guitarist, John Shipley, knew Jerry Dammers of old, and it was their acquaintanceship that saw Dammers popping along to one of their early gigs. "He [Dammers] really liked us and offered us a two-single deal," Shipley explained. "We practised in our drummer Billy Gough's garage, full of canoes and moose's heads; there wasn't enough room to swing a cat, and a name was born."

On signing with 2-Tone, The Swinging Cats recorded 'Mantovani', an off-kilter yet highly infectious instrumental, and 'Away', featuring singer Jayne Bayley's vocals. The single didn't trouble the chart (despite the first 20,000 copies going on sale at the giveaway price of 50 pence), but their association with 2-Tone was sufficient to land the band a spot on the BBC's daytime magazine programme, *Look Hear*, where they performed 'Away' and Connie Francis' 'Never on Sunday'. (The second single, 'Greek Tragedy', had yet to see the light of day.)

CHAPTER

Black viewed inviting The Swinging Cats on to the tour as repaying a favour. The Specials had helped them, so it seemed appropriate to give another home city band a helping hand. The Coventry-based quartet's quirkiness certainly proved a hit with the audiences, however, and with The Bodysnatchers moving up to main support, it was a win/win situation. Or so it might have proved had the headliners all been singing from the same song sheet.

Black was becoming increasingly worried about Brown's mood swings; his unpredictability being fuelled daily with bottles of whisky. She was sitting at the front of the tour bus one morning when Brown took umbrage to the "look" she gave him, Bembridge and Anderson as they came aboard; the three having kept everyone waiting for three-quarters of an hour not coming into the equation. Brown stood staring menacingly at her for several moments, then having shouted something along the lines of, 'Wha'ppen? You t'ink you're the Queen?', he sprang at Black, wrapping his hands about her throat and started strangling her. It took six people to pull him off.

The Bodysnatchers and The Swinging Cats were so traumatised by the attack and the ensuing frosty silence on the tour bus that they took to travelling separately.

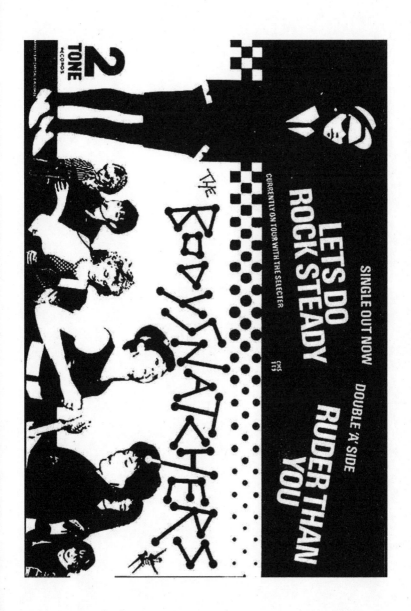

CHAPTER
FIFTEEN

2-TONING AMERIKA

*"Thing was, we were going [to America] with
an attitude. Our 'punk credentials', which were
some- what dubious, given our mean age, meant
that we were supposed to disavow most pre-
1977 music from both sides of the Atlantic
– 'I'm so bored with the USA' and all that –
despite the fact we looked back there for
inspiration. It was something that I always felt
uneasy about, but always seemed to be able to
side-step in the interviews I gave."*

HORACE PANTER

CHAPTER

Horace Panter says that with 1979 having proved The Specials' "year of acquisition", he and the rest of the band were viewing 1980 as one of opportunity. They had proved their worth in the UK, and they'd been rapturously received at the Bilzen Festival in Belgium back in August. They had also visited Munich and Amsterdam, where they'd mimed along to 'Gangsters' on *Top of the Pops*-type music shows that were so excruciatingly naff that *TotP* appeared cool in comparison. The Specials had always viewed themselves as being a British phenomenon, but the time had come to take their Coventry-style ska further afield. The European tour consisted of ten shows in nine cities – a second date being added in Paris due to popular demand. Accompanying them on the tour were The Urge, supposedly Coventry's answer to Joy Division. The five-piece had released the single 'Revolving Boy' on their own label before signing to Arista. Though not a ska band, guitarist and synth player Keith Harrison's familiarity with Dammers and others on the 2-Tone scene would result in support slots with both The Specials and The Selecter. Terry Hall knew the band's drummer, Billy Little, from their time in Squad, while John Shipley of The Swinging Cats was also briefly in the line-up.

Following on from the Ancienne Belgique in Brussels on January 12, the band made their way to Berlin, where they were set to appear at the Metropol in West Berlin. The coach's heater packed in en route. Though chilled to the bone, nothing could dampen the collective mood. Imported copies of *The Specials* were selling moderately well, and thanks to Chrysalis' promotional campaign the band were feted like rock stars wherever they went. This didn't mean to say they didn't suffer occasional uncomfortable experiences. The racism that often plagued their UK shows was just as endemic on the continent, as Staple observed: "There were a lot of racists in Europe – particularly on the streets of

Germany. When we drove through what was then communist East Germany to get to our gig in [West] Berlin, Lynval and I got looks that said it all. I seriously think some of those people had never seen a black man. There was a coldness and unfriendliness that I found totally alien."

The reaction of the West German Jabscos was the polar opposite, of course. Indeed, the adoration was such that ska-influenced bands sprung up in The Specials' wake in each of the cities they played, one or two of which are still performing to this day.

A Euro-pop TV extravaganza in Bremen saw The Specials and Madness appearing on the same bill. 'Too Much Too Young' had just been released in the UK, while Madness' 'My Girl' was riding high in the chart (eventually peaking at #3). Following the final European date in Cologne, the band would have a day's rest before heading out to America.

"I personally thought going to America was a dream come true," says Byers. "We all loved American music. Jerry wasn't so sure. I remember we hadn't been over there long, and during an interview him telling the American press that he'd had more fun in Russia on a school trip. We also had that whole punk attitude, which didn't go down too well with the business people or press. Europe was really good, but we started to get tired early on in the states, and that tour was the one that broke the camel's back.

"Being tired out and cooped up together on the tour bus for weeks on end hardly made us closer as friends. And our all having different tastes in music didn't help much either. I've since heard we didn't make any money on that tour. I know I wasn't told anything about it at the time, but I was hardly in the know about most things. But I wouldn't have cared. We'd gone to America."

The US market had something of a reputation as being the graveyard of English rock and pop aspirations; the more quintessentially "English" the artist, the more the likelihood of failure – regardless of their popularity and success elsewhere in the world. The Specials were the latest cocks of the walk in the UK, and with The Clash's new ska/reggae-fused rock 'n' roll appealing to more and more American teenagers, the band flew into JFK confident in their own ability. According to Roddy Byers' recollections, the strategy was to headline their own show at Hurrahs on West 62nd Street. Since opening its doors four years earlier, Hurrahs had garnered a reputation for booking UK punk and post-punk-related acts, many of which were making their US debuts. (It's also where Sid Vicious assaulted Patti Smith's brother, Todd, with a bottle in December 1978 while out on bail following Nancy Spungen's murder at the Hotel Chelsea. Ironically, the band playing on stage at the time of the assault were called "Skafish".)

Speaking with Paul Morley for *The Guardian* in March 2010, Dammers said he and the other Specials had landed in America brimming with a "passionate belief that their way of singing, dancing and dressing would storm the land", sure that their "combination of ska, protest and pop" was just what America's youth needed. Suited and booted and juiced for action in their shiny tight mod suits, shirts, ties and hats, they were picked up at the airport by a limousine sent by Sire Records. The driver had apparently looked them up and down before asking a Sire staffer if the band were all on day release from a mental hospital.

They arrived at Hurrahs on the afternoon of January 25 for a "meet and greet" with the US press (including a photo session with Britain's leading tabloid, *The Sun*). Paul Rambali and Joe Stevens were covering the tour for the *NME*. The Chrysalis press machine had been busy heralding The Specials as the "next big thing", and the band arrived at Hurrahs to find a huge crowd waiting. They were still trying to shake off their collective jet-lag, however, and this – coupled with problems with the club's stage monitors – resulted in a below-par sound during the performance.

Next stop was New Orleans, where they would be opening for The Police at the city's preferred punk hangout, The Warehouse. It certainly made sense to tag The Specials on to The Police tour – even if the boys had thought the days of opening for other acts were behind them. As with The Clash, The Police had ignored the notion that "only black guys play reggae" and were scoring transatlantic hits with their reggae-flavoured rock.

"New Orleans supporting The Police I remember because I'd always wanted to go there," says Byers. "Bourbon Street, King Creole and all that. The west and east coasts got 2-Tone, but middle America was still hippy flares and Seventies MOR (male-orientated rock). We went down well in Chicago as I remember. LA was weird, having to play two shows a night. We were already tired to start with and we didn't get much sleep. San Francisco was another place that really got us, but America hadn't really got its head around punk rock yet, let alone ska punk with politics."

The Specials went down better than anticipated, but the stark contrast in temperature betwixt New York and the "Big Easy" saw most of the band going down with head colds. The next stop-off on the itinerary was Norman, Oklahoma, where they were again to open for The Police. When Sting and co. cancelled at the eleventh hour without explanation, it was left to The Specials to salve the disgruntlement amongst those ticket-holders expecting to see The Police. "Our gig turned out to be even more interesting [as] the state [Oklahoma] seemed to be in the midst of a Ku Klux Klan uprising," Staple reflected. "There were state troopers in the streets clashing with demonstrators."

"The race thing over there was much worse than anywhere else we'd visited," says Byers. Lynval and Neville did get it bad. This was all over, even though we didn't play the southern states other than the show in New Orleans."

Norman, Oklahoma, might have been a backwater in terms of political correctness, but Oklahomans love their music and were fully appreciative of The Specials – regardless of the skin colour of two band members. The feelgood factor amongst the touring party was cranked into overdrive the following morning when Rick Rogers called to say the 'Too Much Too Young' EP was sitting at #1 on the UK chart, having shot up 15 places from the previous week.

Following further support slots with The Police in Denver, Salt Lake City, Seattle and Vancouver (the Portland show being pulled owing to problems with Sting's voice), The Specials headed straight for Los Angeles, where they were set to play four nights (two sets per night) at the Whisky a Go Go. They were booked into the legendary (and long-since demolished) Tropicana Motel & Motor Lodge on Santa Monica Boulevard in West Hollywood. The boys did all the usual touristy stuff, such as measure their hands in the palm prints of Bob Hope, Humphrey Bogart, Marilyn Monroe and scores of other Hollywood leading lights set in concrete outside Grauman's Chinese Theatre, spend an afternoon at Disneyland, followed by an evening hanging out at the Rainbow Bar and Grill. Another evening was whiled away at the Starwood, another West Hollywood nightclub where Rodney Bingenheimer staged his weekly Wednesday night discos. Bingenheimer was the first American DJ to champion punk rock on his show, and had reportedly been playing 2-Tone solidly in the lead-up to The Specials' arrival in LA.

Panter says the band arrived on US soil pumping "more adrenaline per square inch of body space than we'd ever had in our lives", but coming to America on the back of the

European dates was beginning to exact a heavy toll. "We were knackered by the time we got to LA," says Byers. "'Too Much Too Soon' was at number one back in the UK. You think it would have been one of those 'stand-out moments', and it should have been. But most of us were worn out and not caring that much at the time as we had been on the road non-stop for something like two years."

Local all-girl band, The Go-Go's, were booked to open for The Specials on the opening two Whisky dates – the final two dates being given over to another homegrown outfit called The Alleycats. The Go-Go's' rhythm guitarist was a certain Jane Wiedlin, and it was Terry Hall's subsequent dalliance with Wiedlin that brought about the lyric to 'Our Lips Are Sealed', which proved a hit for Fun Boy Three as well as The Go-Go's.

Had Byers had his way, however, the song might never have come to be written. "I didn't want The Go-Go's playing with us at the Whisky. I wanted The Stray Cats! I've no idea who made the approach to their manager for them to support us on the summer tour. I can't remember them having a manager to be honest! I don't even remember seeing The Go Go's at either of the shows they did with us. I must have been elsewhere, as the band usually splintered off when we weren't on stage. I was certainly spending a lot of time keeping to myself by now. Like I say, we weren't communicating away from the stage. And I was also having problems in my personal relationships, so I was pretty much preoccupied.

"Jerry had decided we needed to change our ska/punk sound around this time. Not all of us were convinced his new 'lounge jazz muzak' masterplan was the way to go, so the second album wasn't an easy ride, as you can imagine. By the time *More Specials* was released during the summer we weren't communicating anymore."

Panter has also gone on record to say the eight-show Whisky stint was the last occasion The Specials played together as a unified, cohesive unit. "The band that [slogged] through the interminable expanses of America had changed from the band that had conquered the Top Tank dance floors of England five months previously. We had run out of energy. Tiredness had made us lose compassion, not just for the people we met, but eventually for one another."

Unfortunately for all concerned, the Whisky burnout came midway through the tour.

While in San Francisco, the band took time out to catch The Go-Go's playing the Mabuhay Gardens, or the "Fab Mab" as the one-time Filipino restaurant was colloquially known. According to Panter, this was the night Hall finally fell for the elfin Wiedlin's charms. The Specials' bassist had nefarious intentions of his own, of course, but seeing his singer helping Wiedlin and the other Go-Go's load up their gear after the show was enough to tell him he should look to cast his net elsewhere.

Wending their way eastwards by coach during the return leg of the US tour only served to widen the fissures within The Specials. The pressure-cooker environment of living cheek by jowl would boil over in Wisconsin when Bradbury lunged at Rogers over the breakfast table and had to be pulled off by Frank Murray. The thrill of playing America had also long-since dissipated, with both Panter and Byers admitting they were simply going through the motions on stage. Even being informed Mick Jagger and David Bowie were in the audience at their New York show failed to raise an eyebrow.

Panter says that by the time the tour rolled into Long Island there had been a "closing down" within the band, and that the tour had all but reduced The Specials "back to seven individuals". News of a last-minute switch to a larger venue (Speaks) owing to ticket demand lightened the mood somewhat. As did having Debbie Harry introduce them on stage.

Prior to their heading out to America, Madness played three consecutive nights (November 16-18) at the Electric Ballroom in Camden Town; the third date being added owing to public demand. Support was provided by Bad Manners – a north London-based ska band fronted by the larger-than-life Buster Bloodvessel (born Douglas Trendle) – and Red Beans & Rice, a Welsh soul band who regularly appeared at the Dublin Castle and were signed to Chiswick Records. What should have been a joyous occasion was once again marred by rogue elements within the crowd chanting racist slurs and making "monkey" noises at Red Beans & Rice's Jamaican-born singer, Lavern Brown, during the band's set. Indeed, the abuse got to the point where Brown fled the stage in tears.

The band had been challenged about the racist leanings within their core fan base in an interview with the *NME*'s Deanne Pearson a couple of weeks earlier in Derby during the 2-Tone Tour. When Pearson asked them why it was that young men with either NF or British Movement affiliations were showing up in greater numbers at their shows, Chas Smash said how it didn't matter as to people's political leanings so long as they were enjoying themselves and not targeting anyone else. "Some of those kids are my mates, and they're good kids," Smash continued, as a way of justifying his stance. "I don't talk to them because they're in the NF. They know I don't agree with their views, and so what if they wear Union Jacks and Nazi swastikas, I don't care about that."

Sensing Smash was getting agitated at her line of questioning, Pearson kept at the Madness MC till he finally snapped. "You just don't understand, do you? They're just a bunch of kids who have to take out their anger and frustration on something. NF don't really mean much to them. Why should I stop them coming to our gigs, that's all they've got." It was a spur-of-the-moment riposte, and one no different to the line chairmen at football clubs up and down the country rolled out when asked about the hooligan elements amongst their club's supporters. Smash would subsequently claim his comments were taken out of context, the article prompting him to pen the lyric to 'Don't Quote Me on That'.

One Step Beyond was riding high on the UK chart when Madness flew out to America on November 21, but Sire were dragging their feet over giving the album a US release date. A relatively unknown act going to America with no product to plug flew in the face of UK music industry protocols, but it nonetheless presented Madness with an opportunity to steal a lead on The Specials. And Stiff hadn't exactly been idle in promoting the band across the pond. "There was a lot of excitement and support for the band on both coasts and in key cities like Boston and Philadelphia," John "Kellogs" Kalinowski explained. His allowing the Nutty Boys too much of a free rein during the 2-Tone Tour had led to his being hauled over the coals by Dave Robinson, and the band had felt it only proper that he be recalled to duty for the two-week US jaunt.

Aside from three dates in New York (including one at Hurrahs), Madness stopped off in the "key cities" (Boston and Philadelphia) before then heading out to California for shows at the Whisky a Go Go in LA, and the Mabuhay Gardens in San Francisco. As with the forthcoming Specials visit to the City of Angels, The Go-Go's were chosen to support Madness at the Whisky, while up-and-coming SF punk band Dead Kennedys were lined up for the Fab Mab date. *Rolling Stone* had thus far proved scathing of the UK ska revival, going so far as to dismiss Madness as being "the Blues Brothers with English accents". The eastern seaboard dates had proved low-key, but with California being home to an ever-increasing number of British ex-pats, it was hoped the Whisky and Fab Mab dates would prove a successful finale.

CHAPTER

How much Madness knew of The Go-Go's prior to their arrival in New York is a matter of conjecture, but sparks certainly flew when Suggs encountered Go-Go's singer Belinda Carlisle during the soundcheck. By Carlisle's own admission, she and Suggs openly flirted with each other throughout the day, watching each other's performances from the side of the stage. As with every other British act of renown, Madness had been sure to book in at the Tropicana Motel, and Carlisle and the other Go-Go's had accompanied the boys back there after the show to continue the party into the early hours and beyond. Carlisle wouldn't be the only Go-Go to fall for a Nutty Boy's charms, however, as Jane Wiedlin would subsequently admit to having a fling with Chrissy Boy Foreman, while drummer Gina Schock became entangled with Bedford.

The Go-Go's' founding bassist, Margot Olivarria, says that while the Madness show was "great", her favourite memory from the band's visit came away from the stage: "We had a wild party after the last gig, at the Tropicana Motel on Santa Monica, where most British bands stayed when they were in town. I remember that party so well because one of the guys threw Ginger [Canzoneri, the band's manager] in the swimming pool. She was incensed. She came out looking like a skinny, wet crow, her make-up running down her face."

Suggs was smitten to the point that on his return to London he began firing off missive after missive professing his feelings for Carlisle. Reflecting on this time in her life in her 2006 autobiography, *Lips Unsealed: A Memoir*, Carlisle said that while she'd enjoyed her dalliance with Madness' charismatic frontman, she wasn't about to allow herself to be lulled into false hope. She also says that her being an avid reader of the UK music press had alerted her to Suggs' relationship with Anne Martin, but she was clearly confusing the timeline of events as Suggs had yet to get together with Martin. Madness would return to LA in March 1980 for a second Whisky date. Yet while Carlisle was hoping she and Suggs might pick up where they left off, the latter maintained a respectful distance.

Upon their return to the UK, Madness appeared on *The Old Grey Whistle Test* performing 'Night Boat to Cairo' from *One Step Beyond*, along with a new composition, 'Embarrassment'; the Nutty Boys' stage show seeming incongruous within the sterile atmosphere of the *Whistle Test* studio.

With *One Step Beyond* still slow-burning its way towards the Top 10 on the albums chart, Madness embarked on a whistle-stop 10-date mini UK tour, culminating with a sell-out show at the Lyceum Ballroom on December 30 with The Bodysnatchers and Bad Manners in support.

Bad Manners have come to be synonymous with the 2-Tone movement without ever being a 2-Tone act. The band had originally come together in 1976 when Bloodvessel recruited several of his more musically minded school friends. As with Pauline Black, Bloodvessel was adopted, and might have remained ignorant of the fact had he not overheard his adoptive mother carelessly explaining the situation to a neighbour over the garden fence.

The band had swelled to a nine-piece by the time they signed with Magnet Records in early 1980. Their debut album, *Ska 'n' B*, would reach a respectable #34 following its April release. The lead single, the nonsensically titled 'Ne-Ne Na-Na Na-Na Nu-Nu', stalled at #28, but the Magnet hierarchy would have no doubt taken solace in the single spending 14 weeks on the chart. The second single from the album, 'Lip Up Fatty', reached #15, its placing no doubt helped by the band's comedic performance on *Top of the Pops*. It is practically unheard of for a third single from an already-charted album to achieve a higher placing than its predecessors, yet Bad Manners were inducted into this select club when 'Special Brew' reached #3 towards the end of September.

Bad Manners also appeared in Joe Massot's 1981 documentary *Dance Craze: The Best of British Ska Live*. The American-born Massot had originally wanted to focus the documentary on Madness after encountering the band on their first US tour while both were ensconced at the Tropicana Motel, before subsequently deciding to include The Specials and other leading ska acts. "My attention was caught by the goings on in the pool," Massot subsequently explained. "They looked strange with their pale skin in the California sunshine. I was interested because they looked like they were having such fun." Massot was so intrigued by the band's poolside frivolities that he went to see them at the Whisky. "They were amazing, and their music was so different from anything in America at that time. By Christmas, I was back in England calling Kellogs to tell him I wanted to make a film of his group.

This led me to Dave Robinson, [who] gave me a lot of encouragement and even offered to supply the mobile to record the gigs."

Just when everyone at Stiff's offices was winding down for the Christmas break, Dave Robinson made the decision that was to change Madness' fortunes – both figuratively and literally. Robinson, and his then partner Jake Riviera, had tongue-in-cheekily come up with Stiff Records for their newly incorporated label as "Stiff" was the slang term within the music industry given to singles that sank without trace. Though Stiff had moved on from the days when one of their act's latest single needed to shift enough copies to allow another act into the recording studio, the label was never more than two steps from financial meltdown. So, Robinson's opting to release 'My Girl' four days before Christmas with no marketing campaign was enough to have some of those in his employ pondering Robinson's sanity, along with their futures.

All the industry movers and shakers, along with the music weeklies, were predicting 1980 would bring ska to the masses – just as 1977 had been the year of punk. Madness might have wanted 'My Girl' to be their first Stiff release, but record labels tend to follow current market trends rather than listen to the wishes of their acts. Robinson could have chosen to cash in by releasing 'Night Boat to Cairo' earlier than the 'Work, Rest and Play' EP, or even have Madness record a couple of catchy ska classics.

Reflecting on his decision with John Reed for the latter's *House of Fun*, Robinson said how he'd seen how more and more young girls were showing up at Madness shows, many of them going moon-eyed whenever Suggs smiled. 'My Girl' – a song brimming with the lovelorn angst any teenager could grasp – would prove a perfect stocking-filler. And so was it was to prove. Aided by a throwaway, light-hearted video hastily filmed at Dublin Castle, in conjunction with heavy rotation on Radio One's daytime playlists and three appearances on *Top of the Pops*, 'My Girl' would climb to #3 on the chart, and in doing so introduced *One Step Beyond* to a whole new audience.

"Things changed with 'My Girl'," Suggs later reflected. "Up until then, I could understand what was happening, but then suddenly it was loads of girls, young girls, screaming, which wasn't what we were after. We became a pop group."

All successful bands are "pop", if only by the term's very definition, yet while 1980 would subsequently come to be viewed as the year of 2-Tone, it would also prove to be the label's high water mark. In hindsight, 'My Girl' wasn't so much Madness' initial move away from ska, but rather their first tentative step towards mainstream longevity.

CHAPTER SIXTEEN

TOO MUCH PRESSURE

"These divisions between us had been brought back to Coventry. The band was unable to go forward until they were resolved. Our problems were brought about by musical differences, exacerbated by the racial and cultural divisions that had brought us together in the first place."

PAULINE BLACK

CHAPTER

Madness and The Specials had both taken their respected cracks at breaking into the American market, so it was perhaps inevitable The Selecter would venture over the ocean blue to test the reaction to their take on the 2-Tone sound. With Chrysalis having released *Too Much Pressure* stateside, the band headed over there in April 1980. Upon learning they were set to tour the US, one might have expected the band to enquire of Neville Staple and Lynval Golding what problems they'd encountered owing to the colour of their skin – especially while traversing America's sprawling hinterland.

Despite having read all about the ongoing struggle for equality facing Afro-Americans – particularly through the writings of counterculture activist Angela Davis – Black says she was willing to give America the benefit of the doubt, believing The Selecter's music and style might "knock some sense into the meanest of ornery hombres". By tour's end, such quixotic notions had been trampled into the dust, as were the illusions of their songs being given an airing.

James Meredith and Rosa Parks had done their respective parts to eradicate segregation in America, but US radio stations in 1980 operated along stark lines of classification: there was black music and white music. Black's argument is that while crossover hits were not uncommon, such antiquated classifications largely held sway. And as such, 2-Tone's being music of Jamaican origin predominantly played by white musicians left the genre open to the risk of slipping between the two stools. It had been the same since Elvis had parked his truck outside of Sam Phillips' Sun Studios, of course, but being white and sounding black hadn't done his career any harm. The overriding problem facing The Selecter in America was their being a predominantly black band playing ska and reggae – two musical genres American ears only seemed to appreciate when played by white musicians.

The Police and The Clash were wowing US crowds with their reggae-fused rock, but while The Specials had fared better than Madness on their respective US jaunts, their being made up of entirely white or predominantly white musicians had proved somewhat confusing. The Selecter, being a predominantly black band playing ska and reggae-fused rock, proved more confusing still.

The further south the band went, the more their simply being black was to prove problematic. Black and Hendrickson already knew what it was like to have silence descend in a room simply because of the colour of their skin from when the band had played Trinity Hall in Bristol the previous September, but suffering such indignities thousands of miles from home in places where good ol' boys could shoot a black person and not worry too much about having to answer any questions would have proved unnerving.

While the band were in LA, Black decided to take a stroll. It was perfectly understandable given the sparsity of palm tree-lined avenues in either Romford or Coventry. With everything being so "first time", she'd wanted to take in all the sights and smells at her own pace rather than have the city flashing past a cab window. She hadn't got far when an LAPD patrol car sidled up to the sidewalk. The officers had received a report of a black woman walking alone in a "whites exclusive" neighbourhood. Their mood changed immediately upon discovering she was British, and having wished her a nice day they'd driven off.

A far more nerve-wracking experience came in Texas during a visit to the Southfork, the ranch that was home to the fictional Ewing clan in the popular US soap *Dallas*. *Sounds*' Gary Bushell had flown out to cover part of the tour, and with *Dallas* gaining an ever-increasing viewing audience back in Britain – especially with the latest season having just ended with the "Who shot J.R.?" cliffhanger – Bushell thought it would be fun to stage a photo shoot there. The ranch was barely visible in the distance, but the arched "Southfork Ranch" sign above the gated entrance would be a kick for the folks back home. Black and the rest of the band were busy striking poses for the camera when a flatbed truck came rolling up the dirt road. Several burly individuals sporting baseball bats alighted from the truck, and on this occasion the band's hailing from little ol' England wasn't going to save them from a beating – or worse – unless they got their asses out of Dodge.

Of course, that isn't to say certain band members weren't above shooting themselves in the foot on occasion. On being asked his opinion of America and its people during an in-store album signing in Greenwich Village in New York, Neol Davis opined: "They're just a bunch of idiots. Posers. They're not interested in our music, they just think they ought to be."

Things took a decided upturn when The Selecter were invited back to the Whisky a Go Go to play eight shows over four nights; the cherry on the cake being all eight shows were sold out. The US tour had ended on an unanticipated high, and it was hoped The Selecter could harness that euphoria for when they returned to England.

It was to prove a chimeric illusion, however.

Immediately upon their return to Coventry, the band returned to Horizon Studios to record four tracks, two of which would be selected for their next single. The four tracks were three Davies compositions – 'The Whisper', 'Cool Blue Lady' and 'Rock and Rockers' – and a cover of The Ethiopians' 'Train to Skaville'. The last single, 'Missing Words' (b/w 'Carry Go Bring Home'), with Roger Lomas having been reinstated as producer, had reached #23 on the chart, and the pressure was on to at least deliver a Top 20 hit this time around.

It was to prove a frenetic session owing to frayed nerves and fragmenting relationships, but amidst the turmoil Black took time out to get married. The breakdown in communication had got so bad that she didn't bother informing the others as to her intentions, and the traces of confetti and rice were still to be found in the cracks in the pavement outside Coventry Registry Office when the inevitable happened. The band had spent an upbeat weekend in Helsinki performing at the Ruisrock festival, but normal service was resumed no sooner had they returned to Horizon. The band were laying down the basic tracks when Brown flew into another of his rages and stormed out of the studio, saying he was done with the band. And no amount of cajoling would see him reconsider.

Within 48 hours of Brown's departure, six became five when Charley Anderson found himself being taken to one side by Black, to be told his presence was no longer required. He and Davies were still at loggerheads over the publishing royalties split, but with Davies penning most of the songs, Anderson's position became untenable.

Speaking with the *NME* soon after his sacking, Anderson presented his side of the story: "The Selecter were earning nothing," he bemoaned. "Everything was going into paying for the costs of touring – we didn't mind too much, because we thought we'd get really strong foundations, and in the end, we'd be a really powerful band."

The Selecter weren't the only 2-Tone act to see their royalties eaten up by touring costs, as The Specials had returned from their extensive US tour barely a penny ahead, but Anderson claimed the £85,000 royalty cheque The Selecter had received for *Too Much Pressure* had been frittered away and the band had still been some £9,000 in the red. Since signing with Chrysalis, each member of the band had been on a £100 weekly wage, but Anderson's gripe regarding the publishing percentage split was that Davies was the only member making any significant money. The way he saw it was that he and the rest of the band had been reduced to little more than session musicians helping Davies make money. Anderson's refusal to let the matter drop had brought about the impasse at Horizon. "The others told me and Neol to go outside," Anderson explained, "out of different doors. Eventually, they asked me to come back in, but none of them could tell me. Pauline's the strongest of them, though. She was the one who said it."

Anderson had long been striving for The Selecter to adopt a more reggae feel to their music, and he finally got his wish in linking up with Brown in the short-lived reggae outfit The People. The People would release one single, 'Musical Man' (b/w 'Sons & Daughters'), before slipping from the radar.

'The Whisper' (b/w 'Train to Skaville') was released towards the end of August 1980. Despite it barely cracking the Top 40 (stalling at a desultory #36), The Selecter's standing was enough to earn them an appearance on *Top of the Pops*. While said appearance failed to elicit much excitement amongst the record-buying public, their visit to the *TotP* studio was to provide a solution to the current plight.

Hendrickson and Amanor had picked up the strain at Horizon to see out the recording of 'The Whisper', but their respective organ and bass skills wouldn't suffice for the recording of the follow-up album Chrysalis were now pressing for. Sensing The Selecter could use a little help, Ian Dury offered them the services of his bass player, Norman Watt Roy. Davies had already penned two new songs that laid the blueprint for the second album – the haunting title track, 'Celebrate the Bullet', and 'Washed Up and Left for Dead'. The multi-faceted Watt Roy sensed immediately what was required on each of the songs. His playing left Black and the others entranced. It not only also served to highlight Anderson's rudimentary style, but brought to light the difficulties they faced in finding a bassist of Watt Roy's prowess.

The band placed ads in the leading music journal classifieds and fumbled on as best they could while awaiting a response. Having whittled the hopefuls to several potentials, a day was set aside at Horizon to hold the auditions. Black could feel the band was moving on both stylistically and musically but, as luck would have it, come the day of the auditions she was invited to sit on Radio One's *Roundtable*, the station's long-running singles review show; the format being two or three guests from the music world discussing the merits of that week's new releases with the host DJ (Black's fellow guests that week were Pete Townshend and Stiff Little Fingers frontman Jake Burns).

Black returned to Coventry anticipating the band would have held off from making their final decision over which of the auditioning keyboardists and bassists best suited The Selecter's new style. Imagine her consternation upon arriving at Horizon to find the decision had been made in her absence, her dismay being compounded with the realisation that the playing styles of Adam Williams (bass) and James Mackie (keyboards) were at complete odds with the band's chosen aesthetic – or at least the aesthetic she'd imagined.

The Selecter parted company with Juliet de Vie around this time, but rather than look to bring in a seasoned manager – one that might prove willing to curb the worst of the band's collective excesses – they instead opted to make all decisions in-house. The Selecter were now barely recognizable from the band that had started out less than 18 months earlier – and not only in the black/white ratio following Williams and Mackie's arrival into the line-up.

The irony surely wasn't lost on Black and the other founding members that in those same 18 months they'd gone from coming close to passing over 'On My Radio' because of its "Eurovision entry" feel to now looking like a Eurovision entry themselves.

2-Tone was still enjoying its fabled "fifteen minutes", but as with all "next big things", the movement's star was on the wane. Pop culture is as much about image as it is music, and even The Specials were beginning to add a splash of colour to their Walt Jabsco wardrobe.

For the first three months of 1977, Covent Garden had served as the spiritual home of punk, and now a new coterie of creative minds had taken to gathering at a new club called Blitz. These "Blitz kids", as they'd taken to calling themselves, included many future luminaries of the New Romantic movement, including Boy George, Steve Strange and Martin and Gary Kemp. Indeed, it was the Kemp brothers' yet unknown band, Spandau Ballet, that was to inadvertently sound the death knell on The Selecter.

Black says she, Davies and Amanor paid a visit to the Chrysalis offices to discuss advances for the new album with Roy Eldridge. It soon became evident, however, that they and Eldridge were at cross-purposes. Not only would there be no moneys forthcoming – at least until the band scored a hit at any rate – but the trio had to sit in silence as the head of A&R slipped Spandau Ballet's debut single, 'To Cut a Long Story Short', on to the hi-fi while proclaiming it the "future of pop music". She'd been struck by how the Chrysalis staff, who had previously worn black and white check, were now sporting tartan scarves or kilts. It wasn't until she saw a promo shot of Spandau Ballet in their tartan finery that the penny dropped. It had been the same with the A&R staff at EMI following the Sex Pistols' appearance on *Today*.

Spandau Ballet might have been heralding the future of pop, but Chrysalis were still harbouring hopes for an upturn in The Selecter's fortunes with the release of 'Celebrate the Bullet' as the lead single from the parent album of the same name. Taken at face value, 'Celebrate the Bullet' was a risqué choice for a song title, but Davies' lyrics were stalwartly anti-war and anti-violence. It was just unfortunate for all concerned that Mark Chapman would gun down John Lennon on a New York sidewalk two days after the single's release. The outpouring of grief in the wake of Lennon's murder was such that any act's latest release would have suffered, but there was little hope of 'Celebrate the Bullet' receiving either promotion or airplay.

Black still stands by 'Celebrate the Bullet' as a song and cites the parent album as being the best Selecter album, but at the time she was savvy enough to recognise there was nowhere left for the band to go; not so much their reaching a crossroads, more of finding themselves in a cul-de-sac. Chrysalis could hardly lay any blame for Chapman's antics at The Selecter's door. It was just one of those unfortunate happenstances that life throws up occasionally. Once the tidal wave of grief from Lennon's murder began to dissipate, the label would look at remarketing *Celebrate the Bullet* in the hope the critics would view the album in its proper context. Black says any hope Chrysalis' strategy might be realised were laid to waste with John Hinckley Jr.'s subsequent shooting of Ronald Reagan, the newly incumbent American President, on March 30, 1981, but by then Spandau Ballet and their New Romantic cohorts were laying siege to the charts. Realizing the futility of swimming against the tide, Black announced she was leaving the band.

The Specials were midway through their inaugural American jaunt when Madness embarked on a second US outing on February 20, 1980. 'My Girl' might have given the Nutty Boys pop star pretensions at home, but Stiff's limited budget restricting their means of travel to wheels rather than wings served as a sobering reminder of how far there was to go in terms of their being idolised stateside. The *NME* had posed the same question of The Specials that faced most British acts facing lengthy tours of the US: who would blink first?

Madness' first visit was more of a busman's holiday than a tour, but this time their endurance would be put to the test. From New York they would be traversing the Midwest, playing blue-collar cities Chicago, Detroit and

Cleveland, then on to the Pacific North West for shows in Portland and Seattle, before crossing the border into Canada for a show in Vancouver, then back down to the West Coast for a three-night, six-show stint at the Whisky a Go Go. Their travelling in two station wagons made for spectacular scenery, but would surely test the firmest of friendships. As Roddy Byers says, the east and western seaboards got 2-Tone just as they had punk rock. This is perhaps understandable given that the majority of American music labels were based on one seaboard or the other. Attracting attention in the vast expanse of land betwixt New York and LA was the difference between making and breaking. "America is like a lot of different countries," Suggs bemoaned in an interview with *Smash Hits*. "2-Tone goes down well in hip places like New York, LA and San Francisco, but Detroit or Cleveland have no idea."

The tour was arranged to coincide with Sire Records releasing *One Step Beyond*. The album failed to crack *Billboard*'s top 100, but reaching #128 was viewed as having made the trip a worthwhile venture.

Madness returned to London to find Dave Robinson wanting to release 'Night Boat to Cairo' as the band's fourth single. They were far from happy as the song featured on the album, and it would be they rather than Robinson who would be open to any backlash from the fans. This was the first occasion they'd had to question signing with Stiff, but a compromise was eventually reached. Taking a leaf out of The Specials' book they would release 'Night Boat to Cairo' as part of an EP that would also feature three new tracks.

To promote the 'Work, Rest and Play' EP – the title borrowed from the unforgettable slogan from TV and billboard ads for Mars Bars – Madness embarked on a UK tour. Surprisingly, the tour didn't include a London date. Following the opening date in Llanelli in South Wales on April 15, the tour would visit far-flung outposts such as Torquay (18th), Margate (21st), Coventry (24th), Blackpool (29th), Carlisle (May 2), Aberdeen (4th) and Belfast (7th), before a final date in the Irish capital, Dublin, the following night. The ads in the music papers made no mention of The Go-Go's' serving as support.

The Go-Go's arrived in London with little or no idea as to what to expect once the tour got underway. As they would be travelling separate to the headliners, and wouldn't be afforded the luxury of hotel rooms, it made sense for the girls to find a base in London. After several nights holed up in a low-rent hotel close to Heathrow Airport, their manager Ginger Canzoneri found a cheap but cheerful five-bedroom house in Belsize Park, north-west London. To meet the rent, the girls shared three of the bedrooms between them, and sublet the remaining bedrooms to two models from LA who were on assignment in London.

"I was pretty off my head at that time so don't remember much," Carlisle told *www.theartsdesk.com*'s Thomas Green in March 2014. "[Madness] gave The Go-Go's their break really. They were pretty instrumental in our success. We quit our jobs, sold everything to come over to [England], thinking we'd go back to the states big rock stars. We were living in a wreck of a house, lived on cough syrup, white bread and Nutella. We each of us lost 50 pounds, and I still don't know how that happened?"

SIXTEEN

There was no money to spare for luxuries such as alcohol. However, with every single bloke — and quite a few that weren't — making a bee-line to north-west London once word got out about a gaggle of good-looking American girls house-sharing in Belsize Park, the house quickly became party central. The parties got ever-more raucous, and though the police were out on occasion by disgruntled neighbours, the landlord was happy to turn a blind eye to what was occurring.

A support slot with one of the UK's most happening acts might have been too good an opportunity to pass up, but opening for Madness would prove something of a double-edged sword for The Go-Go's. The Nutty Boys had attracted a dedicated live following, with kids turning up at concerts emulating the band's quirky dress: tonic suits, Harrington jackets, Crombie overcoats and pork pie hats. Five girls from LA — regardless how attractive — were therefore largely viewed as something to be tolerated rather than appreciated.

Having to collectively get by on a pittance during the tour meant the girls' mood matched the dreary British weather. They were also expected to deal with the large skinhead element that had attached itself to the band. As with ska, punk had brought about a revival of the skinhead subculture that had been prevalent in Britain during the mid-to-late Sixties. "They were young, angry, neo-Nazi extremists who hated everyone, including us," Carlisle reflected. "Once they saw we were five little girls from Los Angeles, they yelled vile things and called us terrible names."

It wasn't only the barrage of crude, misogynistic insults that greeted the girls every time they walked out on stage. Punk had largely been laid to rest by the turn of the new decade, yet its most repugnant trait was still in evidence.

"Gobbing", as the vile practice became known, was supposedly the punk way of showing one's appreciation, when in actual fact it simply gave its proponents carte blanche to engage in one of society's basest of acts.

The stages at most of the venues on the tour were little more than elevated platforms. The audience would literally be within touching distance, making the girls an easy target. "They ran up to the stage, coughed up a wad and hocked it at us," Carlisle explained. "It was unnerving, and downright gross. I never saw the gobs coming, but felt my stomach turn after they hit. We came off stage covered in snot."

Being able to buddy-up with Suggs and the rest of Madness every night meant access to the headliners' tour rider. On rest days, however, they would be left to fend for themselves. "We were living on something like £2.50 a day, which was nothing," says Olivarria. "We were forced to steal milk from the steps of neighbouring houses in the morning, and we'd drink cough syrup from the local pharmacies because it was cheaper than beer."

The 'Work, Rest and Play' EP gave Madness another Top 10 hit, and while it came in three places below 'My Girl', Robinson's decision appeared justified.

Following a clutch of shows across Europe, Madness played several UK dates, including a brace of London shows at the Lyceum Ballroom with Desmond Dekker; the latter having signed to Stiff and recorded *Black and Dekker*. Just as The Go-Go's had discovered, Madness audiences wanted to see Madness. The Lyceum crowd was totally disinterested in what Dekker had to offer, despite his having proved such an inspiration to Madness – a fact sternly pointed out by Chas Smash after Dekker had been roundly booed off stage.

Midway through July 1980, Madness headed into Eden Studios in Chiswick with Clive Langer and Alan Winstanley to begin work on their second album, *Absolutely*. The album would emulate the success of *One Step Beyond* in reaching #2 on the UK chart and would spawn three Top 10 singles, the first of which would finally see Madness shed their ska coil. 'Baggy Trousers' could have been the title of a grainy black and white Ealing comedy Suggs and co. were raised on. Indeed, the song was so quintessentially British and timeless that it wouldn't have looked out of place on *The Kinks Are the Village Green Preservation Society* or, dare we say, worthy of being performed by the fabled Sergeant Pepper's Lonely Hearts Club Band.

CHAPTER SEVENTEEN

IT'S LATER THAN YOU THINK

"Our glory days were beginning to look like they might be behind us – the cracks in the band were starting to show. Brad and Jerry were arguing. Horace wasn't happy with the level of 'professionalism'. Roddy felt his input was being ignored. Jerry wished everyone would do as they were told."

NEVILLE STAPLE

The Specials were close to burn-out, both physically and creatively. Yet while 2-Tone Records gave the band a certain level of autonomy, when Chrysalis told them to jump all they could do was ask "How high?" Madness and The Selecter were recording follow-up albums, The Beat and Bad Manners had released their debut long-players – *I Just Can't Stop It* and *Ska 'n' B*, respectively – and a follow-up album was needed if The Specials were to keep the momentum going. "They [Chrysalis] started pushing for a second album as soon as we got back from America really," says Byers. "It wasn't just a new album, though. There were plans for a return to Europe, shows were being lined up in Japan, and we'd have to get back over to America sooner rather than later. It was exhausting just thinking about what was being expected of us."

The first item on The Specials' post-US itinerary came with a show in Paris at the Pavillon Baltard on Avenue Victor Hugo with The Cure, whose second album, *Seventeen Seconds*, had recently been released in the UK. Their latest single, 'A Forest', had stalled on the chart at #31, but Chris Parry and everyone else at Fiction Records were expecting big things for the West Sussex four-piece fronted by the enigmatic Robert Smith.

Adrian Thrills would be accompanying The Specials over to Paris to do a feature for the inaugural issue of a brand-new music/culture magazine called *The Face*. Thrills had promised the band they would also be given the cover, but when the issue hit the newsstands in May it was a shot of Dammers making his way up the stairwell at the Pavillon Baltard that graced the cover.

The show was marred by fighting between the fans who travelled over from the UK and local skinhead factions who were only there to cause trouble. There was also trouble brewing backstage between Dammers and Bradbury in the lead-up to the show. Panter says the row was over the latter's suggestion for a "2-Tone review, mixing ska, soul and reggae".

He'd thought it a good idea, but Dammers was of the opinion everyone else in the band should get on with doing what they were told. "Not only did The Specials bring together people from very different musical backgrounds," Staple opined, "the band forced several huge talents and egos into close proximity, week after week, month after month. The hatred was starting to bubble to the surface."

Dammers' ire wasn't reserved for his fellow Specials, either. But whereas Staple and the others were willing to put up with their leader's rants – at least for the time being – Staple's rude boy buddies Griffiths and Evans felt no compunction to suffer such tirades and announced they were quitting.

Staple was understandably devastated, but what he hadn't known was that his friends had an ulterior motive of sorts. Evans had been picking up tips watching Dammers night after night, while Griffiths had been teaching himself the rudiments of drums on Bradbury's kit between sound check and show time. The duo would subsequently form their own combo, 21 Guns, with Gus Chambers, the colourful Coventry-based singer/songwriter who had replaced Hall in Squad. (Staple would become their manager, signing them to his newly incorporated Shack Records.)

The Specials returned to America sooner than intended owing to their being invited to appear live in the studio on NBC's flagship entertainment show, *Saturday Night Live*. What should have been another stand-out moment turned sour the moment they arrived in New York. Dammers' aversion to pop star pampering was well known to anyone connected to The Specials, and he complained bitterly to all and sundry about the flash Manhattan hotel and limo trappings that Chrysalis had laid on. By the time the band arrived at the Rockefeller Centre and were ushered into NBC's studios, everyone was in a foul mood; the cramped *SNL* stage only serving to heighten the frisson.

Watching from the wings as The Specials snarled their way through 'Gangsters' and 'Too Much Too Young' was The Rolling Stones' perennially stoned Keith Richards. One can only assume Mick Jagger had passed on how good The Specials were from his having caught a couple of their London shows.

The song ideas the band had been noodling around with over the past few weeks were beginning to take shape. 'International Jet Set' had been born out of a riff Byers had started messing around with on the US tour, and 'Do Nothing' came from a jaunty three-chord reggae refrain. Byers had written a clutch of songs, but the increasing friction between the guitarist and Dammers over song-writing was such that only two – 'Hey Little Rich Girl' and 'Holiday Fortnight' – were deemed worthy by Dammers for inclusion on the new album.

At the beginning of May, the band, with Rodriguez, Cuthell and Dave Jordan in tow, headed into Horizon Studios to start working on the follow-up to *The Specials*. When recording the debut album, the band had played the songs as if they were on stage, but this time around the songs were recorded in piecemeal fashion one instrument at a time, via a Yamaha home organ that Dammers had recently taken receipt of. Panter, for one, felt the new approach to recording the songs alien and soulless.

Some of the songs that appeared on *More Specials*, as the album was to be called, were written at Horizon. 'Pearl's Café' was a reworking of an old song called 'Rock and Roll Nightmare', while 'I Can't Stand It' was fashioned from another long-since discarded tune. Hall presented the band with the lyrics to 'Man at C&A', his first effort since joining them. Dammers then added the second verse before setting the words to music. The band dipped into the Prince Buster back catalogue for 'Enjoy Yourself (It's Later than You Think)', which the latter had himself covered from the 1949 swing singalong.

Panter felt *More Specials* to be "laced with a beyond cynicism vibe", while Staple said how many of the new compositions left him twiddling his thumbs in bewilderment. Staple also commented on Bradbury's frustrations over Dammers using a drum machine on some of the songs, resulting in his stopping coming into the studio, whereas Panter enthuses about his rhythm section partner's willingness to embrace new technology.

Chrysalis were also pressing for a new single. Unlike Dave Robinson at Stiff, Roy Eldridge was happy to abide by the band's decision that the new release wouldn't feature on the new album. The song chosen to hopefully emulate the success of 'Too Much Too Young' was Roddy Byers' song 'Rat Race'.

"'Rat Race' came about from a night out at the Lanchester Polytechnic Students' Union bar," the guitarist explained. "We used to drink in there because the beer was cheaper. It's about a conversation I overheard where some snotty rich kids were talking about having their future mapped out by their parents. I went home and wrote it that night."

'Rat Race' – coupled with Panter's sole Specials composition, 'Rude Boys Outta Jail' – failed to grab the top spot following its release towards the end of May 1980, but #5 certainly wasn't to be sniffed at.

Keen to continue beating to the sound of their own drum, The Specials embarked on a tour of English coastal resorts. The "Seaside Tour", as it was playfully dubbed, was set to commence with a show at Tiffany's in Great Yarmouth on June 4. Although the 14-date itinerary primarily consisted of seaside resorts, the tour would also take in shows in the decidedly landlocked Leeds and Aylesbury. Support would be provided by The Bodysnatchers and The Go-Go's (the girls having stayed on in London after the Madness tour ended).

"The Bodysnatchers were learning to play their instruments on stage," Panter revealed. "Sax player Miranda Joyce was 17 and looked it. Rhythm guitarist Stella Barker was older – mid-twenties, I'd guess. They made a joyous racket, however, and fitted a punk stereotype by being 'only just' able to play their material. Musically, they were held together by bass player Nicky Summers. Their visual presence was provided by Rhoda, who excelled herself night after night with outrageous mini-skirts and tall hair."

Dakar was the first to agree that she and the rest of The Bodysnatchers were still finding their feet as they went along. "We'd never done it before. We all had the same sense of innocence. We all supported each other. [The] "Seaside Tour" was a brilliant experience as regards being a woman in the music business. Including the roadies and crew, it was the only time there were equal amounts of men and women on tour. It felt like a normal job. We weren't marginalised. In fact, as regards artists, women were the majority."

Dakar says her own band learned a lot from watching The Go-Go's on stage. "They were so slick. They'd been playing for some time; their harmonies were really polished. We thought, 'Wow, they can really play well.' We were blagging it basically, whereas they could actually do what they did."

"I was impressed with how tight The Go-Go's were live during that tour," says Byers. "They could really play, and they were also fun to watch. In those days, girl bands weren't very good mostly, but The Go-Go's were great! I still have a copy of the single they did for Stiff, 'We Got the Beat'. What I remember most is how they were all short in height – 'munchkins from the land of Oz', ha-ha. The audiences liked them well enough, but because they weren't 'ska' they preferred The Bodysnatchers."

Neville Staple had his eye on one Bodysnatcher in particular, Stella Barker, with whom he would embark on a fiery two-year affair that neither Staple's infidelity nor a police drugs raid on the toaster's home could dampen.

Barker had been returning to London for a Bodysnatchers show when her erratic driving – caused by her rage at catching Staple out over his womanizing and fuelled with half a bottle of Rémy Martin brandy – saw her being stopped by the traffic police on the M1 outside Daventry. Unfortunately for Barker, the cops found a bag of cocaine in the car's glove compartment. Discovering the identity of her boyfriend, the cops had descended en masse on Staple's home in Coventry and tore the place apart in search of drugs. Luckily, Staple wasn't holding, and the cops went away empty-handed.

Byers says that as he and the rest of The Specials were still based up in Coventry at the time, they were denied the opportunity to visit The Go-Go's in Belsize Park, but remembers plenty of partying out on the road. "Yeah, there was all the usual stuff going on, but sometimes it's best not to say too much if you were living in a glass house at the time – if you get my drift. It's pretty much common knowledge now that Jane was close with Terry – they both got a hit single out of it – but at the time they managed to keep it quiet. I also remember Belinda was lovey-dovey with a friend of Jerry's called John Jostin, who was helping out on the tour.

"It was a bit like a high school holiday trip, so as you can imagine there was quite a bit of romance going on. Seems a lifetime ago now! I have a few good memories from the tour, but it was not a happy time for me personally or for The Specials."

Byers might remember the audiences proving favourable to The Go-Go's, but certain elements within The Specials' fan base cared little for them or their polished harmonies. They just wanted them off the stage. "You can imagine they [the crowds] were not that excited about seeing a punk-rock band with American girls,"Wiedlin subsequently reflected. "We [also] got beer bottles thrown at us every night on these tours and then we would cry, and after the shows we'd go hang out with Madness and The Specials on crazy pub crawls, so there was a lot of drinking."

"Touring with Madness and then The Specials was hard work," says Margot Olivarria. "It was our first time on a tour bus and playing almost every night. It was exciting, even though we were the 'poor cousins' on the tour. I enjoyed meeting the guys, especially Bedders [Mark Bedford] of Madness and Sir Horace of The Specials. But the best was becoming friends with Sean [Carasov], a warm and funny guy who was on the roadie team. We had a drinking contest during a pub crawl in either Bridlington or Blackpool; it definitely began with a 'B' anyways. We were drinking vodka and oranges, and I guess I won as they had to carry an unconscious Sean back to the hotel.

"Sean later moved to New York to work with the Beastie Boys, and he also worked on a couple of Brian Brain tours. We still miss him and will always remember him." (Carasov committed suicide in October 2010.)

The show at Bridlington's Spa Pavilion was memorable for Buster Bloodvessel and the rest of Bad Manners invading the stage during The Bodysnatchers' set, while a stage invasion during The Specials' set at Hastings pier, due to the combined weight of the people on stage, almost caused the pier to collapse into the sea.

Roddy Byers' alcohol-fueled mood swings were getting lower and lower as the tour progressed. "I suppose if anyone was not coping, it was Rod," Panter observed. "It was plain to see he had difficulty handling being a Special and he'd try to blot out the problems with alcohol, which turned him from a likeable lad to an unpredictable and angry young man."

Such was Byers' unpredictability when in his cups that in the north Wales resort of Colwyn Bay he set about Dammers' keyboard with his Les Paul guitar.

The reality was that, as with the Sex Pistols before them, The Specials had become a monster of their own creation. It no longer mattered whether they put on a good show anymore as the music had become a secondary consideration, the shows having been elevated to "must-see" events.

The new album was completed, and with the Seaside Tour at an end The Specials should have taken an extended holiday – from recording, touring and, more importantly, from each other. Instead, however, they were given just seven days off to unwind as best they could before reconvening at Heathrow for a flight (via Anchorage, Alaska) to Tokyo.

Japan is a stratovolcanic archipelago consisting of some 6,850 islands, yet is compact enough to absorb musical subcultures with a fervor that must be experienced first-hand to understand.

"Japan was such a culture shock for all of us," says Byers. "We had toured Europe and America, but this really was something else! I remember we hadn't been there long when Rico got some 'herb' off a Japanese Rasta, which was weird enough in itself, but also very risky as I think Paul McCartney had recently been arrested for bringing some hash into the country around that time. The people were amazing towards us. I came down with a stomach bug and was seriously ill, but the staff at the hotel brought me some traditional Japanese medicine and I was back on my feet in no time."

This was The Specials' first visit and no other 2-Tone act had toured here, and yet there were so many kids bopping about town in tonic suits and pork pie hats that the band could have been forgiven for thinking they were back in the UK. The opening show at Tokyo's 2,000-capacity Konen Hall was a near sell-out.

Taking to the stage at 6.50 p.m. was a unique experience, as was the end of each song being greeted by polite applause as opposed to the lager-fuelled yelling they could expect in Britain and elsewhere. It wasn't that the audience weren't enjoying themselves, it was just the way things were done in the Land of the Rising Sun. It wasn't until the familiar jaunty D/G/C/D intro to 'Too Much Too Young' filled the air that the audience finally got into the swing of things, many of the kids vaulting over seats and surging to the front of the stage. There was even a stage invasion during the opening number of the first encore ('Nite Klub'), but even this is carried out with polite uniformity, with the kids leaving the stage at the song's end as if by remote control.

The shrine-like ambience that had greeted The Specials' arrival on stage had long since given way to a party atmosphere, but while the band were happy to repay the rapturous ovations with three encores, all was not well behind the scenes. The venue's owners were mightily displeased by the audience's behaviour. So much so, that it seemed this would be The Specials' one and only performance in Japan. Rick Rogers was far from perturbed by the threat as the press mileage he could garner from the band being unceremoniously "kicked out of Japan" would more than make up for the tour having to be aborted. Fortunately, the owners backed down from their threats to have The Specials expelled and the tour was allowed to continue on to Kyoto, Japan's former imperial capital.

Despite Dammers feeling under the weather, the outdoor, Hollywood Bowl-esque show was another rip-roaring success – even surpassing the previous night's show, according to Panter's diary entries – with the 1,500-capacity crowd's enthusiastic ravings proving deserving of four encores. Next on the itinerary were two consecutive nights at the Expo Hall in Osaka.

Regardless of the Kyoto show passing without incident, word of what occurred at the Konen Hall had preceded the band's arrival in Japan's second city. Panter describes the Expo Hall as being a "Sixties exhibition complex [with a] football-pitch-sized stage". Directly in front of the stage was a hydraulic orchestra pit, which could be raised to the level of the stage if so desired. 2-Tone hadn't yet extended to the Kansai region of the country and ticket sales were poor, but after much chin-stroking the hall manager begrudgingly consents to allow 50 from the audience to occupy the orchestra pit.

The band were slightly downhearted at walking out into a near-empty hall on the back of two fantastic shows, but they quickly shook off their despondency. However, the show must always go on, and what the crowd lacked in numbers they more than made up for with their enthusiasm. Their fervor soon got the better of them, and, ignoring the manager's decree, they began swarming into the orchestra pit. The pit was soon rocking… alarmingly so from the manager's viewpoint.

"I think the idea was to allow a limited number on to the stage but then stop the rest," says Byers. "As the gig went on, the kids ignored the restrictions and started piling on to the stage with us. Everyone was having a great time, but the guards started to get really heavy with the fans. Terry and Jerry were shouting at the guards, telling them to stop, but I guess something got lost in translation."

The band were helpless to do anything as the hall security stepped in and began manhandling the fans from the orchestra pit. When the house lights suddenly came on, the band stopped playing, downed their instruments, and vented their frustrations by hurling a few mic stands about before departing the stage.

The house lights were still on, but The Specials returned to the stage determined to finish the show. They blasted their way through 'Gangsters' and 'Skinhead Moonstomp' before ending with a monstrously cynical version of 'Enjoy Yourself', during which the majority of the audience joined the band on stage. The crowd refused to leave, however, and as the house music coming over the PA was barely audible, the band returned to the stage and burst into 'You're Wondering Now'.

The band returned to the dressing room to find that their promoter, Massy, had been bundled off to the nearest police station, having been charged with allowing 800 people to dance. Dancing at a rock 'n' roll concert – whatever next? This was only the start of the honourable promoter's problems, however, as the owners of Konen Hall had imposed a 12-month ban on his staging any shows there. The *Daily Mirror*'s over-the-top expose on the incident had The Specials facing deportation "following a concert riot", and the band had been detained at their hotel in Osaka after a "wild stampede by fans".

"The Japanese kids loved the band and were only imitating what they'd seen on our videos on television," Byers says of the stage invasions. "The local authorities did get upset, but I'm not sure how serious it was. I do remember the promoter getting down on his hands and knees and begging Jerry not to ruin his life, though. Me and a few of the others in the band were very annoyed with Rick for telling the British press that we were in jail, as our families back home got very upset reading about it."

The band arrived at the Expo Hall the following afternoon with obvious trepidation. And not without reason as the hall manager's over-the-top response to ensure there could be no repeat of the previous evening's orchestra pit-shaking frivolities was to draft in 40 local police officers to provide extra security. This wasn't going to wash with the band, however, and another compromise was reached whereby the officers would wear Specials T-shirts. The band agreed to the hall manager's insistence that the 40 officers sit at the front of the stage in the orchestra pit; the trade-off being this allowed the audience to come as close to the stage as they wished. "That was down to Jerry," says Byers. "The cops brought in to make sure the crowd behaved were actually paramilitary police. Jerry told them they would have to wear Specials tees and kneel in front of the stage so that the fans could still see us."

The band started off sluggish, but eventually got into their stride and a good time was had by all. The audience might not have been allowed in the orchestra pit, but no one had said anything about the ruling applying to the band. During the encore, Panter and Golding leapt down into the pit while Hall and Dammers made their way to the rear of the hall. The Specials brought the show to a climactic finale with a storming version of 'Nite Klub' (replete with newly incorporated extended intro) and 'You're Wondering Now', but with the crowd baying for more they played 'International Jet Set' before taking their leave. The crowd had made no move to leave, so The Specials returned to the stage for a blinding version of 'Man at C&A' before retreating for the final time. That's all folks. Oyasumi, Sayōnara. Even the hapless Massy came away smiling.

Upon their return to Tokyo, The Specials did an in-store album signing in a huge department store that sold musical instruments as well as records. Following the signing session, the band made their way upstairs to peruse the instruments. Byers and Golding checked out various guitars, Rodriguez and Cuthell amused themselves trying out various cornets, trumpets and trombones, while Staple made a grab for anything he could lay his hands on. Panter tried his hand at a double bass, but it was strictly eyes rather than hands when it came to the £12,000 Alembic bass.

The Yamaha rep who had dutifully followed the band in the hope they would come round to the company's proposal – to use Yamaha guitars for live work and recording for 12 months – was once again left frustrated, but Byers did come away with a blood-orange Gretsch semi-acoustic guitar. That he could pick up an identical model on his return to the UK for a fraction of the price didn't come into the equation. "I didn't care about the cost, I just had to have it," says Byers. "It was a Chet Atkins. I'd rediscovered my rockabilly roots – even before hearing the Stray Cats. This was mostly through early country and western, which I related to from spending too many nights alone in hotel rooms with a bottle. Funnily enough, I gave the guitar to my younger brother not long after we got back to England."

The Specials were set to play two shows over consecutive nights at the Shibuya Hall, which, like the Expo Hall, had a hydraulic orchestra pit. Given the problems the band had experienced in Osaka, they were left somewhat bemused by the hall manager's insistence the pit be raised to stage level. The Specials played best with the fans up close and personal, but with the raised orchestra pit creating a 30-foot gap betwixt band and audience, the performances suffered as a result; the second show being marred by the hall's security getting heavy-handed with some of the fans. The Specials, already jaded with how things were going, stopped playing and left the stage, refusing to return until the offending security guards had been removed.

The following night's show was to have been at the Sun Plaza, but the hall's management got cold feet and cancelled with something like 18 hours to go before show time. The band were happy with the alternate venue – a dance club called The Tsubaki House – but this venue fell through on the afternoon of the show. A second alternate is located, but while the Carnival was also a dance club, it lacked a stage. It was shades of the Hammersmith Palais benefit show of the previous August, with the staging arriving ten minutes before the doors opened.

The Specials played two sets at the Carnival; the first being filmed for Japanese TV. In his book, Panter bemoans why the powers that be at Chrysalis chose to film one of the London shows at the end of the 2-Tone Tour when the bands were worn out, rather than shoot one of the shows midway through the tour when everyone was on top form. History was now repeating itself as the band were leg-weary and beyond raising a smile, let alone their game.

When reflecting on the Japan tour, Panter believed the orchestra pit fiascos and inflexibility of the Japanese touring circuit gave the band a renewed sense of purpose on their return to the UK. Staple, however, says he felt the polar opposite; that the band were now merely going through the motions and bereft of any sense of purpose. "There was a feeling that we were definitely into an end game. I felt the light was slowly but steadily going out of the band. It had started to lose its soul – the very reason for being."

CHAPTER
EIGHTEEN

NO MORE SPECIALS

"Everything was a drama. Getting picked up at the airport was a drama, checking into the hotel was a drama, leaving the hotel was a drama. You couldn't get any space, not even for an hour or two, because wherever you went there were these lads who'd travelled 9,000 miles to see you live and didn't have anywhere to stay, so you had to put them up in your room and then you had to sit up all night with them - talking about the fucking Specials."

TERRY HALL

CHAPTER

The Specials were the vanguard of the 2-Tone movement, carrying the torch lit by Prince Buster, Duke Reid, "Sir Coxsone" Dodd et al two decades on. They had driven Japanese audiences to distraction, causing an excitement not seen since The Beatles' visit of 14 years earlier. British audiences had lost none of their fervor, and yet Jerry Dammers had decided the time had come for The Specials' trademark sound to take a left oblique. Their dropping older songs such as 'Little Bitch' and 'Do the Dog' from the set in favour of new material is the natural order of things in any band, but Dammers' wanting to experiment in what Roddy Byers calls "lounge muzak" left others in the band perplexed.

Staple says the aimless direction *More Specials* was taking the band in left him pondering his future, but the lead double A-sided single, 'Stereotype' / 'International Jet Set', reaching #6 on the UK chart following its September release helped to keep such musings in check.

Following its release in October, *More Specials* received largely positive reviews in the music media. The band's moving away from their ska/punk roots proved somewhat confusing to the fans, but their unwavering loyalty to the 2-Tone cause was enough to see it reach #5 on the UK chart (*More Specials* would reach a respectable #98 on the *Billboard* 200).

More Specials had failed to match its predecessor on the chart, but a second Top 5 ranking should have brought the fragmenting Specials together. Yet as they headed out on a 27-date UK tour in support of the album, relations within the band had reached an all-time low, the rival factions barely able to speak to each other; the copious amounts of booze and drugs that were now a constant feature backstage playing their respective parts in fuelling the deep-seated resentment. To add to their misery, several of the shows were marred by violence in the audience.

At an outdoor show in Cambridge, on the university city's Midsummer Common, Dammers and Hall were arrested for trying to intervene to stop unruly fans battling with security guards. The pair were charged with incitement to riot and subsequently fined £400 each (and £130 costs). The Cambridge debacle was enough for the band to consider whether to give up touring. "You're in this amazing, fantastic group making this wonderful music and you can't play it any more because people are hitting each other," Panter told *The Guardian*'s Alexis Petridis in March 2002 for the paper's Specials retrospective. "What started out as a big party ended up like *One Flew Over the Cuckoo's Nest*," Byers dryly observed in the same feature. "It seemed the police and local authorities had it in for us in Cambridge," the guitarist says today. "Even the hotel we stayed in asked the band to prove that the ladies accompanying us were either our wives or girlfriends – which they were!

"The [hotel] manager let himself into the room me and my wife were in and shouted at us for making a noise the night before – which we hadn't as we weren't even staying there the night before. I ended up throwing the bedside lamp at him. I guess they just didn't like young, socialist, working-class kids from up north in Cambridge."

Panter says he struggled trying to think of anything positive or uplifting about the *More Specials* tour while penning his memoirs. The bassist was living in Exeter at the time with his girlfriend, Jackie, and with the opening date coming in St. Austell in neighbouring Cornwall, he elected to book a hotel close to the venue (Riviera Lido) and have the tour bus pick him up en route to Bristol for the following night's show. Dammers apparently turned up at the hotel announcing he didn't want to do the tour. It was, of course, way too late to pull it now, as Panter was at pains to remind him. With the halls booked, and tickets sold, the promoters would take great delight in suing the band. "The inevitability of it all was, for me, very frightening. I coped by keeping myself to myself. On the previous year's 2-Tone Tour the band seemed to consist of three

separate tribes – hedonists, herbalists and sensibilists. Now
we had seven. We were adrift in a sea of our own celebrity –
promoting our new product."

A "product" he says took 20 years to appreciate. To his mind,
it was akin to The Beatles' *Let It Be* – the sound of a band
breaking up.

The auguries appeared ill-fated from the off. The support for the
tour was supposed to have been The Swinging Cats *and* The Stray
Cats, whose debut single 'Runaway Boys' would soon give the
bequiffed New York-based trio a UK Top 10 hit at the first time
of asking. Byers had finally got his wish, but with the T-shirts and
tour posters already printed, The Stray Cats gave backword. Byers,
for one, was left disappointed, and not for reasons one might have
anticipated: "I was kinda hoping Brian [Setzer] might need a second
guitar player as I was sick of the way The Specials were going. I was
also disappointed that they pulled out of the tour as I was looking
forward to seeing them play. But I doubt the skinheads and mods
would have given them an easy time. Their first single broke not
long after so they wouldn't have needed to support us anyway."

The music was now more secondary than ever. The Specials had
welcomed – even encouraged – stage invasions, but the invasions
were coming earlier and earlier in the shows. And there was
also the risk of injury or worse, with 200 or more drunken yobs
jumping about on stages that weren't designed to take such loads.
Such unruly behaviour could have been easily deterred, but the
band didn't want to resort to having a row of bouncers at the front
of the stage.

The second single from *More Specials*, 'Do Nothing' (b/w
'Maggie's Farm'; released as The Specials featuring Rico with the
Ice-Rink String Sounds), would get a mauling at the hands of the
music weeklies, yet nonetheless charted at #19 following its early
December 1980 release, eventually peaking at #3.

The Specials were invited to appear on the Christmas edition of *Top of the Pops*. In an attempt to inject some festive bonhomie into the occasion, Dammers presented each member of the band with hideous Christmas jumpers. The Beat were also appearing on the show, performing their latest single 'Too Nice to Talk To'. Panter and his opposite number in The Beat, David Steele, thought it amusing to swap bands for the duration of the filming. On a more serious note, as the two bands had yet to share the same bill, it was decided to get together at a later date to look at remedying this oversight.

In January 1981, The Specials and The Beat headed over the Irish Sea for four shows – Belfast, Dublin, Galway and Cork – with the profits going to various local charity organisations. The opening show at Belfast's Ulster Hall proved a memorable occasion, if only for the absence of violence in a city wracked with troubles.

Normal service was resumed at the following night's show at Dublin's dilapidated Stardust Ballroom, however. The Beat's set was marred by "sieg heiling" morons gathered at the front of the stage, and The Specials barely got through their opening number, 'Concrete Jungle', when those same boneheaded morons started lashing out at each other and anyone else slow in getting out of harm's way, resulting in the first of many interruptions. Hall and Dammers tried to restore order from the stage; the memories of what had occurred in Cambridge serving to temper their admonitions. The lull following the by now habitual stage invasion was longer than anticipated owing to some light-fingered scallywags making off with the microphones.

The *Record Mirror*'s Simon Ludgate, who was covering the show, noted how the strain of working themselves to death over the last two years was beginning to take its toll on the band; the energy was still there, but only on "reserve". It was Ludgate's tenth Specials show, and while he felt the performance somewhat lacklustre, the crowd were going nuts, their overexuberance finally bringing a stack of speakers crashing down on to the stage. Fortunately, except for a girl suffering a broken jaw, no one else was seriously injured.

The standout show came at Galway's Leisureland. Reversing the running order, The Specials went on first, and both bands went down a storm. The final show in Cork, however, proved a case of "after the Lord Mayor's ball", with the poor sound merely adding to the dispirited vibe. In total, the four shows raised in excess of £8,000, and yet the charities to which the cash was intended wouldn't see any of the money. Unbeknown to the bands, they had inadvertently contravened some Irish currency laws; the £8,000 was confiscated by officials at the airport in Cork and then passed on to the Irish government, where it was to languish for some 15 years before being split between the band members.

The Specials and The Beat hadn't long been back in England when *Dance Craze* received its official release with a lavish party at the Sundown Club on Charing Cross Road (later The Astoria). Panter says that while there was a "very negative vibe" towards the film from the "London 2-Tone posse" (i.e., Madness), he thought – and still thinks – *Dance Craze* to be a brilliant document capturing the very essence of 2-Tone.

Byers, however, has yet to see the film. "No, never seen it. It came out a bit late as the scene was changing by then, and most of us didn't even bother going to the screening."

Madness' lack of enthusiasm for *Dance Craze* might stem from Massot originally intending to focus the film on them rather than the 2-Tone movement. "My son, Jason, was 15 and very much into the music scene," Massot explained. "It was [he] who thought up the idea of filming all the bands. He told me about the 2-Tone movement, that ska came before reggae, and all about the fashions – pork pie hats and two-tone suits. I saw right away the impact that the bands and the music were having in England."

Ultimately, the band that was to have been the sole focus of the film ended up having no input with the project, as Suggs reflected while speaking with *Jamming* magazine. "We just didn't have any say in that film. That made us all a bit sick. Jerry Dammers did, [but] when we were watching the premiere, Jerry walked out and said he wouldn't have anything to do with it – and he'd been up to the editing every day.

"They should have taken one number from each band and given it to the groups to do something with. We'd have gone out and talked to a few people and had a bit about the history of the band. We could have done something a bit more varied than a live show."

Pauline Black's recollections about the *Dance Craze* premiere is that it took place at the Dominion Theatre, on the corner of Tottenham Court Road, but her confusion most likely stems from the Dominion standing directly opposite the Sundown Club. She also has the premiere coming the same day she, Davies and Amanor heard the "future of pop" at Chrysalis' offices. The Selecter attended the premiere, and Black was soon regretting her decision as the band sitting in the theatre stalls was a pale imitation of the one on screen.

The *Dance Craze* soundtrack album, featuring 15 of the 27 songs featured in the film, was released a week after the premiere. Thanks to the blaze of publicity surrounding the film, the album reached #5 on the UK chart.

The one-time Scottish promoter Andi Lothian is credited for coining the term "Beatlemania" while talking to a reporter at a Beatles show at Dundee's Caird Hall in October 1963. There had been other pop "manias" since the Fab Four, notably The Osmonds, David Cassidy and the Bay City Rollers. The mania surrounding The Specials was somewhat different. Instead of hordes of teenage girls driving themselves into a frenzy, The Specials' shows were being disrupted by mobs of "sieg heiling" skinheads.

a film by
JOE MASSOT

featuring

BAD MANNERS

THE BEAT

THE BODYSNATCHERS

MADNESS

THE SELECTER

THE SPECIALS

DANCE CRAZE

THE BEST OF BRITISH SKA... LIVE!

As with the Sex Pistols before them, the media's fixation on the violence surrounding The Specials had turned them into a travelling circus. Panter says that he and Dammers mooted the idea of having seven stages strategically situated around a particular venue, with each band member having his own spotlight. It was as preposterous as it was impracticable and didn't get beyond the ideas stage. Another plan was for the band to play occasional weekends, but this was also quickly discarded, if only because the thugs who were ruining the shows for everyone else were hardly likely to behave themselves because they fell on a Saturday or Sunday. One idea that might have proved more successful would have been to introduce identity (or membership) cards to gain entry to live shows, similar to those Thatcher's Tory government would contemplate issuing to football supporters at the end of the decade in the wake of the Heysel and Hillsborough disasters. It would have proved both costly and time-consuming, but would have nonetheless eradicated the problem.

The irony of *Dance Craze* being released just as the 2-Tone whirlwind appeared to be blowing itself out wouldn't have been lost on The Specials. Indeed, at the time of the film's release, the only acts signed to the 2-Tone label were the soon-to-be-defunct Bodysnatchers, The Swinging Cats and Rico Rodriguez. Rodriguez's debut album, *That Man is Forward*, was released in March 1981 (Rico's final solo album, *Jama Rico*, was released in 1982).

The filth and fury of punk had been assimilated into the mainstream within two years of the Pistols hitting the headlines, and two years on from 'Gangsters', the industry was gearing itself up for the latest pop phenomenon, the New Romantics. 2-Tone's black and white style had replaced the bondage strap and safety pin, and now it was Walt Jabsco's time to be consigned to the pantheon of pop fashion.

CHAPTER

Back in late October and early November, while Panter was exploring America and Dammers was holidaying elsewhere, Bradbury booked time at a London studio to record demos ostensibly intended for a third Specials album. With the multi-faceted Dick Cuthell switching betwixt horns, keyboards and bass, the sessions were to prove quite productive. Aside from cover versions of U-Roy and The Paragons' 'Wear You to the Ball' (later covered by UB40 on their 1989 album *Labour of Love II*) and ? and The Mysterians' 1966 US #1, '96 Tears', Byers' 'Sweet Revenge' and Golding's 'Why?' were laid down. Golding had penned 'Why?' after being set upon by racist thugs outside a Modettes show in London the previous July.

Two reggae instrumentals were also recorded, one of which would be worked up to become 'Racist Friend', which subsequently appeared on *In the Studio*.

Panter says he got the feeling the session was more of a power play, that the band could move forward without Dammers.

Byers had no intention of letting his new songs wither on the vine, however. "While The Specials were having a break from live work, I'd formed my own rock 'n' roll roots band, The Tearjerkers, with my brother Mark and a couple of old friends. So, without officially quitting The Specials, I started playing my new songs with The Tearjerkers. We were signed to Chiswick Records and released our debut single, 'Desire', the following year. We were together for about seven years but split in 1987 because we couldn't get a recording deal with one of the majors."

Although The Specials were taking an unofficial break from touring, they played sporadic shows here and there when the mood suited. A double headline show with Madness in an Amsterdam ice rink was followed with a festival appearance in Oslo alongside Ian Dury and The Blockheads and Toots and The Maytals, amongst others. A proposed show playing with Bob Marley and The Wailers in St. Lucia sadly came to naught owing to Marley's death from cancer in May 1981.

Panter remembers these shows serving to bring back the in-band bonhomie of their pre-'Gangsters' Heath Hotel days, if only fleetingly before each of them retreated back into their respective shells.

Britain was now in the grip of New Romantics fever, but The Specials still had to dance to Chrysalis' tune. The label thought it time to test the band's popularity against Spandau Ballet, Duran Duran et al with a new single. In an attempt to bring some of the feelgood factor the band had enjoyed while venturing over to Europe, they convened at the General Wolfe pub on Foleshill Road to work on song ideas. It was a magnanimous gesture, but one doomed to failure. The atmosphere soon became unbearable, with the seven musicians going to great pains to keep as far away from each other as humanly possible for the duration of the recording. Dammers got so frustrated at how things were going that he stormed out close to tears on one occasion and had to be coaxed back into the room by Panter.

Much of the first day was wasted sifting through the sample sounds on the Simmonds electric drum kit he'd taken receipt of, but the old magic eventually returned. Golding's 'Why?' was already earmarked for what was to be another EP, and so the first song to be worked up during the sessions was Terry Hall's 'Friday Night and Saturday Morning', set to a simple keyboard motif that the singer had come up with while noodling around on a keyboard at home.

The other song worked on was Dammers' brand-new composition, 'Ghost Town'. Panter remembers their playing the haunting melody for the first time, which had sent shivers down his spine; the changing key of the middle eight, from a minor to a major, then back to the minor key again for the next verse, proving inspired. "Neville began scat-singing over the descending chords of the chorus, and soon Lyn and Terry were joining in, wailing like banshees. It made the song moodier and very spooky indeed."

'Ghost Town' didn't set everyone's spine a-tingling, however. "I didn't even see it as a single to be honest," says Byers. "I thought it was more of an album track as it was slow, and you couldn't dance to it. But Jerry was adamant it was the best thing since sliced bread – and so did the rest of the band. But our days were already numbered as Jerry wanted everyone to sing and play exactly how he told them, unlike before when everything was a group effort."

The three tracks that were to make up what would prove to be the "classic line-up" Specials' seventh and final single were recorded and mixed at Woodbine Studios in Leamington Spa, with Woodbine's owner, John Collins, producing alongside the studio's in-house engineer, John Rivers.

As with the rehearsals, however, the recording sessions weren't without incident, with Byers getting so angry that he took his pent-up frustrations out kicking a hole in the studio door.

"I wasn't happy with things in my life or the band," the guitarist says in reference to the door incident. "Being treated like a session player brought out the worst in me."

The end product more than compensated for the friction, or perhaps the friction served to get the best out of the band. "The Specials had ultimately become a job," says Panter. "Turn up, tune up, play and go away. Jerry seemed more and more despondent, Brad blustered away [and] Roddy snarled. Lyn, Terry and Nev sat together looking miserable, which is why Dave Jordan named them the 'Fun Boy Three'."

"The recording of the three songs for the EP took about ten days," John Rivers told *The Independent* in July 2011 (to mark the thirtieth anniversary of the single's release). "I remember John Collins making only one suggestion throughout the session, but he did do the mix, which is great. I had all the misery – there were problems with people being 'incapable'.

"I remember vividly that crazy vocal bit in the middle – when Jerry started humming that at us we thought he'd gone lunatic. But he was a determined man, and he was right. It's genius. Horace, Brad and Lynval were the greatest rhythm section I've worked with."

Speaking about the recording process, Dammers said how certain members of the band had resented the "weird, diminished chords" he was using, and "wanted the simple chords they were used to playing on the first album. It's hard to explain how powerful it sounded. We had almost been written off and then 'Ghost Town' came out of the blue."

"'Ghost Town' created a lot of resentment in Coventry at the time," Pete Waterman chimed in. "There were outraged letters to the local paper saying, 'Coventry isn't like that', which, of course, it bloody was! I remember if we put prices above 50p [at the Locarno], nobody would come in, because they couldn't afford it. Jerry's lyrics were modern poetry."

While Collins got on with mixing the tracks at his home studio in north London, The Specials embarked on a mini European tour that was set to culminate with a sell-out show at the Rainbow Theatre in Finsbury Park on May 1. Finding herself a free agent again having been expunged from The Bodysnatchers, Rhoda Dakar would be accompanying the band out on the road to duet with Hall on 'I Can't Stand It'.

With unemployment spiralling uncontrollably towards the three-million mark, the Rainbow show was a benefit to raise moneys for the forthcoming Liverpool-to-London March for Jobs, which would see 500 people setting off from Liverpool's Pier Head and marching the 280 miles to the capital to deliver a petition bearing 250,000 signatures at 10 Downing Street. The show was a success for all concerned, with £3,000 being raised for the protest march.

Another benefit show – the "Peaceful Protest Against Racism" benefit show, staged several weeks later in Coventry at the city's Butts athletic stadium – was rather less enthusiastically received. There had been a spate of racially motivated attacks in Coventry in recent weeks – most notably the murder of 21-year-old Asian student Satnam Singh Gill in the city centre on April 18 – and The Specials headlined a bill that featured local ska act The Reluctant Stereotypes (now viewed as being the "nearly men of Coventry's ska scene"), The Bureau (basically the first incarnation of Dexys Midnight Runners sans Kevin Rowland) and "local girl done good" Hazel O'Connor, a 25-year-old singer/songwriter who had scored a UK Top 5 hit with 'Breaking Glass', the title track of the film of the same name in which she'd starred alongside Phil Daniels.

The event needed to pull a crowd of 5,000 or more for The Specials to break even, but an overcast sky coupled with anxieties over further racial attacks meant that only some 3,000 turned up on the day. The band were left some £8,000 out of pocket, but they could at least take consolation from the praise heaped on them by the city council.

The benefit show passed without incident, but by then inner-city Britain was riven with civil unrest following a series of race riots, the main trouble hotspots being Brixton, Handsworth (Birmingham), Chapeltown (Leeds), Toxteth (Liverpool) and Manchester's Moss Side. This wasn't the first occasion tensions had spilled over into violence in Britain's inner cities, of course, but with Thatcher having failed to take heed of the stirrings of dystopian unrest the Sex Pistols had warned about some five years earlier, anarchy in the UK seemed a distinct possibility.

"There are songs that capture the mood of a people at a certain point," Staple reflected. "Like a photo snapshot. 'Ghost Town' did that brilliantly. We released the song on June 20, 1981 [sic] and it went to number one for three weeks. During that time, Liverpool, London and Manchester burned."

Britain was indeed burning, but the pop charts kept a-churning and The Specials found themselves taking to the *Top of the Pops* stage yet again. But scoring a second #1 when the music weeklies were beginning to write them off failed to unite the warring factions within the band. The Specials were still occupying the top spot when they played what would prove to be their last-ever UK show, at Liverpool's Royal Court Theatre on June 24, 1981.

"I don't remember much about that night to be honest," says Byers. "We went through the motions on stage and no one was talking to each other. I do remember how most of the band were dressed in Jerry's new jazz beatnik-style clothes, and me being in my rocker gear."

The Beat had also changed musical tack on *Wha'ppen?*, the follow-up album to *I Just Can't Stop It*. While keeping ska and reggae at its core, the new album saw Wakeling and co. experimenting with steel band, dub and African tribal rhythms. The new album also saw a surprising toning down in tempo, a decision that didn't meet the approval of some fans.

Speaking with *Louder than War* in January 2018, Ranking Roger revealed the decision to write songs at a more relaxed tempo came from reading a fan club letter sent in by an American woman who had been driven to exasperation when trying to exercise while listening to the first album. "It was a lovely-written letter, so we decided to tone it down a bit in the way that the beat became what we call 'one-drop', where the rim shot and snare hits at the same time and that's the main emphasis."

The Beat had been amassing ideas for the album whilst touring with The Pretenders across Europe promoting *I Just Can't Stop It*, predominantly interesting headline news stories happening in the towns and cities they passed through. Unlike The Specials, where the dictatorial Dammers' approach to song-writing held sway, everyone in the band was free to pitch in. "Everybody would write on to somebody else's thing and a lot of the lyrics from the second album came in that way," Ranking Roger explained in the same *Louder than War* interview. "It was a great way to get stuff together and say, 'Well, that's a band effort.' Cause even like the smallest line from the drummer could get into the song. We used a lot of bits from headlines and stuff like that. It all came together and made sense."

For reasons no one can quite fathom, The Specials thought they could quell the mounting disharmony by flying out to America to play a string of dates in support of *More Specials*; the irony being, of course, the unrest that had riven the band asunder would be amplified a hundredfold within the cramped confines of a tour bus. The opening date was in New York at Pier 84 on August 13, with The Go-Go's in support. Bernard Rhodes, who was back overseeing The Clash's fortunes by this time, reportedly dropped by to say hello.

From New York the band flew out to California for a show at Perkins Palace in Pasadena, before then heading up to Toronto to be reunited with The Police at the latter band's "Police Picnic", lending their weight to a bill including Iggy Pop, Killing Joke and The Go-Go's.

At some point after the show, Dammers got embroiled in a row with Rick Rogers and sacked him on the spot. Rogers was soon reinstated, however, and back at the managerial helm by the time The Specials headed back to the east coast for three shows, the final one coming at the Bradford Ballroom in Boston.

There'd been no sit-down discussions as to what the immediate future held for the band once they returned to the UK, but Hall, Staple and Golding had been doing some plotting of their own over recent weeks. The first hint as to what was occurring came during the penultimate US show in Long Island when Staple walked off stage towards the end of the set. "The ill-feeling, the seething, the years of personality clashes, arguments, sarcasm, cynicism, egos and conflicts had finally made it to the stage," Panter observed. "The only place where the band made any sense at all."

Panter had no inkling as to what was occurring; he only knew The Specials had reached the end of the road. "Some of us knew it was the end; some of us wished it was the end; some of us just didn't seem to care."

"The fun had really gone out of it by the time we went back to America," says Byers. "I no longer cared about being a Special anymore, that's for sure. I just wanted to write and record my own stuff without being told how to play and what to wear.

"We were late going out on stage at Boston because Dave Jordan's heroin problem had surfaced again, and he couldn't be reached. The mood of the crowd began to sour the longer they were kept waiting. In the dressing room we were all getting a bit anxious, hearing bottles and glasses smashing on stage as we waited for Dave. We ended up going on with the monitor guy doing the 'out-front' and we managed to win the crowd over."

Dammers had stayed on in New York for a few days, and it wasn't long after his return that Hall called round to announce he, Staple and Golding were quitting the band. Within days of the music weeklies breaking the news about The Specials' split, Fun Boy Three were signed with Chrysalis. Rick Rogers would be acting as their manager, and Dave Jordan had signed on to produce their debut single, 'The Lunatics (Have Taken Over the Asylum)'.

Staple says a piece of him died the day he quit The Specials, and that the direction in which Hall would be taking with Fun Boy Three hadn't really been to his taste. He was also quick to point out that he hadn't plotted to break up The Specials; seeing as both he and Hall were leaving, it's hard to see how he could justify such a statement. He argues that Hall had merely showed him and Golding "a way forward", and that it was the steadily worsening politics within The Specials that had finally forced his hand.

When giving his version of events in the *NME* (the paper's February 13, 1982 issue), Hall said that while the breakaway had been planned in advance, there had been "no real point in telling the others [as] it would only have caused friction", and that some of the others had harboured suspicions as to what was happening anyway.

Staple says that once he'd settled on throwing in his lot with Hall he'd sought out Dammers to drop the bombshell. Dammers had remonstrated with him that things would be different if the band stayed together, but Staple wasn't for turning. Byers didn't even bother with goodbyes and threw himself fully into The Tearjerkers.

The Specials were over, and yet they weren't. Dammers still retained the Specials name, the band were obviously still contracted to Chrysalis, and he, Panter and Bradbury agreed to continue working together on a "suck-it-and-see" policy; the first lick of which came with recording Rhoda Dakar's song, 'The Boiler', with one-time Bodysnatchers bassist Nicky Summers taking Panter's stead in the studio. The "Rhoda with The Special AKA" single was released in January 1982 but stalled at #35. In contrast, Fun Boy Three's debut, 'The Lunatics (Have Taken Over the Asylum)' reached #20 following its November 1981 release, with the eponymously titled parent album peaking at #7 several months later.

The dismal showing of 'The Boiler' left Dammers, Panter and Bradbury floundering on the rock 'n' roll reef of ambiguity. When Rico Rodriguez threw the trio a lifeline to serve as their rhythm section on a forthcoming European tour – with the ever-attendant Dick Cuthell also coming along for the ride – they grabbed it with six hands.

What started out as a rejuvenation of sorts was soon to turn sour, however. There were problems over people getting paid, and the final tour dates being cancelled for reasons unspecified.

Back in Coventry, two songs from the tour – 'Jungle Music' and 'Rasta Call You' – were recorded at Woodbine Studios and released as a single. 'Jungle Music' received a sizeable amount of airplay owing to The Specials' standing, but the single's poor showing in the chart was a litmus test to how the music world was already moving on. Dammers didn't help matters with his sideswipes at Panter over his ongoing involvement with the Exegesis Programme.

Exegesis was Robert D'Aubigny's remodelling of Werner Erhard's controversial EST programme – the "programme" being a series of self-awareness seminars aimed at making those who signed up for the courses more self-assertive in their everyday lives. Panter had seen the effect the seminars had on his then girlfriend, amongst others, and while still dubious decided the £230 fee was worth satisfying his curiosity.

When explaining Exegesis in his book, Panter describes it as a "mental boot camp" designed to turn the negative traits within a person's psyche into positives. While admitting to participating in "quasi-religious techniques" during the weekend seminar, he insists he was never once offered Kool-Aid and was riled by Dammers' quips in the media of his supposedly "giving away all his money to a cult".

Relationships with Dammers became ever-more strained, but Panter and Bradbury dutifully turned up at Woodbine each day to work on songs intended for what would be the *In the Studio* album. Ex-Swinging Cats guitarist, John Shipley, was now a full-time Special, but Dammers' tunnel vision determination to outdo Fun Boy Three made the atmosphere in the studio unbearable.

Panter was becoming more and more concerned about Dammers' mental state and tried to get his friend to postpone the sessions. When Dammers refused, Panter used his new-found self-assertiveness and announced his departure. Though unable to shake the feeling he'd stabbed Dammers in the back, he knew quitting was the only means of keeping his sanity.

Dammers and Bradbury would see *In the Studio* through to completion and the album was released in June 1984 – under the familiar guise of The Special AKA. The album peaked at #35 on the UK chart despite it receiving positive reviews, with the *NME* subsequently placing it at #3 in its end-of-year "Albums of the Year" rankings.

As with other seminal bands that had left an indelible mark on British subculture, however, The Specials as a whole proved greater than the sum of its parts. The writing on the wall that was perhaps now obvious to all except Dammers was evidenced with the single 'War Crimes (The Crime Remains the Same)' reaching no higher than #84 on the chart following its release in August 1983, and the album's lead single, 'Racist Friend'/'Bright Lights' stumbling in at #60 several weeks later. Dammers' protest song, 'Nelson Mandela', brought a return to former glories, but this was to prove another false dawn when the follow-up, 'What I Like Most About You is Your Girlfriend' failed to break into the Top 50.

Ghost Town

Words & Music by Jerry Dammers

CHAPTER NINETEEN

NEW TRENDS AND OLD FRIENDS

"In the same way that we had crossed ska with some punk and rockabilly influences, the American bands cross-fertilised ska with stuff that was going on around that time. But the end result was, like 2-Tone, a brand of music that had serious messages, but you could also dance to it. It was pop with a conscience."

NEVILLE STAPLE

Rather than face the inherent embarrassment promoting an album that had failed to crack the Top 30 would surely bring, Dammers dissolved The Specials in order to pursue other interests – primarily helping create Artists Against Apartheid in the US. He would also be involved with the "2-Tone alternative" to Bob Geldof and Midge Ure's Band Aid supergroup in aid of famine relief in Ethiopia. Conspicuous by their absence from both the Band Aid single, 'Do They Know It's Christmas?', and the subsequent Live Aid extravaganza, Madness collaborated with UB40, General Public, Dammers, Rico Rodriguez, Dick Cuthell and The Pioneers to record the latter band's hit 'Starvation'. The flip side featured a host of African musicians, including King Sunny Ade and Manu Dibango, performing 'Tam Tam Pour L'Ethiopie'.

Though no less worthy than the squillion-selling 'Do They Know It's Christmas?', the 'Starvation' single was met with an indifference bordering on apathy by mainstream radio and only reached as high as #33 following its release in February 1985. The following year saw Dammers participate in the inaugural Red Wedge Tour alongside Billy Bragg, Paul Weller and The Communards' Jimmy Somerville, in support of the Labour Party campaign in the lead-up to the 1987 general election.

Horace Panter continued playing with his friends in The Mosquitos, the ad hoc R&B outfit he'd formed with friends while still in The Specials, before turning his back on music for several months to help his wife run her punk clothing cottage industry. Like all musicians, however, he eventually got itchy fingers, and upon hearing Dave Wakeling and Ranking Roger were setting up General Public (along with ex-Dexys Midnight Runners keyboardist Mickey Billingham) in the wake of The Beat's demise he called Wakeling to say they needn't bother advertising for a bass player. (The Beat's David Steele and Andy Cox would subsequently team up with Roland Gift to form Fine Young Cannibals.)

General Public were signed with Miles Copeland's I.R.S. Records in the US (and Virgin Records in the UK) and released their debut album, *All the Rage* (featuring a post-Clash Mick Jones on guitar). The lead single from the album, the eponymously titled 'General Public', would stutter to a halt at #60 in the UK while being completely ignored stateside. This came as something of a surprise given the success enjoyed by The Beat – or "The English Beat", as they were known in the US. When the follow-up single, 'Tenderness', also proved a flop at home, it seemed General Public's brief time in the spotlight was over. However, thanks to director John Hughes using 'Tenderness' in both *Sixteen Candles* and *Weird Science*, the single broke into the *Billboard* Hot 100. Not only that, but its success also propelled the album into the Top 30 (#26) on the *Billboard* 200.

The sun was suddenly shining again and the band made hay while they could, touring the US throughout 1984 and '85. There were high hopes at I.R.S. and Virgin that the renewed interest in General Public would auger well for the band's second album, 1986's *Hand to Mouth*. Panter says he wasn't surprised when the "rather sterile" follow-up failed to meet expectations, and though General Public limped on for a few months, when Wakeling announced his departure it effectively called time on the band.

'Ghost Town' had proved there was method to Dammers' lounge muzak madness, but Neville Staple says Terry Hall was already looking beyond the New Romantics with his vision for Fun Boy Three. He'd effortlessly morphed from punk to ska on joining The Specials, and so changing musical directions to mainstream pop hadn't fazed him in the least. Staple, however, says while he kidded himself at the time, ditching edgy, punk-fused ska for staid bubblegum pop had stuck in his craw.

Though speaking with the benefit of hindsight, Staple's claim isn't without substance given the somewhat mediocre reaction to 'The Lunatics (Have Taken Over the Asylum)'. But FB3's teaming up with sassy all-girl trio Bananarama on the band's follow-up record, a reworking of the 1939 jazz standard 'It Ain't What You Do (It's the Way that You Do It)', was to prove a masterstroke as the single was a smash hit, reaching #4 on the UK chart following its February 1982 release (simultaneously launching Bananarama into the spotlight). Bananarama would subsequently repay the favour by inviting Fun Boy Three to make a guest appearance on 'Really Saying Something' later that same year. The girls would also go out on tour with FB3 alongside The Go-Go's.

Fun Boy Three's eponymously titled debut album reached a very creditable #7 on the UK chart, but the release was marred somewhat by Lynval Golding getting caught in a crossfire between two rival Coventry gangs and ending up in intensive care with a life-threatening knife wound to the throat.

Further chart success came with 'Tunnel of Love' (#10) and the aforementioned Hall/Wiedlin composition 'Our Lips Are Sealed' (#7). The band's second album, *Waiting*, produced by Talking Head's David Byrne, received positive reviews yet failed to match the success of its predecessor, stalling at #14 on the chart.

Coventry's pop chameleon was already looking to a future that didn't include Staple and Golding, and it wasn't long after the trio arrived back from a US tour that Hall made his intentions known.

Ten years were to pass before a chance encounter on the streets of Coventry brought Pauline Black and Neol Davies back into each other's orbits. The Eighties had proved a cliched roller-coaster ride for Black. Shortly after leaving The Selecter she'd relocated to London on the advice of her new manager. The move was to put a strain on her marriage, but with the Blitz Kids having handed London back the bragging rights for the country's pop epicentre, the longer she remained in Coventry, the more likelihood of her morphing back into her former guise of Pauline Vickers and a return to radiography.

Black was still signed to Chrysalis, and so was happy when the label thought her talents worthy of a solo deal. In hindsight, however, she recognises that going with another label might have proved more rewarding. She began writing songs with Simon Climie, who would go on to enjoy a modicum of mainstream success later in the decade as one half of pop duo Climie Fisher. The songs were duly recorded with rising producer Bob Sergeant, whose production credits included The Ruts' *Crack* and The Beat's *I Just Can't Stop It*. Chrysalis, however, were unhappy with the results and Black's musical career stymied.

In what was to prove a prime example of Alexander Graham Bell's adage of "when one door closes, some window opens", Black got involved with the Black Theatre Co-operative, a radical new black theatre company formed in 1979 by playwrights Mustapha Matura and Charlie Hanson. She was invited to write the lyrics and music for the company's latest play, *Trojans*. Though the play received dreadful notices, Black's singing was singled out for praise. This led to her landing a speaking role in a play called *Love in Vain*, based on the life of the near-mythical blues musician Robert Johnson.

Having been at the forefront of 2-Tone, Black was enjoying being at the vanguard of an emergent black theatre group, finding "travelling from theatre to theatre like a travelling troubadour doing semi-political black plays" infinitely more satisfying than writing songs for a disinterested record company. Had she followed Horace Panter's lead in signing up for an Exegeses seminar, she might have possessed sufficient self-assertiveness to ignore her manager's insistence that she accept the gig as presenter on Granada TV's toe-curlingly hideous kids quiz show, *Hold Tight*, which was recorded in front of a live audience at the Alton Towers theme park in Staffordshire; the show's premise pitting two teams of school children against each other on a giant snakes and ladders board for free rides on the park's attractions.

No kids quiz show is complete without musical guests. Bad Manners had written the show's title music, and Black had to suffer the ignominy of interviewing Buster Bloodvessel (whom she had last seen at Horizon Studios three years ago) on the opening show. She also had to endure introducing Kevin Rowland's "raggle-taggle gypsy-esque Dexys Midnight Runners, performing their UK #1 'Come On Eileen'. She'd last seen Rowland on the 2-Tone Tour, and the latter's condescending glances were more than she could bear.

Dumping her manager and reuniting with Juliet De Vie brought a satisfying change in career tack, and Black got back to what she did best – writing songs of import rather than throwaway ditties in the Climie Fisher mould. Slowly but surely, she amassed an album's worth of material and headed into the studio with up-and-coming producer Adam Kidron with renewed confidence. A version of American soul and R&B singer Betty Wright's 1975 hit, 'Shoorah Shoorah' (coupled with the self-penned 'Call of the Wild'), was released as a single in 1983. Despite significant airplay, however, the single failed to dent the chart.

Black remained unbowed and returned to Basing Street Studios with Kidron and got on with completing the album. However, when the lead single from the album, 'Threw It Away' (b/w 'I Can See Clearly Now') sank without trace, Chrysalis shelved the album indefinitely.

Black turned her back on the industry and moved back to Coventry to salve her wounded pride. Once again, the storm cloud hanging over her came replete with a silver lining as she soon landed the role of Lola Lola in a new adaptation of Josef von Sternberg's 1930 film *The Blue Angel*, at the Liverpool Playhouse. Lola Lola, of course, was the role made famous by Marlene Dietrich, and so receiving a good luck telegram and a bouquet of flowers from Dietrich on opening night meant as much as the ensuing plaudits.

Imbued with renewed confidence, Black auditioned as presenter for the second series of Channel 4's fortnightly show, *Black on Black*, which focused on issues directly impacting on black communities – especially in the wake of the Scarman report.

While enjoying her second stint in front of the television cameras, Black was still contracted to Chrysalis and so had to play ball when the label looked to recoup the outlay on her shelved album by teaming her up with the newly redundant Neville Staple and Lynval Golding (Terry Hall having now formed The Colourfield with ex-Swinging Cats duo Toby Lyons and Karl Shale).

Calling themselves "Sunday Best", Black, Staple and Golding released the self-penned 'Pirates on the Airwaves'; the lyric centring around the return of pirate radio via illegal home-made MW/AM transmitters secreted in biscuit tins in tower blocks throughout Coventry and many other inner-city areas. A promo video was filmed at Coventry's most notorious high-rise, 9C Pioneer House in Hillfields, where The Selecter had pointedly abandoned their dilapidated Bedford van before boarding the 2-Tone Tour bus some five years earlier.

Chrysalis were so excited that they released the single (backed by Black's 'Streetheart') on both seven inch and twelve inch formats, but with Radio One and other

mainstream stations turning a jaundiced blind eye to a song championing pirate radio, the single stalled at #93. Chrysalis finally washed their hands of 2-Tone and dropped Sunday Best – both collectively and individually – from their roster.

1985 also started on a high with the third series of *Black on Black* being screened, even if Black found herself relegated to covering "youth and light entertainment" issues following the return of the show's original host, Beverly Anderson. However, Channel 4's subsequent decision not to commission a fourth series of the show left Black bereft of ideas or hope. Indeed, her melancholy was such that she fleetingly contemplated suicide by throwing herself under an approaching Tube train.

Black hadn't fully forgiven Davies over his dictatorial indulgencies having brought about her departure from The Selecter, but she was happy to look at seeing if they might reconnect musically. Davies had recently acquired a rehearsal space within the basement of the local Marks & Spencer, and the two got together to write songs.

News of Black and Davies' collaboration quickly spread, and they were invited to appear on *Later with… Jools Holland*. This led to their being invited to join Buster's All Stars, basically a travelling assortment of one-time Bad Manners line-ups fronted by Buster Bloodvessel. Following an appearance at Nottingham's Rock City (only their second outing with the All Stars), Bad Manners' rhythm section, Nick Welsh and Perry Melius, along with keyboardist Martin Stewart, offered their services should Black and Davies be contemplating reforming The Selecter.

Black maintains she wasn't privy to the behind-the-scenes intrigues that left Bloodvessel temporarily bereft of All Stars. However, given the memory of how Bloodvessel had taken great delight in making her look stupid on the *Hold*

Tight set by repeatedly referring to "grimble" (the band's codeword for amphetamine sulphate, aka "speed") during their interview, it's unlikely she carried the guilt beyond the one day of rehearsals the newly regenerated Selecter undertook before hitting the road.

By the time of Black and Davies' happenstance encounter, ska was enjoying another renaissance of sorts in the US thanks to bands such as The Mighty Mighty Bosstones, Goldfinger, Reel Big Fish and The Toasters.

Perhaps the best known of ska's so-called "Third Wave" bands are Rancid, fronted by Tim Armstrong and Lars Frederiksen. Rancid formed in 1991 following the break-up of Operation Ivy, the Berkeley-based Californian four-piece credited with being the first US band to fuse elements of hardcore punk and ska into the new musical amalgam, ska punk. Taking their name from the once highly secretive series of nuclear tests carried out by the US military in late 1952 at Eniwetok Atoll in the Marshall Islands, Operation Ivy released just one full-length studio album yet come to serve as the yardstick against which every other band to emerge from the Orange County ska scene is measured. Armstrong and Frederiksen's continuing championing of ska would see The Specials Mk II inviting the pair to provide backing vocals on *Guilty 'Til Proved Innocent*. Returning the favour, Rancid invited Staple, Golding and Byers to appear on their 1998 album, *Life Won't Wait*.

Though ultimately responsible for the latest stateside resurgence, Staple and the other 2-Tone pioneers were in total ignorance. That was until Ranking Roger was invited over to San Francisco in 1990 to perform with Beat International at the Greek Theatre.

The Beat's implosion back in 1983 had left Saxa and drummer Everett Morton at something of a loose end. They eventually teamed up with ska-loving singer/ songwriter Tony Beet. By this time, General Public were no more, so the trio invited Mickey Billingham to help form The Elevators. Saxa and Morton were clearly not ones for bearing grudges as they approached both Ranking Roger and Dave Wakeling to join them on stage on occasion. The Elevators had since undergone a name change to Beat International, and were on the road promoting their new album, *The Hitting Line* (released via Buster Bloodvessel's Blue Beat Records label).

Ranking Roger had produced the album, but as far as he was concerned the Greek Theatre show was simply another

opportunity to get together with old friends to relive
former ska glories. Walking out on to the Greek Theatre
stage and seeing some 15,000 ska-crazy kids rise up in
unison was enough to convince Ranking Roger that the
time had come to perhaps call upon some other old friends
back in England.

Staple says he couldn't believe what his friend was
telling him upon his return, but being at a loose end he
was happy to get on board. "America had gone bonkers
for ska," he reflected. "The surfing community in [Orange
County] California were all into 2-Tone, and in New York
there was a massive scene. Boston had some great bands,
and even Texas had its network of ska fans. We had blinked
and missed all of this."

Time was of the essence, and as Staple was the first
person Ranking Roger had approached, they quickly
decided to concentrate on bringing in musicians to play
Beat and Specials numbers, while calling themselves
Special Beat. Bradbury and Panter both readily agreed.
(Golding would also get involved at a later date.)

The US tour proved such a success that Special Beat decided
to continue. "We made a good living playing our old repertoire
to [mainly] Americans who had finally got wise to the music
we had played ten years previously," says Panter. "It was really a
glorified tribute band, but we had a lot of fun and played some
very exciting concerts. We toured America for three months
solid in 1991."

With ska making waves again, it was inevitable that record
companies would get in on the action. In 1993, Trojan Records
called on Roger Lomas to give Desmond Dekker's latest
album a ska twist. Lomas hit upon the idea of having Dekker
collaborate with The Specials and record an album of ska and

reggae covers. The Specials hadn't been in the same room together since their being backstage at the Bradford Ballroom in Boston twelve years earlier, so Lomas was deluding himself if he thought he could tempt the seven into working together again. And so it proved. Hall wanted nothing whatsoever to do with the project as he was occupied working with Dave Stewart. Staple, Golding, Byers and Panter (even though he'd recently graduated from a teacher-training course as a qualified teacher) were amenable to burying past differences, but Dammers remained unmoved, going so far as to seek legal advice over ownership of the Specials name.

Though happy to play with Special Beat, Bradbury surprisingly opted out of the "reunion", deciding to give up drums altogether to work in the regular "9-5" world as a computer programmer.

Staple says that having four out of the seven Specials on board justified the decision, but Trojan remained unconvinced as to Staple's logic and issued the album, *King of Kings*, as Desmond Dekker and The Specials.

The album didn't do Desmond Dekker's career any favours, but its tantalising title caused something of a stir in Japan. Lomas called Staple and the other Specials who had featured on the album to say a Japanese promoter was offering a sizeable chunk of money to bring the band over to Japan. With Hall and Dammers still steadfastly disinterested, and Bradbury happy living a life of normality, Aitch Bembridge was drafted in on drums, and Mark Adams and Adam Birch joined on keyboards and trombone, respectively.

It was originally decided to go out as The Coventry Specials so as to minimise the risk of Dammers renewing his legal challenge. It was perhaps to be expected that promoters would drop the "Coventry" from the billing, and with their one-time leader maintaining radio silence, the band were happy to throw caution to the wind (though between themselves they referred to the band as "The Specials Mk II").

The reconstituted Specials were content wowing audiences by running through classics and crowd favourites, but in 1996 they returned to the studio to record an album of covers – *Today's Specials*. It was to prove an eclectic mix: Ewan MacColl's 'Dirty Old Town', Desmond Dekker's 'Shanty Town 007', The Clash's 'Somebody Got Murdered', and perhaps strangest of all, Neil Diamond's 'A Little Bit Me, A Little Bit You'. The band signed a deal with Kuff Records, a Virgin subsidiary set up by UB40's Ali Campbell.

The Specials returning to the recording studio should have been a mouth-watering prospect for fans both old and new – even without Dammers, Hall and Bradbury – and would surely have proved one had the band thought to pen some original material to go alongside the covers.

"I'd formed a punk/rockabilly outfit called The Bonediggers, and I was doing that right up to when The Specials reformed," says Byers. "Well, four of us from the classic line-up did anyways: Neville, Lynval, Horace and me. We toured for four years, mostly in the states, and recorded two albums. The first, *Today's Specials*, was a covers album, but the second, *Guilty 'Til Proved Innocent*, was made up of new songs, four of which were mine. When we called it a day in 1998, I formed The Skabilly Rebels. I've been playing with the Rebels ever since, even while I was playing with the last Specials line-up between 2009 and 2013. I quit for all the usual reasons.

"Looking back now it does seem that 2-Tone broke overnight, but we played anywhere and everywhere for two years before it broke, mostly the back rooms of pubs and small clubs. We also got occasional support slots with whoever would have us – Generation X, Sham 69, etc., etc. I suppose it was once we became The Specials and switched to a more ska-based sound and a mod/rude boy image that things really started happening. We were in the right place at the right time, but it also took a lot of hard work. There was also a bit of luck involved. There was a mod revival going on around the same time because of *Quadrophenia*, so we fitted nicely into that scene as well. We also had John Peel, a few other DJ's, and some other music rebels pushing 'Gangsters' for us, which gave us our first hit and set us on our way."

Today's Specials was roundly criticised following its release in May 1996, yet despite this, Trojan Records commissioned Roger Lomas to take The Selecter into the studio to record three covers albums from the label's back catalogue. By this juncture, The Selecter had undergone further line-up changes – primarily the departure of Neol Davies and Gaps Hendrickson's return. The band had recorded two more studio albums, *The Happy Album* (July 1994) and *Pucker* (August 1995). Neither had troubled the UK chart, but with the band still pulling sizeable crowds wherever they played, Trojan were convinced the covers albums would bring a profitable return given that they owned the licences on the original recordings. The resulting albums were *The Trojan Songbook* (1999), *The Trojan Songbook II* (2000) and *The Trojan Songbook III* (2001).

Lomas would subsequently call upon The Specials to dip into the Trojan goody bag for *Skinhead Girl* (October 2000) and *Conquering Ruler* (February 2001). Golding had little interest in recording ska standards and pulled out of the recording to spend time with his girlfriend in Seattle. His replacement in the studio was Neol Davies. Sandwiched betwixt the two run-of-the-mill covers releases, however, the band (with Golding returning for duty) recorded an album of original material via a one-off album deal with MCA. *Guilty 'Til Proved Innocent* would also fail to trouble the chart, but was treated kindlier than either of the covers albums by the critics.

Staple takes credit for his songs proving sufficient to garner MCA's interest, and says that after the injustice of not having received rightful recognition for his contribution to The Specials' canon, he was now ready to put his song-writing talents in the firing line. Given that his composition 'It's You' was the sole single culled from *Guilty 'Til Proved Innocent*, his boast is somewhat justified. What wasn't quite so defensible, perhaps, was his assuming the mantel of band leader.

Golding's loyalty towards Staple was probably to be expected, but for Panter and Byers – especially Byers – being dictated to a second time around quickly became a bone of contention. Careful not to name names, Staple says taking control "kicked off a bit of a whispering campaign" against him, which soon escalated to heated face-to-face confrontations. The Specials Mk II were on tour in the US at the time, and the pressure finally got to Staple in Chicago. According to *Rolling Stone*'s version of the truth – accompanying its "Specials Singer Gets Rude & Arrested in Chicago" banner headline – Staple got into an argument with one of the production crew, which boiled over into his attacking the crew member with a bar stool and grabbing him by the throat. Staple was charged with a "simple battery misdemeanour" and was facing the possibility of jail time had the case not been eventually dropped for lack of evidence.

Staple's arrest, coupled with the lingering court case, did little to ease the internal wrangling and matters finally came to a head in late 1998 when Panter, Byers and Golding announced they were quitting.

Staple set up an operating base in California, primarily so that he could check out the emerging talent on the Orange County ska scene. He missed performing, however; the thrill of walking out on stage to the adoration of the crowd. When he returned to Britain in 1999 he had just one thing on his mind: to seek out musicians for his own band. The musicians were soon located, if only because they were all playing together in the same band. And so, for the second time in five years, the hapless Buster Bloodvessel was powerless to stop his All Stars abandoning him for the greener pastures of the Neville Staple Band.

Ska's "third wave" riptide was showing little sign of dissipating anytime soon in the US, but it was a different story in the UK. 2-Tone was seen – if it was seen at all – as an archaic throwback, with Walt Jabsco's tonic suit akin to Miss Havisham's fabled wedding dress.
As such, carrying the 2-Tone flame singlehandedly into the twenty-first century initially proved a daunting and thankless task, but gradually interest and audience numbers began to swell.

Year after year, Staple toured the world introducing 2-Tone to a whole new audience, occasionally sharing the billing with Ranking Roger's reconstituted line-up of The Beat.

By 2007, Golding had turned his back on music and was enjoying life in Seattle as a stay-at-home father when Lily Allen called out of the blue, asking if he'd like to join her on stage at that year's Glastonbury. The initial idea was for Golding to perform 'Blank Expression' with Allen, but it ended up with Terry Hall getting in on the action for an airing of 'Gangsters'. And it was seeing the reaction of those festival-goers too young to remember The Specials first time around that got him to thinking maybe it was time to look at reforming the band. Later in the day the two got together with Damon Albarn for a beatbox rendition of 'A Message to You, Rudy'. Following the official announcement that The Specials were reforming in May 2009, Golding paid tribute to Allen for playing a "massive part" in bringing about the reformation.

Behind the scenes, Golding quietly set about sounding out the other ex-Specials about the possibility of an anniversary reunion. According to Staple, all seven ex-Specials got together for "clear-the-air" talks in September 2007. He hadn't spoken with Hall since their Fun Boy Three days, and his having to drop his publishing battle with Dammers because of spiralling legal costs had also left a bitter aftertaste. The meeting was doomed from the off, largely due to Dammers' insistence that any reunion should be to take The Specials forward by playing new material rather than churning out the classics. Unsurprisingly, finding themselves on the receiving end of another of Dammers' high-handed edicts had stirred up old and unpleasant memories. Further meetings followed, but again, nothing of any consequence was resolved.

Nothing sells quite like nostalgia, as the saying goes, and although nothing had come of the get-togethers, the "will they, won't they" stories about a Specials reformation persisted in the media. In March 2008, Specials fans finally heard the news they'd been waiting for. Speaking with the BBC, Hall confirmed the band would be going out on the road some time during the following autumn. "We're still trying to put dates together," he revealed, "but hopefully September/October time. We need to spend the summer rehearsing. I think it's taken me 30 years to realise we could do it really well. You do it with dignity or don't do it at all."

Staple, of course, was already working with Dammers again by this juncture. There'd been no fuss or fanfare when Dammers began DJing at Staple's shows. To the uninitiated, the unobtrusive bearded and beshaded figure manning the DJ booth was applauded for his impressive and wide-ranging collection of ska records, but to those in the know, the trademark gap-toothed grin needed no introduction.

Dammers' continuing refusal to countenance a Specials "greatest hits" tour was the sole stumbling block holding back the reunion, but Staple says he was honoured when Dammers agreed to join Staple's band on stage at a July show at the Astoria (the same London venue where *Dance Craze* had received its premiere 27 years earlier). Imagine Staple's surprise when instead of taking his place behind the keyboards as expected, Dammers grabbed a mic and proceeded to rant about Terry Hall to the bemused crowd.

Dammers' public dissing of Hall at the Astoria killed any notion of the classic Specials line-up ever taking to a stage again. Despite having his stage stolen that night, Staple remained on cordial terms with Dammers. He also continued to believe the mooted thirtieth anniversary reunion wouldn't be complete without Dammers' involvement.

There would be plenty of soul-searching, and not only regarding his loyalty towards Dammers. The Neville Staple Band was pulling in the crowds, and while he was predominantly performing Specials and Fun Boy Three numbers, he felt he had come into his own as a frontman, and the prospect of being relegated to second fiddle again didn't sit lightly. However, when Hall and Golding called to say the band would be getting together for the anniversary tour, Staple knew the time for fence-sitting was at an end. The decision would weigh heavily on his conscience for some time to come, but in the end there really was only one way to go.

In the wake of the news that The Specials were to reform for a thirtieth anniversary tour without him, an official statement was issued to the media on Dammers' behalf, in which he hit out at one-time bandmates for attempting to "rewrite history". Having pronounced Dammers as having been the "main songwriter and driving force" behind the band's success, the statement then revealed the true situation: that not only had he not been invited to take part in the tour, he'd been purposely kept out of all negotiations, before going on to say that while the other band members had insisted the "door was still open" to Dammers, they had "failed to mention his being driven out every time he has attempted to get involved".

The statement concluded by saying how Dammers didn't believe the reunion shows represented what the "real Specials" stood for "politically, or in terms of creativity, imagination or forwardness of ideas".

The Specials' thirtieth anniversary tour was the most anticipated reunion since the Sex Pistols' Filthy Lucre Tour of 13 years earlier, but a taster of what the fans could expect on the tour came with the band making a surprise appearance on the main stage at the 2008 Bestival on the Isle of Wight. Owing to the ongoing legal wrangling with Dammers over the Specials name, they were billed as "Terry Hall and Friends". It was the first time the band had been on the same stage in 27 years.

The 2009 tour commenced with a show at Newcastle's O2 Academy on April 22. The clamour for tickets was incredible, and each show could have been sold three times over. Speaking with the *NME* following the announcement, Hall said how the band had talked about getting together to mark the twenty-fifth anniversary but had decided against it; they "weren't together enough, [but] now we're all getting on and it feels comfortable again". When asked to comment on Dammers' absence, Hall said the door "remained open".

Speaking with *entertainment.ie* in November 2009, Golding said how he'd read an article in that month's *Word* magazine in which Dammers had seen one of the shows and had come away again unimpressed. "I think he's the only one in the country who's seen us who's saying we're not as good as we should be. We just laughed at that. I think the band has been absolutely fantastic. It's been great. From a musical point of view, we've all grown so much, y'know? It's absolutely brilliant."

While his one-time comrades in arms got on with rehearsing for the reunion shows, Dammers looked to his own Specials-related project, The Spatial AKA Orchestra, which would boast

MOBO award-winning tenor and soprano saxophonist Denys Baptiste, flautist Finn Peters, the multi-faceted Terry Edwards on baritone sax, Trinidadian poet Anthony Joseph, Jamaican crooner Cornell Campbell, and vibraphone virtuoso Roger Beaujolais.

It truly is a spectacle to behold, with Dammers and the other musicians rigged out in African robes and Egyptian masks, sharing a stage with sphinxes, futuristic mannequins and what appears to be a spaceship fashioned from a motorcycle sidecar. There is logic behind Dammers' seemingly bizarre taste in costumery and stage props as the music of Saturnian avant-jazz polymath composer and bandleader, Sun Ra (born Herman Poole Blount), features heavily in the set, along with interpretations of Alice Coltrane, Cedric Brooks, Erik Satie and orchestral offerings of Specials numbers, of course.

"The instrumental side of ska was pretty much Jamaican jazz over a popular street rhythm, so we're joining a lot of dots and maybe for the rock fan it's giving a slightly alternative history of what became known as psychedelic music," Dammers told *The Scotsman* in March 2010. "The purpose of this exercise is not to alienate Specials fans," he continued. "I'm not trying to sever the links with my past. The thing I've always done is mix elements of the past with the present and the future. I hope from seeing this people will maybe see the original Specials slightly differently – although it was a ska band, it was also what I might call a 'cutting-edge retro band'. Ska was the thing we happened to revive, but it could have been anything in a way. This is all part of a progression. It's not supposed to be a battle with anybody."

Dammers had let it be known that any mention of the Specials reunion of the previous year would bring an immediate curtailment to the interview, and yet during the *Scotsman* interview he freely broached the subject himself – even if he was still doggedly refusing to acknowledge his erstwhile friends going out on the road a "reunion".

"What they did wasn't real," he said. "They're trying to exactly reproduce the past and you're always going to fail if you try and do that. They basically did the first album and I think The Specials moved beyond that and the best stuff was at the end. By the time we got to 'Ghost Town', we'd actually become a classic British pop band."

Dammers was obviously casting a "rose-tinted" glow on his high-handed diktats having proved largely responsible for the demise of The Specials, as he went on to opine that he'd thought it "completely unnecessary" for the band to break up when it did, and that fans had got a taste of the musical direction the band was taking at the time of the split in the songs he and John Bradbury released as The Special AKA and what Hall, Staple and Golding were doing with Fun Boy Three. "This [The Spatial AKA Orchestra] is where the real Specials have ended up," he added. "It might seem like a long journey, but then people have missed out on 20 years of my musical activities. But there is a strong link – it's what I've learned about music. So, I hope people will understand what I do a bit better from this."

When The Specials walked out on stage at the 2,000-capacity Newcastle O2 Academy and burst into 'Do the Dog', it was as if those thirty years rolled back in the blink of an eye. And with Britain in the grip of another recession, the songs – notably 'Ghost Town' – had as much resonance as they did in 1979. The critics were universal in their acclaim, with *The Guardian* declaring that picking any song at random from the band's heyday run of seven consecutive hit singles would serve as "a running commentary" on modern-day Britain.

The high point of the tour was, of course, the "homecoming" show at Coventry FC's Ricoh Arena on May 15. The Specials had never been a stadium act, but 9,000 delirious fans serving as an ad hoc chorus line more than compensated for any flaws in the performance.

Rico Rodriguez didn't partake in The Specials' reunion but would occasionally sit in with Dammers' orchestra. He was also a long-standing fixture of Jools Holland's orchestra, and continued playing with Holland until having to give up owing to ill health. In 2007, he was awarded an MBE for services to music.

Following his death in September 2015, Holland said of Rodriguez: "I first met and worked with Rico in the early 1980s. He was an originator and a unique person in the twentieth century. He bridged the gap between early Jamaican music and modern British ska pop music."

There were countless other tributes, of course, but the most poignant eulogy came from Jerry Dammers: "It's hard to express how sad I feel," he said via a statement released to the media. "He taught me so much about what a proper musician is supposed to try and do. For me, getting to play with him was one of the greatest things about The Specials." Having praised *Man from Wareika* as being one of his all-time favourite albums and a great inspiration musically, Dammers went on to praise Rodriguez's "immeasurable" contribution to The Specials in providing the all-important link to authentic Jamaican ska and reggae. "He took us to the next level and helped offer the band a possibility beyond the confines of punk."

Upon hearing the news of Rodriguez's passing, legendary Jamaican producer, Bunny Lee, compared his playing to that of Don Drummond, in "creating the iconic sound which for a while made the trombone virtually the national instrument of Jamaica".

Reflecting on the reunion tour, Staple said The Specials had been a "contradiction" for far too long; their failure to unite themselves making a mockery of their espousing unity between black and white. "We were riding a thirty-year wave of nostalgia – a lot of people wanted to be transported for a single night back to 1979. They wanted to hear me toast "Bernie Rhodes knows, don't argue", Roddy's guitar soaring over the crowd, Horace's bass thumping out the ska rhythm, and Prince Rimshot and Lynval getting the punters skanking to the music."

Hall's contribution is glaringly absent from Staple's self-acclamation, but in November 2010, the singer admitted to having enjoyed the reunion shows and confirmed there would be further Specials dates some time during the following autumn. "It's a celebration of something that happened in your life that was important, and we're going to do that again next year, but then maybe that'll be it."

True to Hall's word, The Specials took to the road in September 2011, first across Europe and then the UK, tracks from selected European dates featuring on the live album, *More… Or Less – The Specials Live*. And nor would that be it, as February 2012 brought the announcement that The Specials would be performing at the Olympics' closing ceremony in Hyde Park on August 12. "We have been keeping it under our pork pie hats for a month or so now," an excited Golding said. "I think it is going to be the only chance people get to see The Specials performing in the UK this year."

Staple was jumping the gun a tad, for when The Specials arrived in London to bring the 2012 Olympics to its climactic finale, they did so on the back of a string of dates in Australasia and European festival appearances. The Hyde Park show did prove to be Golding's Specials swansong. In January 2013, the band announced his departure owing to ongoing health issues via their website.

Roddy Byers would take his leave the following February. His replacement on the forthcoming 2014 UK and European dates, which kicked off with an appearance at the Isle of Wight Festival on June 14, was ex-Ocean Colour Scene and Paul Weller mainstay Steve Cradock. "Steve has brought a totally different thing to it," Hall told the *Shropshire Star* in April 2017. "He's got free reign to do what he wants. There's a total mutual respect. We're not here to tell him what to do. It's nice to have people involved who we can trust and not say, 'Here's the chord sheet.'"

Plans were underway for more Specials shows in 2016 when Bradbury died suddenly at home on December 28, 2015. He was 62. The news left the rest of the band distraught.

"We started working on these dates last October," said Hall. "Everyone was really looking forward to them and then just after Christmas Brad passed away. It was devastating, but in our heart of hearts we know he would want us to continue with the plan he helped to put together."

Having recruited The Libertines' jobbing stickman, Gary Powell, The Specials got the 19-date UK tour underway at Nottingham's Rock City on 19 October. In honour of Bradbury's memory, The Specials incorporated Louis Armstrong's 'We Have All the Time in the World' into the set. "It was really weird for us at first after 30 years of turning round and seeing Brad on the drum stool and then he wasn't there," said Hall. "But Gary's done a really lovely job. He's a lovely bloke and easy to get on with. The new members keep it fresh. They bring something to it."

As for whether The Specials would go back into the studio to record a new album, Hall said while it wasn't off the table, they were realistic enough to know what was bringing people through the door. "People love our set," Hall continued. "If you go and see a band, you want to hear the songs you know. I've seen bands who've reformed and played stuff that nobody wanted to listen to. The defining moment for me was seeing the Pixies performing 'Dolittle', that's what I wanted, and I never got to see it the first time. Another time, I saw Patti Smith performing 'Horses'. It's a generational thing, whether we're in the UK or America and Japan."

It remains to be seen whether the surviving Specials will mark their fortieth anniversary in 2019 with either a tour or a new album, but with the world the way it is, songs like 'Too Much Too Young', 'Stereotype' and 'Ghost Town' will surely prove as relevant as they ever did.

Born in Jamaica and nurtured in Britain, ska is music of the streets. It had lain dormant for more than a decade until The Specials gave its infectious rhythmical tropes a renewed lease of life, and yet even Jerry Dammers came to recognise the band would have to draw their inspiration from other wellsprings of creativity and diversify for their sound for the second album if the band was to move forward.

Except for Vivienne Goldman, it's fair to say the music journos writing for *NME*, *Sounds*, *Melody Maker* et al at the time of 'Gangsters' being released would have been able to comment on Coxsone Dodd, Duke Reid or Prince Buster without reaching for a copy of the *International Who's Who in Music and Musicians' Directory*. Nor would they have immediately recognised Neville Staple's "Bernie Rhodes knows, don't argue" opening gambit on 'Gangsters' being a play on Buster's "Al Capone's guns don't argue", or that Buster had also penned Madness' 'One Step Beyond'. In today's twenty-first-century digital world, such details are but a mouse-click away, and as such it's therefore unlikely that a single subculture niche such as punk or ska could possibly flourish as in years gone by.

Regardless of whether The Specials – with or without Jerry Dammers – reconvene in 2019 for some fortieth anniversary frolics, ska will continue skanking to its off-kilter beat in one guise or another; be it ska jazz, ska pop, ska-core or ska punk. Indeed, at the time of writing, The Selecter and The Beat are set to get together with punk perennials Stiff Little Fingers and Buzzcocks for a clutch of UK dates, and who's to say these shows won't serve to inspire some like-minded kids in the crowd to pick up the baton and give rise to a fourth ska wave…?

NINETEEN

TOP
100

SKA & SKA PUNK SONGS

"It's never easy compiling a Top 100 list of any musical genre. If I had my way, I'd do away with the placings and say these songs struck more of a chord than others while writing the book."

MICK O' SHEA

1. 'Too Much Too Young' – The Specials

2. 'Rudy, a Message to You' – Dandy Livingstone/The Specials

3. 'Train to Skaville' – The Ethiopians/The Selecter

4. 'Mirror in the Bathroom' – The Beat

5. 'Guns of Navarone' – The Skatalites/The Specials

6. 'Too Much Pressure' – The Selecter

7. 'The Prince' – Madness

8. 'Carry Go Bring Home' – Justin Hinds and The Dominoes

9. 'It Mek' – Desmond Dekker and The Aces

10. 'Long Shot Kick de Bucket' – The Pioneers

11. 'Madness' – Prince Buster

12. 'Tougher than Tough' – Derrick Morgan

13. 'Bellevue Special' – Don Drummond

14. 'Ghost Town' – The Specials

15. 'One Step Beyond' – Prince Buster/Madness

16. 'Tears of a Clown' – The Beat

17. 'Rudie Don't Go' – Dandy Livingstone

18. 'Gangsters' – The Specials

19. 'Life Could Be a Dream' – The Maytals

20. 'Ska Killers' – The Toasters

21. 'King of Ska' – Desmond Dekker and his Cherry Pies

22. 'On My Radio' – The Selecter

23. 'Blazing Fire' – Derrick Morgan

24. 'Let's Ska' – Dandy Livingstone

25. 'Rudie Got Soul' – Desmond Dekker and The Aces

26. 'Street Corner' – The Skatalites

27. 'Man in the Street' – Don Drummond

28. 'Praise and No Raise' – Prince Buster

29. 'Rock Steady' – Laurel Aitken

30. 'Three Minute Hero' – The Selecter

31. 'Concrete Jungle' – The Specials

32. 'Al Capone' – Prince Buster

33. 'Lorraine' – Bad Manners

34. 'Return of Django' – The Upsetters

35. 'Monkey Man' – Toots and The Maytals

36. 'Night Boat to Cairo' – Madness

37. 'Man from Wareika' – Rico Rodriguez

38. 'Think of the Good Times' – Dandy Livingstone

39. 'You're Wondering Now' – Andy and Joey

40. 'Rudie Gone a Jail' – The Clarendonians

41. 'We Are Rolling' – Stranger Cole

42. 'Slow and Easy' – The Silvertones

43. 'Everything Crash' – The Ethiopians

44. 'Independent Woman' – Jackie Brenston

45. 'Dance Crasher' – Alton Ellis and The Flames

46. 'Out on the Streets' – The Selecter

47. 'Hands Off … She's Mine' – The Beat

48. 'Too Hot' – Prince Buster/The Specials

49. 'Sound System' – Operation Ivy

50. 'Special Brew' – Bad Manners

51. 'Phoenix City' – Roland Alphonso and The Soul Brothers

52. 'Low Down Dirty Girl' – Laurel Aitken

53. 'Let's Do Rocksteady' – The Bodysnatchers

54. 'They Make Me Mad' – The Selecter

55. 'Cool Smoke' – The Skatalites

56. 'Rock and Shake' – Prince Buster's All Stars

57. 'Roos Radicals' – Rancid

58. 'The Selecter' – The Selecter

59. '(Dawning of a) New Era' – The Specials

60. 'I Feel the Spirit' – Prince Buster

61. 'Musical Communion' – The Skatalites

62. 'See the Blind' – Derrick Morgan

63. 'Two Swords' – The Beat

64. 'Sell Out' – Reel Big Fish

65. 'El Pussycat' – Roland Alphonso

66. 'Ska'd for Life' – The Akrylykz

67. 'Wash Your Troubles away' – Prince Buster

68. 'In the Middle of the Night' – Madness

69. 'Here We Go Again' – Operation Ivy

70. 'Unstoppable' – The Planet Smashers

71. 'My Boy Lollipop' – Millie Small

72. 'The Little that You Have' - Justin Hinds and The Dominoes

73. '007 Shanty Town' – Desmond Dekker and The Aces

74. 'Just a Feeling' – Bad Manners

75. 'Over the Mountain' – Rico Rodriguez

76. 'Hey Boy, Hey Girl' – Dandy Livingstone

77. 'Freedom Sounds' – The Skatalites

78. 'Try Me One More Time' – The Clarendonians

79. 'Rough and Tough' – Stranger Cole

80. 'Nite Klub' – The Specials

81. 'Rudie Boy Train' – Desmond Dekker and The Aces

82. 'Hey Boy, Hey Girl' – Dandy Livingstone

83. 'Oh Carolina' – The Folkes Brothers

84. 'Look into That' – Justin Hinds and The Dominoes

85. 'Run Rudy Run' – The Toasters

86. 'Thorough Fare' – The Skatalites

87. 'Spyderman' – The Akrylykz

88. 'Time Bomb' – Rancid

89. 'El Pussycat Ska' – Roland Alphonso

90. 'Teenage Ska' – Baba Brooks

91. 'Why Should I Worry' – Justin Hinds and The Dominoes

92. 'Rudi's In Love' – Locomotive

93. 'Dance Crasher' – Alton Ellis and The Flames

94. 'Take on Me' – Reel Big Fish

95. 'This Day' – Rico Rodriguez

96. 'Get Up Edina' – Desmond Dekker and The Four Aces

97. 'Judgement Day' – Laurel Aitken

98. 'The Impression that I Get'–The Mighty Mighty Bosstones

99. 'Take Me as I Am' – Jackie Edwards

100. 'I'll Get Along Without You' – The Melodians